ORTHODOX JUDAISM IN BRITAIN
SINCE 1913

D1593384

ORTHODOX JUDAISM IN BRITAIN SINCE 1913

An Ideology Forsaken

MIRI J. FREUD-KANDEL

University of Oxford

VALLENTINE MITCHELL
LONDON • PORTLAND, OR

First published in 2006 in Great Britain by
VALLENTINE MITCHELL
Suite 314, Premier House, 112–114 Station Road,
Edgware, Middlesex HA8 7BJ

and in the United States of America by
VALLENTINE MITCHELL
c/o ISBS, 920 NE 58th Avenue, Suite 300
Portland, OR 97213-3786

Website: www.vmbooks.com

Copyright © Miri Freud-Kandel 2006

British Library Cataloguing in Publication Data

Freud-Kandel, Miri
    Orthodox Judaism in Britain since 1913 : an ideology
    forsaken
    1. Orthodox Judaism – Great Britain – History – 20th
    century 2. Chief Rabbinate – Great Britain – History – 20th
    century 3. Jews – Great Britain – History – 20th century
    I. Title
    296.8'32'0941'0904

ISBN 0-85303-713-2 (cloth)
ISBN 978-0-85303-713-2 (cloth)
ISBN 0-85303-714-0 (paper)
ISBN 978-0-85303-714-9 (paper)

Library of Congress Cataloging-in-Publication Data
A catalog record has been applied for

Typeset in 10.5/12pt Palatino by Vitaset, Paddock Wood, Kent
Printed in Great Britain by MPG Books Ltd, Bodmin, Cornwall

Contents

List of Abbreviations

CAJP	*Conference of Anglo-Jewish Preachers*
HWE	Louis Jacobs, *Helping With Enquiries: An Autobiography* (London: Vallentine Mitchell, 1989)
JC	*Jewish Chronicle*
JJS	*Jewish Journal of Sociology*
JTS	Jewish Theological Seminary
LMA	London Metropolitan Archives
MBJ	Geoffrey Alderman, *Modern British Jewry* (Oxford: Oxford University Press, 1992)
RWC	Robert Henriques, *Sir Robert Waley Cohen 1877–1952: A Biography* (London: Secker & Warburg, 1966)
SAS	J.H. Hertz, *Sermons, Addresses and Studies*, 3 Vols. (London: Soncino Press, 1938). References are by volume, followed by page number, e.g., *SAS*, II, p.48.
TJHSE	*Transactions of the Jewish Historical Society of England*
UOHC	Union of Orthodox Hebrew Congregations

Foreword

This year will be 40 years since Chief Rabbi Hertz passed away. He held the Chief Rabbinate for 33 years, the longest time a chief rabbi held this office. Surprisingly, until now we did not have a comprehensive study of his life and activities. Dr Miri Freud-Kandel has written the first serious study of the theological writings of Chief Rabbi Hertz. You have to appreciate him from many angles: from demographic, political, religious, rabbinic and Zionist perspectives.

He was the first to graduate from the Jewish Theological Seminary in New York. The name of the seminary aroused a lot of opposition from Orthodox Jews. In this title Jewish Theological Seminary there is no mention of the Talmud, of rabbinic law, of which there was general incomprehension among the various groups of Jews that came to the United States. Theological seminary are two words that are in contrast to rabbinic Judaism. Through the nineteenth century, from Rabbi Solomon Hirschell to the death of Chief Rabbi Hermann Adler, Anglo-Jewry did not have a single intellectual. Even rabbinic learning was considered of a very limited value. The first intellectual chief rabbi was Dr Hertz. In this and other respects it is interesting to compare Britain and Central Europe. In the most democratic country in Europe, the Jews were divided into three categories, East European, very religious, but with very few leading scholars; a small group of Jews had already become highly anglicized; and those cultured in English life and English language, very few of whom converted.

In 1860 there were roughly 50–55,000 Jews in the whole of the United Kingdom. By 1910, 30 years after the assassination of Tsar Alexander III, the Jewish population had tripled, and there were nearly 180,000 Jews in the United Kingdom, mostly strict Orthodox and highly suspicious of anglicized Jewry, forming their own community in the East End of London. They were opposed to Chief Rabbi Adler and they fought the established Jewry led by Lord Rothschild. Hermann Adler was a man of limited intellect, of conservative manner, and he believed he played a similar role to the Archbishop of Canterbury among Christians. He considered he had the only right to be called rabbi; other ministers were to be called reverend.

When he died there were three candidates for the job of chief rabbi

– R. Moses Hyamson, R. Bernard Drachman, and Dr Hertz, a rabbi in South Africa after graduating in New York. He was in South Africa when he supported the British in the Boer War, and he was deeply respected by Lord Milner. This helped Lord Rothschild to appoint him to the chief rabbinate. We have now a demography. Dr Hertz visualised himself as a bridge-maker between strict Orthodox Jews, mildly conservative Jews and mildly Reform Jews. Hertz made many approaches to East European Jewry. He wanted them to become more anglicized; he also wanted them to become more lenient towards the United Synagogue. But paradoxically the East European Jews in the East End of London were led by Lord Swaythling, the rival to Lord Rothschild, who led the United Synagogue. He called this group of Jews the Federation of Synagogues, which continues to the present day. Hertz became known as a brilliant orator. He gave lectures on Maimonides, Bachia Ibn Pakuda, the author of the Duties of the Heart. Then he wrote a very competent commentary of the Five Books of Moses and on the Prayer Book, the Siddur. In these essays and commentaries he takes a middle road between strict Orthodoxy and conservative Judaism.

Dr Freud-Kandel has written a pioneering study of the religious ideas of Chief Rabbi Hertz. It is the first major study we have about him and goes much further than Hertz's life. It reaches the controversy between Louis Jacobs and Chief Rabbi Dr Israel Brodie. There have been major changes and shifts in the Jewish community in Britain. First, the decline of the Jewish community in numbers, from half a million to 300,000, and the community's division into at least three sections, the Orthodox round the United Synagogue, the move to the right from children of East European Jews born in Britain, some of whom moved to the Hasidic groups, especially the Lubavitch, and the major break to the left of Reform and Liberal Judaism. At the moment the Orthodox Jews have larger numbers than the secular Jews. In many ways Dr Freud-Kandel's book is a major contribution to the intellectual history of the Jews in Britain. It may be a bit too early to judge and to understand the follow up to the controversy between Jacobs and Brodie. It is still a very important contribution to the discussion going on among British Jews. Her contribution is a major development in the study of Anglo-Jewry after the Second World War. She has read voraciously and I warmly recommend her book to the study of Anglo-Jewry in the twentieth century.

Professor Chimen Abramsky
May 2006

Preface

The Jewish community in England exists as a minority religious community located in the midst of a host society that, where it is not dominated by secular values, espouses the values of a different religion. The theological position of the Anglo-Jewish community has shifted during the twentieth century as attitudes have changed regarding the dilemma of how Jewish identity is to be maintained intact in these surroundings. Fear of the potential ill effects of inter-action with the host society, with its alternative sources of wisdom and truth, has heightened. The expediency of allowing meaningful inter-action has increasingly been questioned as it has come to be viewed as a danger to the preservation of Orthodox Judaism. This work seeks specifically to examine the role of the Chief Rabbi in Anglo-Jewry, analysing the influence that holders of the post have been able to exert over the theological outlook of the community. The focus falls on the three chief rabbis whose tenures began and ended within the twentieth century: Joseph H. Hertz, Israel Brodie and Immanuel Jakobovits.

The year 1913 provides the starting date for this study, since it represents the year in which a new Chief Rabbi was appointed in the Anglo-Jewish community. It may be viewed as the beginning of a new era in the history of the community. By the following year, with the outbreak of the First World War, the mass immigration of East European Jews into Britain that had exploded in the 1880s was brought to a halt, allowing Anglo-Jewry to become a more stable entity. The years that followed represent the period in which the community sought to readjust and progress in the aftermath of the enormous changes that it had experienced. The influence that the Chief Rabbi was able to exert over the religious direction of the community through this period provides a focus for this work.

The Chief Rabbi represents and defends Orthodox Judaism, the religious position that is dominant in Anglo-Jewry. Various forms of Orthodoxy are present within the community, in addition to pro-gressive movements, but it is centrist Orthodoxy to which the greatest proportion of the community affiliate. This religious position is exemplified in the United Synagogue, which along with the Chief

Rabbinate represents the main religious institutions of the community. The two are closely inter-related, particularly in the religious sphere, since the United Synagogue recognises the Chief Rabbi as its ultimate religious authority. Although it has considered broadening its geographical scope, the United Synagogue is a London institution; the model of its congregations extends into the provinces and the authority of the Chief Rabbi is recognized by many provincial communities, but it is London that has always taken the lead in the Anglo-Jewish community. Following the suggestion of Aubrey Newman, reference to 'Anglo-Jewry' is therefore taken predominantly to refer to the London Jewish community, for as he has observed 'it is, I think, sufficient to indicate that there is a wider community outside London and yet leave it at that'.[1]

The historical development of the Anglo-Jewish community has been studied elsewhere. The work of Cecil Roth has been followed by more revisionist readings of the community's history by Geoffrey Alderman, Todd Endelman, David Ruderman and others. The history of the United Synagogue has been extensively covered by the work of Aubrey Newman. This work is not intended as a history; rather, it represents an attempt to examine the theological development of Anglo-Jewish Orthodoxy, assessing how and why it has altered, examining the influence of changing circumstances and key individuals, and especially focusing on the role of the Chief Rabbi. It is an attempt to extrapolate theology from what is essentially, as we shall see, an unthinking community; the voluntary nature of communal membership heightened the importance of synagogue affiliation without concomitant acceptance of religious principles or practices that could have been expected to exist alongside identification with Orthodoxy. It has traditionally proved difficult to speak of theology in the context of Anglo-Jewry. You do not often find religious functionaries of Anglo-Jewish Orthodoxy seeking to grapple with theological issues and their congregations rarely require it of them. Reference to theological thought in this study and to the theological development to which the community was subject does not therefore refer to dogmatic theology. The term is used more broadly, to incorporate the sense that the religious community has its own distinctive approach to the various issues of modern life. Not all of its values are shared with the wider community and a religious leader may therefore construct a method for advising Jews on how to approach their religious life.[2]

It should be acknowledged that in a religion in which praxis has always been emphasized over dogma, Jews often engage in ritual activities without fully considering the principles upon which such actions rest, or the implications that the practices may suggest regarding belief.

This is perhaps particularly true of Jews in the modern world as the notion of adjectival forms of Judaism developed in which 'Jewish identity', or 'Orthodox Jewish identity', formed only one component of an individual's sense of self. Postmodern considerations of the multi-layered identities developed by Jews have further highlighted the gap that develops between principle and practice.[3] The perception that Anglo-Jewry marginalizes the function of theology could therefore, in fact, be said to be true of many communities in which a sociological survey is undertaken rather than an examination of the thought of its communal religious leaders. Nevertheless, the theologies constructed by religious leaders in an attempt to influence their communities provide an indicator of the strategies adopted to address changing times and situations. This work focuses upon shifts that have occurred in the principles promulgated and attempts to understand why these changes have taken place in Anglo-Jewry.

In arguing that Anglo-Jewish religious leaders can provide a theology worthy of study, this work fits into the school of thought which argues that a Continental European or Germanocentric assessment of the development of modern Judaism provides an incomplete picture that studies of Anglo-Jewry can enhance. Todd Endelman, by focusing upon the contribution Anglo-Jewish studies can make to understandings of social and political history, has been pivotal in highlighting the significance of Anglo-Jewry for work on modern Judaism. David Ruderman has gone further to suggest that beyond social history, studies of Anglo-Jewry can in fact contribute to intellectual history. Querying the prevalent assumption that Anglo-Jewry is a generally unthinking community, he has argued that it provides an important alternative insight into the development of modern Jewish thought. However, as Ruderman himself acknowledges, his examination of late eighteenth- and nineteenth-century Jewish thinkers in Britain, engaging in scholarly work that could be construed as part of 'Jewish enlightenment thought', found that this never led to the emergence of a Haskalah movement in Britain. Although Ruderman provides various explanations for why this may be, it seems fair to assert that whilst the common presumptions about Anglo-Jewry's intellectual vacuum, as evidenced by Endelman among others, may go too far, it can nonetheless be assumed that the majority of British Jews devoted little effort to thinking about their Judaism. This work seeks to steer a middle path between the presentations of Anglo-Jewry found in the writings of these two historians.[4]

A particular advantage of examining Anglo-Jewish thought is the manner in which it provides a distinct setting for the development of modern currents. Although British Jews may often have been aware of the events that were occurring in Jewish communities outside Britain, primarily thanks to their Jewish press, this is different to being intellectually influenced by such knowledge. The generally poor levels of Jewish and particularly Hebrew literacy in Anglo-Jewry tended to prevent the widespread influence of ideas that were developed beyond British shores. Ruderman notes that the thinkers he studied often worked in glorious intellectual isolation in the eighteenth and nineteenth centuries, independent from continental European Jewish influences, constructing peculiarly British models of modern Jewish thought. As we move through the nineteenth century, external influences certainly come to play a more prominent role, especially as immigration introduced into Britain a critical mass of individuals schooled in foreign ways of thinking about Judaism. However the primarily Anglocentric focus of this work reflects the manner in which Anglo-Jewish theologies were required to address particular Anglo-Jewish needs.

The sermons, addresses and writings of Chief Rabbis Hertz, Brodie and Jakobovits provide the main source for an examination of their religious thought. They facilitate an analysis of their theological programmes and the underlying factors that moved their theology. They offer a means of assessing whether and in what ways their religious positions were altered across the span of their leadership. Moreover, they highlight the central issues on which they concentrated as religious leaders in the Anglo-Jewish Orthodox community.

A number of interviews undertaken with various persons who were either themselves directly involved in the events described or were close to some of the leading characters examined, provide an additional resource. Able to provide first-hand knowledge of the history of the period and the influences that were at work, they offered an invaluable insight. Two of the interviewees are the offspring of major figures in this study, who have been able to contribute to an understanding of the personalities involved. Chimen Abramsky, emeritus Professor of Hebrew and Jewish Studies at University College London, is the son of Yekhezkiel Abramsky, who was a dayan on the London Bet Din from 1935, exerting considerable religious influence over the community even beyond his retirement in 1951. Jeremy Schonfield is a grandson of Hertz and son of Solomon Schonfeld, head of the Union of Orthodox Hebrew Congregations, which stood on the right wing of Anglo-Jewish Orthodoxy. Their personal recollections enabled them to provide a penetrative 'behind the scenes' account of various events related to our study. A central figure in the history of the theological development of Anglo-Jewish Orthodoxy in the twentieth century is Louis Jacobs. In the course of my discussions with him, he provided his own version of the events known as the Jacobs Affair and offered his perspective on the roles of Hertz and Brodie and the changes that have occurred in the community. Interviews with United Synagogue ministers who served at the time of the Jacobs Affair have also contributed to an analysis of events.[5] I am grateful to all these interviewees for their help in the research for this book.

Two additional sources of considerable importance in an analysis of the period covered have been the *Jewish Chronicle* and archival material of the United Synagogue and office of Chief Rabbi, including archives from the London Bet Din. The *Jewish Chronicle*, particularly through its editorials and letters pages, captured the concerns of the age and offers a means of understanding public perceptions of the major events in twentieth century Anglo-Jewish history. I am grateful to Charles Tucker, Record Keeper of the United Synagogue and Chief Rabbinate, for granting me access to the archives of these institutions. Containing the official records of events and including personal correspondence between the various offices and individuals, the archives provide invaluable source material. I would also like to extend my thanks to Ezra Kahn, librarian at the London School of Jewish Studies, and the librarians of the Jewish National Library at the Hebrew University of Jerusalem, for the assistance they offered during my research of additional materials on the Chief Rabbinate and United Synagogue held in their collections.

The constant help, encouragement and support provided by Nicholas de Lange, who has guided me since my time as his student, has proved invaluable throughout the research for this project. This work originally formed the basis of my doctoral dissertation, completed under his supervision in the Faculty of Divinity at the University of Cambridge. I approached my studies as a product of the Anglo-Jewish community, equipped with certain levels of 'insider' knowledge, but also encumbered by certain assumptions that he never allowed me to leave unquestioned. I owe him an enormous debt for forcing me to strive to engage in rigorous analysis of my subject matter. I am also grateful for the time laid aside, advice offered, and sometimes lively discussions that ensued with friends and colleagues including Jeremy Wanderer, Daniel Rynhold and Debra Chopp, and my fellow members of the Oxford University Teaching and Research Unit in Hebrew and Jewish Studies, particularly Martin Goodman. I would also like to extend my thanks to the President and Fellows of Wolfson College, Oxford, and to Tony Kushner who helped bring this work to publication. In addition, I would like to thank my parents for the support that they have always provided me with over the years, and Livia for allowing me the time to complete this work. Finally, while it may be clichéd to suggest that without the constant help and encouragement of my partner this work could never have been produced, it is, however, the only accurate way of acknowledging the gratitude that I owe Jonathan. He has found a way of living with me when my mind was wandering elsewhere. He may now have a far greater understanding of Anglo-Jewish Orthodoxy than he ever wished to attain, but more than anyone else he has been the constant sounding board for my ideas. He has battled to strengthen the coherence with which I constructed my arguments and has engaged in more proof reading than could possibly be appropriate, and all that at the end of his own long days at work. My own innate stubbornness means that any errors and misjudgements that remain are entirely my own. I dedicate this work to him, and to the memory of Mark Silverman, whose model of progressive conservative Judaism truly provides an inspiration.

The story of the modern Anglo-Jewish community, introduced into British society from a variety of different original areas of settlement, is the story of a community's accommodation into the environment that the host society provided. Throughout its history, its members have been free to engage in both realms in which they were located: the Jewish world provided its own specific values and dictates whilst the British world offered an alternative source of ideas. Whether consciously or otherwise, the Anglo-Jewish community has been engaged in an attempt to reconcile these two realms so that Judaism is not undermined by its interaction with the ideas of its host society. Meaningful interaction in the non-Jewish world has been a characteristic ideology of the community for pragmatic reasons if nothing else. An examination of how this ideology came to be forsaken as a theological shift occurred in Anglo-Jewish Orthodoxy provides the focus of this work.

1
Introduction: Anglo-Jewish Orthodoxy in 1913

At the time of Joseph H. Hertz's election to the office of Chief Rabbi in 1913, Anglo-Jewry, concentrated in London and its immediate environs, was a divided community. It consisted of an eastern European immigrant community, which had its origins in mass immigrations that had been increasing since the mid-nineteenth century before exploding around the 1880s. In addition, it contained the resident community that, in contradistinction to the newcomers, represented what was characterized as the 'native' community in Anglo-Jewry. In truth, all members of the modern Jewish community in Britain are of immigrant origin. Members of the so-called native community had begun to arrive in the country from the late seventeenth century. In the interim period they had become highly acculturated to their English setting so that they differed considerably from the newcomers in practically every sphere: religious, social, cultural, linguistic and economic. The Anglicization process to which the native community had been subjected reflected their experience of toleration in England. Both the native and immigrant communities had been introduced to England from Continental Europe, where attitudes towards Jews, legislation dealing with them, and the pro-cesses of acculturation and emancipation contrasted to the situation in England. Jews in England were subject to very few discriminatory laws and were largely free from persecution. The few civil disabilities that were suffered generally had not been designed to discriminate specifically against Jews. They were primarily the result of legislation directed against Christian non-conformists who did not follow the rites of the established Church of England. Consequently, the earlier settlers had been able to interact in numerous ways with the host society and be influenced by the customs, attitudes and values that they encountered, all of which affected the nature of the Anglo-Jewish community.[1]

The original Jewish settlers, whose official residence in England dated back to 1656, had been of Sephardi origin and had arrived either directly or indirectly from Spain and Portugal. They practised a form of religious worship and had developed traditions that differed from those practised by Ashkenazi Jews who came from central and eastern Europe. In 1690 the Ashkenazim established their own synagogue in Duke's Place. Although at that time they represented only a small minority of the Anglo-Jewish community, by the middle of the eighteenth century additional immigration had increased their numbers. In 1750 the Sephardi community contained approximately 2,000 members whilst the Ashkenazim had grown to a community of around 6,000. Henceforth they became the dominant group in Anglo-Jewry, at least in terms of population size. References to the Anglo-Jewish community in this study therefore refer solely to the Ashkenazi community unless otherwise stated.

The manner in which a number of the community's religious institutions developed reflected the particular circumstances of Jews in England. In contrast to the political situation on the Continent, where membership of the Jewish community was generally required by law, from the beginning of the resettlement identification with the Anglo-Jewish community was entirely voluntary. In speaking of Anglo-Jewry therefore one can only refer to those Jews who consciously chose to affiliate with their religious community. Those who wished to abandon their Jewish identity were able to sever all ties with Anglo-Jewry, suffering no legislative requirement from the state to associate with their religious kin. Consequently, since it provided the principal means of identifying with the community, the importance of synagogue membership was greatly heightened. By way of further contrast to the various models of Jewish communities in continental Europe, the leaders of Anglo-Jewry had no authority to collect taxes from their members, and were reliant instead on voluntary contributions. Aside from charitable donations, the collection of synagogue membership fees thus provided the community with a primary method for raising the funds required to sustain various institutions of the community: synagogues, welfare organizations or other religious facilities.[2] The absence of state legislation discriminating against Jews and controlling the organization of the religious community highlights the tolerance in religious matters that was enjoyed by Anglo-Jewry. However, by the same token, the community's leaders possessed no access to legal sanctions over its members, impeding their ability to impose uniformity in religious standards across Anglo-Jewry. As we shall see, despite the heightened importance of synagogue membership, affiliation did not necessarily accurately reflect levels of religious observance amongst members.

The creation of strictly hierarchical and essentially oligarchic structures for the community can, in part, be seen as a response to the voluntary make-up of the Jewish community in Britain. The concern to preserve the religious identity of the community intact, and secure the funding to provide for Anglo-Jewry, necessitated the creation of a strong organizational framework that centralized authority. The influence of an established church was another crucial factor.

The growth of Anglo-Jewry led to the emergence of three separate major synagogues in the City of London. The original Ashkenazi synagogue, in Duke's Place, became known as the Great Synagogue and was followed, in 1706, by the establishment of what became known as the Hambro' Synagogue. Formed as a result of a religious dispute with the Great, the synagogue's name was intended to designate the new community's adherence to the rites of Jews in the city of Hamburg. In 1761 an additional synagogue was founded to secure its members' independence from the Great. As a result of its junior status it was known as the New Synagogue.[3] A number of additional independent, smaller and often more religiously-committed communities were established in subsequent years, but by the beginning of the Victorian age the members of the three dominant congregations had agreed to cooperate with one another and with the Sephardim on a number of religious and communal matters to improve organization and management of the community. In 1804 the London Shechitah Board had been created by both the Ashkenazi and Sephardi communities to facilitate the sharing of religious and economic responsibility over the provision of kosher meat for Jews in the capital. They had also agreed to form a joint Board of Deputies of British Jews which, although it had its background in the accession to the throne of George III in 1760, only began to hold regular meetings in the 1830s and did not adopt a constitution until 1835.[4] As will become clearer below, by the early 1800s the Ashkenazim had joined together to acknowledge a single religious leader at their head, distinct from the Haham, the title given to the religious head of the Sephardi community. By 1834 the three main synagogues had produced a Treaty that clearly defined the roles and responsibilities for each, establishing, *inter alia*, the means for sharing the burden of burying poor unaffiliated Jews. In addition, this Treaty recognized each synagogue's reliance on its membership to provide the funds that enabled it to sustain its institutions; it was therefore agreed that no attempt would be made to poach members from one congregation to another.

The creation of a Reform congregation, which established a synagogue in 1842, involved a secession from both the Sephardi and Ashkenazi communities and undermined the tendency towards centralization.[5] Nineteen Sephardi and five Ashkenazi Jews joined together to form the new congregation, which was named the West London Synagogue of British Jews. Two main influences had been at work in leading to this secession. One was the concern to reform Anglo-Jewish synagogal services, the other was an interest in providing a synagogue for Jews who had relocated to the West End of London. The concerns of the original seceders were laid out in a signed Declaration that outlined the reforms they intended to institute.

> We think that a remedy may be applied by the establishment of a Synagogue in the Western part of the Metropolis, where a Revised Service may be performed at hours more suited to our habits, and in a manner more calculated to inspire feelings of Devotion, where Religious Instruction may be afforded by competent persons, and where to effect these purposes, Jews generally may form an United Congregation under the denomination of British Jews.[6]

Each of these issues reflected a growing tendency in Anglo-Jewry to judge Judaism against the standards of the host society.

The design and location of the community's institutions began to reflect English sensibilities and focused on areas of importance perceived by Jews in the arrangements of the Anglican Church. The synagogal reforms carried out in the formation of the West London Synagogue focused on the form rather than the content of the service.[7] A primary concern was to increase levels of decorum, to match more closely the atmosphere found in an English church. To this end a choir was introduced and the service shortened, through the removal of a number of *piyyutim* (liturgical poems). The transferral of Jews out of the City into the West End of London also reflected more general population shifts that were occurring among the middle and upper-middle classes of London society. The desire to move away from the City, despite the fact that the centres of Jewish life were located there, was influenced by the popular movement westwards. Those who moved however, still wanted to attend a synagogue and therefore wished to establish one that was within reasonable walking distance from their homes, since Jews are forbidden to travel on the Sabbath. The centralization process which had been designed to protect the long-term survival of the community was not attuned to this new problem. The creation of new synagogues was expressly forbidden by the *ascamot* – regulations – of the Sephardi community and the main Ashkenazi synagogues were keen not to lose their members on whose payment of membership dues they relied for their maintenance.

The inherently conservative religious temper of Anglo-Jewry was demonstrated by the limited reforms introduced by the West London Synagogue. In truth, the more far-reaching theological issues raised as a result of Jewish engagement in a non-Jewish society, which required the later formation of the Jewish Religious Union (JRU) in 1902 to address, were not particularly prevalent amongst members of Anglo-Jewry at the time of the West London's creation. Lily Montagu, daughter of Samuel Montagu, about whom we shall learn more below, was the guiding force behind the JRU, assisted by Claude Goldsmid Montefiore. Initially, the Union was merely intended to provide a forum for Sabbath afternoon prayer meetings at which a more spiritualized, more universalist, and less ritualistic interpretation of Judaism was promoted. These services were designed to appeal to English Jews who were drifting towards Christianity, to attempt to retain their religious allegiance. However, the JRU was unable to find a home in which to hold its services. The West London Synagogue, further demonstrating its conservatism, objected to the mixed seating of the services, the absence of a Sefer Torah, and the predominance of prayers recited in the vernacular.[8] By 1903, the JRU had produced a prayer book which removed all references to the hopes for a return to Zion, the restoration of a Jewish state, and the reinstitution of the sacrificial system. Closer in theology to Classical Reform Judaism, it was also influenced by the liberal principles of the Unitarian church. It emphasized individual autonomy, rejected divine authority, particularly as the source of Hebrew Scriptures, and focused upon the prophetic message of Jewish teachings. In 1909 the JRU became explicitly constituted as a Movement for the Advancement of Liberal Judaism, firmly establishing its independence as a new religious movement in Anglo-Jewry. A synagogue was created in 1911, and Israel Mattuck, a graduate of the Hebrew Union College in Cincinnati, was appointed rabbi the following year. By 1915, the Liberal Jewish Synagogue had 416 members.[9]

The concerns which had originally led to the formation of the West London Synagogue, an interest in increasing decorum and the need to create synagogues to serve Jews in the West End, were not merely issues of importance for those who joined the Reform congregation. There had been agitations from both Ashkenazi and Sephardi Jews for some time on these matters. They reflected the changing patterns of the community as a whole, particularly as the now dominant Ashkenazim grew in wealth and status to match their Sephardi counterparts more closely. By the middle of the nineteenth century, V.D. Lipman has calculated that in terms of income, 5 per cent of London's 20,000 Jews were upper or upper middle class and an additional 30 per cent belonged to the middle classes. Of the remaining London Jewish population, 35 to 40 per cent, whilst classified as lower class, were self-reliant and the percentage in need of either occasional or regular aid from charitable organizations had dropped to between

25 and 30 per cent of the community.[10] In 1882, Joseph Jacobs calculated that more than half of London Jewry could be classified as middle-class or above: 14.6 per cent had entered the upper or upper-middle-class strata; 42.2 per cent were middle class; 19.6 per cent were lower class; and 23.6 per cent were poor.[11] Prior to the mass immigration from eastern Europe that would radically alter the size and nature of Anglo-Jewry, more than half the community was now native-born and was moving away from peddling and hawking to become stall-holders, shop-keepers or manufacturers of the goods they had previously sold on the streets. No more than one-fifth of London Jewry was involved in hawking.

Aside from the relatively small numbers who joined the West London Synagogue, the movement to the West End of London did not lead to widespread disaffiliation from the main synagogues, despite the inconveniences. There were a number of reasons why identification with Orthodox Judaism remained dominant. As has already been noted, Anglo-Jewry experienced toleration; religious identity did not act as a real barrier to interaction with other Englishmen and women. The temptation to discard it to facilitate contact with English society was therefore small. In addition, in the Victorian age the host society in fact placed considerable emphasis on the practice of religion. As Endelman has explained:

> The outlook of prosperous native Jews bore the impress of these patterns of Victorian religiosity. Well-to-do Jews, as members of a minority group eager to secure social acceptance, took their cues from respectable society, especially Anglican upper middle-class society, and, just as they adopted the fashions of those circles in matters of costume, entertainment, display and decoration, and recreation and leisure, so too they conformed in the area of religion. Religious observance being a necessary part of respectability, they adhered to the established conventions of the faith in which they had been raised.[12]

As has been noted, affiliation with Anglo-Jewish Orthodoxy did not necessarily reflect strict adherence to its beliefs and practices. Stephen Sharot has argued that for Jews who had moved out of the predominantly Jewish enclave of the East End, into areas in which they had far greater contact with gentiles, continued membership of a synagogue provided a relatively easy means of identifying with the Jewish community without directing too much attention towards the practicalities of religious observance.[13] Endelman has insisted that '[t]hey were not in any sense Jews in name only, nor was their Jewish identity merely a lingering ethnic allegiance'.[14] Observance of the

Sabbath and Festivals was maintained, some of the laws of *kashrut* were heeded; however Endelman acknowledges that these practices were not followed in strict accordance with Jewish teachings. The more prosperous Jews who had moved to the West End were influenced by contemporary Christian practice and 'were indifferent to or ignorant of philosophical and theological distinctions and quite content to observe traditions that did not overly inconvenience them'.[15] This form of religious observance is classified in this work by the term 'spiritist Orthodoxy'. The term points to the tendency amongst such Jews to focus on the spirit rather than the letter of the law. It is defined here as a distinct religious position in Anglo-Jewish Orthodoxy that may be contrasted with centrist Orthodoxy. Influenced by the experience of being members of a voluntary Jewish community, it concentrates on the importance of maintaining Jewish identity intact and preserving inherited traditions without directing too much attention to the minutiae of religious practices. Despite its lax attitude to observance, those who may be termed 'spiritist' continue to identify with Orthodox Judaism but are concerned that it should not greatly inconvenience other aspects of their lives, keen to find a method for accommodating Judaism within their existence in British society. It should not be viewed as a principled theological position on the left wing of Orthodox Judaism, which is demarcated by the Reform movement and Masorti Judaism, whose theology will be analysed below.

The term right-wing Orthodoxy is interpreted in this work to refer primarily to Jewish groups with western and central European origins who allow some limited form of integration into modern society. The more stringent attitude towards interaction with the modern world, willingness to submit individuality to religious authority, and interpretation of ritual, most clearly mark the boundaries between right-wing and centrist Orthodoxy; they also serve to differentiate both groups from ultra-Orthodoxy. This latter group, whilst also functioning on the right wing of Orthodoxy, is primarily made up of Jews of eastern European background, both those of *hasidic* origin and their opponents, known as *mitnagdim*, whose worldview is dominated by the yeshiva. Ultra-Orthodoxy is also often characterized by the Hebrew term *haredi*, meaning fearful, pointing to the awe of God they maintain.[16]

THE UNITED SYNAGOGUE

In 1855, the Great Synagogue sponsored the establishment of a new synagogue in the West End of London, in Portland Street, known as the Central Synagogue. This was created specifically as a branch synagogue of the Great rather than a new independent congregation and it enjoyed no real autonomy. The Great had invited the leaders of the Hambro' and the New to join them in the creation of this branch but they declined, concerned, according to Aubrey Newman, at the financial burden it would have imposed. Subsequently, membership of the Central was restricted solely to members of the Great Synagogue. In considering the emergence of this new congregation Newman has suggested:

> As so often with Anglo-Jewish institutions, there was a close parallel with non-Jewish institutions, and here the parallel was with the relations between a parish church and a 'chapel of ease', the chapel having no ecclesiastical independence and its curate being normally unlicenced for such things as marriages ... this branch was so much under the direct control of the Great Synagogue that it was not permitted its own honorary officers, nor was it allowed to allocate seats to any members of the others in the Conjoint.[17]

By 1859, the three main City synagogues had met to discuss the building of another West End synagogue that would be open to all their members. They produced a resolution suggesting that to achieve this end it would be wise to consider 'an amalgamation'. The Bayswater Synagogue was, in fact, only sponsored by the Great and New Synagogues, financial concerns once again influencing the ability of the Hambro' to cooperate in this endeavour. However, the organization of a new congregation under the joint sponsorship of more than one synagogue provided a model for the future creation of the United Synagogue.

All three of the City Synagogues were involved in the creation of the United Synagogue. Newman has suggested that the emergence of this institution received its impetus from the expansion of London Jewry, the financial problems encountered by the Hambro', and the considerable cooperation that was already practised between the congregations, which made a stronger and more formal union seem appropriate.[18] The establishment of the Bayswater Synagogue had provided one precedent for a new synagogal union; the manner in which the Great agreed to help fund the construction of the North London Synagogue in 1865, provided another. The possibility of supporting the creation of an independent congregation that retained strong connections with a City synagogue and therefore maintained the principle of centralization had been established.

By the end of 1866, the leaders of each of the three City synagogues had agreed to the amalgamation in principle, approving the formation of the United Synagogue under its original title: the United Metropolitan Congregation of Jews. Negotiations continued over the following two years before it was decided that the new institution should be officially brought into being through a private Act of Parliament: 'confirming a scheme of the Charity Commissioners for the Jewish United Synagogues'. The Act was finally passed in July 1870.[19] Newman has highlighted the significance of the decision made by the leaders of London Jewry to attain a Parliamentary Act 'to give the outward appearance its spiritual life'.[20] This reflected an interest in giving Jewish institutions an English gloss and pointed to the manner in which the community's leaders 'were less concerned with religious life itself than with what might be termed the "envelope", the outward appearances of religious life'. Nonetheless, in forming the United Synagogue they established a centralized religious institution for the Ashkenazi community in London that would provide for its continued expansion. The delegates who finally achieved the passage of the Act, in a report signed by Lionel Louis Cohen and Asher Asher, declared it to be an action 'calculated to increase the harmony and stability of the whole community, and to assist in the fulfilment and development of its sacred duties. They are convinced that union is strength'.[21] The schedule to the Act had outlined the role of this new synagogal organization:

> The objects of the institution to be called 'The United Synagogue' shall be the maintaining, erecting, founding, and carrying on, in London and its neighbourhood, places of worship for persons of the Jewish religion who conform to the Polish or German ritual, the providing means of burial of persons of the Jewish religion, the relief of poor persons of the Jewish religion, the contributing with other bodies to the maintenance of a Chief Rabbi and of other ecclesiastical persons, and to other communal duties devolving on Metropolitan congregations, and other charitable purposes in connection with the Jewish religion.[22]

As Lipman has noted, through the specific wording of the formula explaining that the new institution was 'for persons of the Jewish religion who conform to the Polish or German ritual', the founders of the United Synagogue ensured that

> no test was demanded [of worshippers] other than that the member should be Jewish and prepared to accept the orthodox ritual in its German or Polish form (i.e. Ashkenazi, not Sephardi).

Thus the degree of personal observance or commitment of individuals could vary widely but the institution – certainly as manifested in its form of worship – was to be orthodox. Hence the United Synagogue, the embodiment of mainstream Judaism in Britain by its numerical predominance in London and its example to the provincial communities, set a pattern.[23]

The creation of such an institution, in which the observance of specific religious practices by its members was not prescribed, would appear to be in keeping with the membership that the United Synagogue would serve. The emphasis on externals rather than more spiritual affairs, and the fact that synagogue membership was viewed more as a social than religious requirement, was demonstrated by the seating arrangements in the synagogues. The allocation of the most prestigious seats was made according to social status, moving away from the more traditional practice of according status to Jews qua Jewish learning rather than qua economic success.[24] Another example of the middle-class bias in services was the demand that men wear a 'high hat', an outward sign of respectability, in order to be permitted to be called to the Reading of the Law. Alderman has suggested that in its development of new congregations the United Synagogue focused its attention on

> erecting in north, west, and north-west London imposing ecclesiastical edifices in which the alumni of Jews' College could ply a uniquely English brand of Judaism, within a liturgical and organizational framework that had come to resemble the class distinctions then to be found in the Anglican Church.[25]

Within a decade another five congregations had joined the United Synagogue, bringing the number of synagogues affiliated to the union up to ten with over 2,500 male seat holders. Notwithstanding the concern to cater for middle-class Anglicized sensibilities, the United Synagogue's disinclination to prescribe strict adherence to religious practice from its members was also reflective of the community's interest in sustaining unity in Anglo-Jewry. The United Synagogue was intended to function as an umbrella organization in which all Jews who were prepared to identify as Orthodox, regardless of their practice, could be encompassed. The impetus for centralization demonstrated a concern to create mirrors of the Anglican Church in Anglo-Jewish institutions. Yet it also provided a means for unifying the community and thereby helped to preserve the religious identity of its members intact, despite the fact that they were a minority group interacting in a host society that espoused the values of an alternative religious system.

THE CHIEF RABBINATE

The influence of Anglican Church models and the concern to centralize authority and construct clear hierarchies were also important
aspects of the role of the Chief Rabbi, a position whose authority had
been considerably enhanced by the formation of the new synagogal
institution.[26] In the Deed of Foundation and Trust, the constitution of
the United Synagogue, the Chief Rabbi had been established as the
unfettered religious authority of the congregations joined under its
union. The official Act by which the United Synagogue was brought
into being had been altered in a number of clauses in order to gain the
approval of the charity commissioners.[27] The Deed of Foundation and
Trust was therefore specifically designed to remedy the exclusions that
had been made since 'it was declared that it was an essential part of
the Contract between the said Synagogues that the said provisions
should form part of the constitution of the said United Synagogue'.[28] It
stated that:

> The form of worship in each of the Constituent Synagogues,
> and all religious observances in the Constituent Synagogues,
> and all matters connected with the religious administration of
> the United Synagogue and of its subsidiary charities, shall,
> subject to the provision in the Scheme requiring such form of
> worship to be in accordance with Polish or German ritual, be
> under the supervision and control of the Chief Rabbi ...
>   In all cases in which religious duties are to be performed in
> connection with any office, other than that of a Chief Rabbi,
> the duties of which relate to the United Synagogue generally
> ... [and] specifically to a Constituent Synagogue, ... no person
> shall be approved of as a suitable candidate by the Board of
> Management of such Synagogue, unless the Chief Rabbi
> certify that he is a fit and proper person to perform the same.[29]

The incumbent in the office at the time of the United Synagogue's
formation was Nathan Marcus Adler, who had been elected to the post
of Chief Rabbi in 1845. Adler's appointment had been significant
in the history of the development of Anglo-Jewry, since it represented
the first time that delegates from more than one synagogue joined
together to choose a chief rabbi for the community. The evolution of
this office, which in some senses had its origins in the rabbinate of the
Great Synagogue, is to be viewed as another example of how Anglo-
Jewry's experience of toleration exerted a considerable influence on
the structure of the community. We have already noted how Anglo-
Jewry accorded little status to Jewish learning; the community had set

up no yeshivot from which there could have emerged a rabbi whose religious scholarship would have demanded the respect of the community, establishing him as their natural leader. At the same time, no religious leader was imposed on the community by the State, as a Crown Rabbi, whose authority would have been sustained by government statute.[30]

The earliest Ashkenazi settlers had acquired the services of a rabbi, Judah Loeb Cohen, around the time that they established their own synagogue in Duke's Place. As small congregations of Jews became established in provincial towns they were neither large enough nor sufficiently prosperous to secure their own rabbis, and since a number of Jews in these settlements retained their ties to the London community, they turned to the Rabbi of the Great Synagogue for the resolution of religious problems. Between 1704 and 1756 Aron Hart was rabbi of the Great, and it was in this period that there are records showing how the Portsmouth community turned to him to register their *shochetim* (ritual slaughterers) and license their marriages, as well as resolve any questions of ritual. He was succeeded by Hart Lyon who served from 1756 to 1764 and whose authority was also recognized by the Hambro', whose members contributed towards his salary. When the New Synagogue was founded during his tenure in 1761, it too accepted the overall religious leadership of the rabbi of the Great, seeking his approval before proceeding with the appointment of its own rabbi. Roth has pointed to the authority that the rabbi of the Great was able to exert over the three main London synagogues as a clear sign that his powers must also have extended to the lesser communities in the provinces. However this period of apparent harmony was short-lived, since Hart Lyon chose to take up a post in Halberstadt, and although the Great and Hambro' had resolved to cooperate in the appointment of his successor, the members of the two synagogues were unable to reach agreement on who should be chosen.

Subsequently, two rabbis entered Britain, each seeking to assert overall religious authority over the community. Roth has described how the dispute between these two rabbis was played out in the Portsmouth community, the most significant provincial congregation at that time. Ultimately the Portsmouth Jews acknowledged the authority of David Tevele Schiff, the rabbi of the Great, and in 1780 Israel Meshullam Zalman, the Hambro' rabbi, left England, frustrated at his inability to secure control. Roth asserts that this ensured that until his death in 1791 Schiff's authority 'was henceforth unchallenged … and he was able to transmit to his successors the unquestioned prestige that he himself enjoyed'.[31] However, when his successor came to be appointed, only the members of the Great participated in this election. Nonetheless, the authority of their appointee became firmly established. Solomon Hirschell, the son of Hart Lyon, was appointed in 1802, and in 1808 when his portrait was published he was described as 'The Rev. Solomon Hirschell, Chief Rabbi of the German and Polish Jews in England'.[32]

Hirschell remained in office for forty years until his death in 1842, and during that time he established the authority of the office so that its powers extended across the British Empire to congregations in Australia, New Zealand and South Africa.[33] The fact that his successor came to be elected by representatives from a number of provincial and London communities fully demonstrated the influence that the office had achieved during his tenure. An article in the *Voice of Jacob* at the time of Hirschell's death further attests to the status and role that the Chief Rabbinate had come to enjoy. It noted

> The provincial and colonial synagogues, scarcely one of which had, forty years since, a status in the Jewish world, have since grown into importance, and though independently minded enough sometimes, they have found reference and subordination indispensable in *shehita*, marriages, divorces, etc., etc., and hence, not from design or system, but from inevitable necessity, the late Rabbi was recognized as the spiritual head of most Jews claiming British origin.[34]

The Great Synagogue took the lead in associating together all those congregations who agreed to provide a nominal share of the upkeep for the office of Chief Rabbi. Subsequently, the new Chief Rabbi was the first to be elected to his office, by a Committee of Delegates representing five Ashkenazi London Synagogues (including the Western and Maiden Lane synagogues) as well as twenty-one provincial communities.[35] A United Synagogue report from 1871 confirmed these figures and noted the participation of an additional representative from one of the colonial communities. Focusing its attention on the financial obligations for the office of Chief Rabbi, that the newly formed United Synagogue had agreed to oversee, this report identified five additional provincial communities who had begun to contribute to the office in the interim. Demonstrating the growing extent of the Chief Rabbi's authority, whilst also highlighting the United Synagogue's abiding fixation on financial matters, it recorded that: 'There are no fewer than twenty-one Provincial and fifteen Colonial Congregations participating in the benefits of the Chief Rabbi's supervision who have never contributed to the Fund.'[36]

The decision to appoint Nathan Marcus Adler to the office of Chief Rabbi in 1845 provides a useful means of assessing the community he was to serve. The traits that Anglo-Jewry sought in their religious representative reflected the concerns of the community. Born in 1803, in Hanover, a subject of the British Crown, he had a doctorate from the University of Erlangen, in addition to being learned in Jewish studies.[37] Anglo-Jewry wanted a chief rabbi who could share a platform with representatives of the Church, suitably attuned to western culture and sufficiently educated in secular subjects to enhance their public image. At the same time, they gained a leader who would act to centralize the religious life of the community, further establishing the Chief Rabbinate as an office that was more or less equivalent to that of an archbishop. Following his appointment, Adler carried out a survey of all the communities supposedly under his religious leadership and used this material to assess the nature of the Anglo-Jewish community. In 1847, his response to the results of this survey were embodied in his *Laws and Regulations for all the Ashkenazi Synagogues in the British Empire*, a document that sought to centralize religious authority strictly within the office of Chief Rabbi. In addition to making the Chief Rabbi the sole religious authority of the community, it built on the authority that the office had gained from the Marriage Registration Act of 1836. This devolved authority for the registration of marriage secretaries for synagogues into the hands of the President of the Board of Deputies. The Board, in recognizing only the Sephardi *Haham* and the Chief Rabbi as the religious leaders authorized to provide it with guidance on religious matters that would enable it to determine whether to grant such certification, secured an authoritative voice for the Chief Rabbinate in this realm. In his *Laws and Regulations* Adler took this principle further by asserting that

> The erection of a new synagogue must have the sanction of the Chief Rabbi; and the formation of a new Congregation must have the sanction of the Chief Rabbi, besides that of the Board of Deputies.[38]

The officers of the Bet Din, the religious court of the Chief Rabbi, were explicitly relegated to the position of religious underlings subservient to him. Moreover, the appointment of new religious functionaries by any synagogue under his control also came under his supervision, an area of religious authority that would prove to be most significant in the history of the United Synagogue following that institution's decision to uphold this principle in its constitution. As Newman has noted, an appointment to a pulpit in Manchester was recorded by the *Voice of Jacob* to have been 'very properly made subject to his obtaining a letter of licence from the Revd. Dr. Adler'.[39] An advertisement for a chazzan (cantor) at the Hebrew Congregation of Dublin similarly stated: 'It will be indispensable that moral character and qualifications be certified by the Revd. The Chief Rabbi.'[40] In order to create suitably trained ministers for Anglo-Jewish congregations, Adler was also instrumental in establishing Jews' College in 1855. This was an educational institute that did not seek to produce traditionally trained rabbis; religious authority rested in the hands of Adler. Rather, it was designed to create English preachers who could oversee the daily pastoral needs of a community. Whilst clearly differing in origin from the models for Jewish religious leadership that existed on the Continent, the authority that the Chief Rabbi came to exercise over the Anglo-Jewish community was considerable. The willingness exhibited by both the United Synagogue and the Board of Deputies, in vouchsafing religious authority to the powerful Chief Rabbinate that Adler was establishing, demonstrated the concern of each of these institutions to impose unity in the Anglo-Jewish community through the practice of centralization. The emergence of umbrella organizations in Anglo-Jewry, that sought to be all-encompassing in their representation of the community, reflected the exigencies perceived by the leadership as essential to the survival of a minority religious community.[41]

THE IMPACT OF THE IMMIGRANTS

Analysing the nature of the office of Chief Rabbi in his book *Troubled Eden*, Chaim Bermant suggested that:

> In Eastern Europe there were Rabbis, like Elchanan Spector, who through their scholarship, piety, sagacity and force of character could establish their ascendancy over a whole region, and even beyond. Further West, Chief Rabbis were appointed by the Crown and therefore enjoyed the backing of the civil authority. In Britain, where the office had neither civil nor always spiritual authority, there were the Rothschilds.[42]

Whilst the more light-hearted element of this statement should not be overlooked, it does point to the power wielded over Anglo-Jewry by a small number of inter-related wealthy Jews, led by the Rothschilds, to whom Bermant gave the title 'the Cousinhood'. Lionel de Rothschild was the first Anglo-Jew to take up his seat in Parliament, in 1858, and four of the first five United Synagogue presidents were members of the Rothschild family. Newman has argued that during the presidencies of Sir Anthony and Nathaniel (later Lord) Rothschild '[d]espite their rank as Presidents, they were very much nominal figures, brought into the arena only when their immediate involvement was essential'.[43] Israel Finestein has insisted that the vice-presidency was 'a position which has often in the United Synagogue been the effective office of power'.[44] Nonetheless, he suggested that

> In the 1880s there opened what may fairly be described as the age of Lord Rothschild. He was president for 36 years until his death in 1915. It was an age marked by increasing deference inside the United Synagogue to its lay head. In its earlier phase, the age coincided with the high point of Victorian England.

However, whilst the period in which the United Synagogue entrenched its position might have represented the zenith of the Victorian Age, whose influence in the community was considerable, Alderman has identified it as 'the Indian summer of emancipated Anglo-Jewry'.[45]

Anglo-Jewry had evolved into a well-established community, highly organized and Anglicized. It had adapted to the temper of the host society with a number of different institutions designed to cater for the various religious, political and charitable needs of the community. Immigration from eastern Europe began to increase in the 1860s, a consequence of various natural and political disasters that befell the region in this period and a generally growing sense of financial insecurity. There was famine in Lithuania between 1866 and 1869, cholera in Poland in 1869 and 1870, a pogrom in Odessa in 1871 and the introduction of conscription in Russia in 1874.[46] However from the 1880s onwards there was an immigration revolution. Czar Alexander II was assassinated in March 1881, setting off a series of pogroms. These were followed by the May Laws, issued the following year, which imposed strict limitations on Jewish life in Russia, further restricting the livelihood and areas of settlement of Jews.[47] As a consequence of this immigration the makeup of the community was radically and irrevocably altered as a massive influx of immigrants arrived on British shores. The community into which these immigrants were absorbed was, in short, ill prepared for this predicament. Newman has argued that Anglo-Jewry was better equipped to cater for this immigration than the Jewish community in New York, where far greater numbers of immigrants arrived. Organizations were in place to help the immigrants and prevent 'fragmentation'. Nevertheless, the contrast between the attitudes of the established community and the newcomers, in social, religious, and economic terms, was to produce a conspicuous split in Anglo-Jewry, leading to the formation of distinct native and immigrant communities.

In 1880, the Anglo-Jewish population was estimated to number approximately 60,000, of whom 46,000 were resident in London. More than half this community was native born. By 1900 the London community had exploded to 135,000, of whom 120,000 were resident in the East End. An analysis of data from 1904 of weddings registered in Anglo-Jewish synagogues found that 71 per cent of the participants were immigrants.[48] By 1914 London Jewry had expanded further to 180,000 and Anglo-Jewry as a whole had grown to more than a quarter of a million, with provincial Jewry having grown from 20,000 to roughly 100,000.

Each community looked at the other with considerable horror. The native community was shocked by the foreignness of the immigrants and what they viewed as their uncivilised social and religious demeanour. The immigrants, for their part, could not comprehend the Jewish identity that the native community had evolved. The Anglicized religion they encountered appeared as utterly alien to their eyes as their practices appeared in the eyes of the native community. Alderman records that by 1870 there were already at least forty minor synagogues in London representing possibly as many as 10,000 people.[49] The phenomenon of the *chevrot* (guilds) was nonetheless to grow still further with the arrival of so many more immigrants. These *chevrot* were small prayer groups, often comprising of Jews from the same neighbourhoods in eastern Europe, which were established to provide a religious environment that maintained the religious norms to which Jews had been accustomed in eastern Europe.[50] They offered an alternative to praying in the cathedral-like synagogues belonging to the United Synagogue, where the emphasis on decorum, in particular, was alien to the immigrants' approach to prayer. The *chevrot* fostered an atmosphere that was more reminiscent of Jewish life in the shtetl than in a westernised Anglo-Jewish community. If the native community had been distressed by the appearance and manners of the immigrants, they were horrified by what they perceived as the wretched and unsanitary conditions in which these *chevrot* were established. They were concerned at the negative image that was being attached to Jews as a whole as a result of the practices of the immigrant section of Anglo-Jewry. Their response was to institute a programme of Anglicization to reduce the differences between the two communities.[51]

The methods of Anglicization focused primarily on the education of the children of the immigrants, in Jewish schools such as the Jewish Free School (JFS), originally founded in 1822, and others provided by the local councils. The inculcation of English mannerisms amongst the children was expected to exert an influence on the parents. In addition, adult English classes were provided without charge and a number of clubs and societies were created for both the children and adults. Through these groups the established leadership of the native community sought to impart different aspects of English culture and leisure activities, even including the introduction of the pleasures of cricket to the immigrants.[52] An interest in Anglicization was also evident among the immigrants themselves and the many Friendly Societies that they created served as additional vehicles of acculturation to English mores. However, although the lay leaders of the native community achieved some success in acculturating the immigrants to their new social surroundings, they encountered considerable difficulties in Anglicizing the religious attitudes of the immigrants. Lipman asserts that 'if it was a linguistic, social and cultural assimilation, it was not necessarily thereby a process of de-Judaization. The vital fact about this "anglicization" was that it was not "assimilation" in the religious sense.'[53]

In the religious sphere, the creation of the Federation of Minor Synagogues, later to become known simply as the Federation of Synagogues, represented an alternative method of Anglicization aimed at improving the conditions in which the immigrants prayed. A number of the smaller *chevrot* were amalgamated in more suitable buildings and through their federation they were able to secure services that each community could not have afforded individually, most notably cheaper provisions for burial, and representation on communal bodies. Unlike the model of the United Synagogue, each congregation retained a large measure of autonomy and there was no strict centralization of funds.[54]

Samuel Montagu was the driving force behind the creation of this new institution. Born in 1832 in Liverpool, he established himself as a banker in London and through his marriage to the sister of Lionel Louis Cohen became a member of the 'Cousinhood'.[55] However, in some ways he was an uneasy member of Anglo-Jewry's lay elite. A Liberal in politics, he was conscious of a sterility in the community's Jewish life and was attracted to the religious fervour of the *chevrot*. He sought to sustain certain aspects of this in the new institution that was founded in October 1887, by federating together sixteen *chevrot*. By the time of his death, in 1911, the Federation consisted of fifty-one London congregations, representing more than 6,000 male seat holders. Montagu was accused by some of having created the Federation in order to improve his own position amongst the lay leadership of Anglo-Jewry, setting himself up as a rival to Lord Rothschild and establishing the Federation as a schismatic movement. Alderman utterly rejects this view, recording how at the time of its foundation Rothschild was installed as president of the institution. Montagu also shared many of the aims of the Anglo-Jewish leadership to which he belonged. He was conscious of the need to Anglicize the immigrants, bringing them into the overall framework of the community and improving their places of worship and the *chedarim* (basic Jewish schools) attached to the *chevrot*. Lipman has stated that

The Federation of Synagogues provided a means of adjusting the *hebroth* to the physical standards required of Anglo-Jewish places of worship and associating the immigrants with the main religious institutions of the community, notably the Chief Rabbinate.[56]

In bringing the immigrants affiliated to the Federation under the overall umbrella of Anglo-Jewry, Montagu insisted that the authority of the Chief Rabbi be accepted in the organization. Its chief minister was expected to exercise his religious authority under the overall control of the Chief Rabbi and when Avigdor Chaikin was appointed to fill this role, Hermann Adler's approval was sought. The Federation also decreed that the examination of pupils in the *chedarim* under its supervision should be 'under the sanction of the Chief Rabbi'. The difference was that Montagu effected reform in the religious lives of the immigrants from within the world of the *chevrot*, without seeking to weaken the religious intensity that characterized their worship.

Notwithstanding the successes of Montagu and the Federation, there were some immigrant groups that remained outside the religious umbrella of the native community. They were concerned not only by the external Anglicization they observed in the practice of Judaism by Anglo-Jewry, but at the laxity that was permitted in this practice under the supervision of the Orthodox religious authorities. The focus fell specifically on the Chief Rabbi's superintendence of the provisions for kosher food, in particular, the practices surrounding the ritual slaughter of animals. Bernard Homa has examined the concerns of some elements of the immigrant community in his *A Fortress in Anglo-Jewry*, which records the activities of members of the 'Machzike Hadath Society', formed in 1891.[57] This society was created through an amalgamation of the Machzike Shomrei Shabbat in East London and members of the North London Beth Hamedrash in Canonbury, which was primarily a community of Jews of central European origin. Its title was associated with a grouping of Orthodox Jews in Galicia who in 1878, led by Simeon Sofer and Joshua Rokeach, established a society with this name to join Jews together to defend Orthodox practices and beliefs. As Homa has explicitly stated, it was created in England in order to provide an organization that would 'function as vigilantes within the Community'.[58] Their intention was not to create a separatist community but rather to improve conditions for religious observance throughout the Anglo-Jewish community.

> It was noted that many butchers openly desecrated the Sabbath; it was also discovered that it was possible to obtain unporged hindquarter meat as well as kidney suet. Both are Trefa and may not be eaten ... As for 'Petticoat Lane', the position there was also

most unsatisfactory. Jewish stall-holders in that famous street market sold allegedly kosher-killed poultry without any visible sign to indicate that Shechita had been performed … other breaches of the kashruth laws were soon discovered … Yet all these infringements were taking place ostensibly under the eyes of the Board for the Affairs of Shechita which, in turn, was under the religious control of the Beth Din …

The sole purpose for which the Machzike Hadath Society was established was to secure an improvement in the facilities for religious observance particularly in regard to kashruth, and every effort was made to achieve this objective by peacefully reminding the Chief Rabbinate of their responsibilities and duties in this direction.[59]

Alderman has suggested that it was no coincidence that the creation of the Machzike Hadath and their appointment of Rabbi Aba Werner as their leader coincided with Hermann Adler's confirmation in the office of Chief Rabbi as successor to his father.[60] Hermann had been educated in England before being sent back to Continental Europe to continue his studies and receive his rabbinical training. In 1862 he received his doctorate from the University of Leipzig and obtained *semikhah* (rabbinical ordination) from Solomon Judah Rapoport, the Chief Rabbi of Prague, the following year. In many ways he could be viewed as an archetype of the English Jew in the Victorian age, as he had acknowledged in his Installation sermon when he acceded to the post of Chief Rabbi:

I have grown up in your midst. I have endeavoured to draw my mental nurture from the rich stores of our dear England's thought and learning. In my paternal home, as a disciple and student, and subsequently, during a period of gradually increasing responsibilities, every detail has become familiar to me of the exalted office which I have been called, by the Providence of God and the voice of the community, to occupy.[61]

It was with this full awareness of the duties of his office and the ideals of the community that Adler, in this sermon, issued an appeal: 'Let not your divergence of opinion lead to schisms and divisions, to discord and disruption.'[62] The inherent temperament of the native community, to maintain an image of unity, was well known to Adler and it was a principle that he sought to uphold whilst Chief Rabbi. Like his father he viewed himself as the sole religious authority of the community, regardless of the other prominent rabbinical leaders that had arrived in the country with the immigrant influx. This perhaps explained Alderman's suggestion that:

No one, in truth, had suffered more from the immigrant presence than Hermann Adler himself. For if it was true that the immigrants posed a challenge to the English way of life, it was even truer that, by their very presence, they constituted an affront to the Adlerian way of Judaism, and an assault upon the acculturative tendencies promoted so vigorously by those who felt themselves privileged to lead the community in the post-emancipation era.[63]

Hermann Adler's refusal to implement the more stringent supervision sought by the Machzike Hadath over *shechitah* (ritual slaughter) and the provision of kosher meat led Werner to authorise the creation of an independent body that supplied its own butcher shops. The Anglo-Jewish authorities were incensed by such a display of disunity that undermined the Chief Rabbi's authority and raised questions about his religious competence. It also undercut an important source of revenue. They responded by issuing a statement declaring that the meat sold by the Machzike Hadath was not kosher. The two sides, as Homa noted, subsequently became engaged in 'open warfare' in a dispute that continued for some fourteen years. It was not finally resolved until the Machzike Hadath agreed to bring all the facets of its *shechitah* organization under the overall authority of the Chief Rabbinate and the Board of Shechitah, whilst the leaders of the native community were forced to allow the Machzike Hadath to retain religious control and overall supervision of their activities.[64]

When this resolution was reached there remained a section of the Machzike Hadath who were unwilling to accept this conclusion. The members of the North London Beth Hamedrash were perturbed by the decision to recognize the authority of the Chief Rabbi. The fact that these members had come from the *Austrittsgemeinde* (separatist communities) of central Europe rather than from eastern Europe, as will become more evident below, was of considerable significance; they were more positively inclined to the benefits of secession rather than inclusion.[65] However they were in a minority and the agreement was therefore able to go ahead. The re-imposition of some degree of unity across the native and immigrant communities had been achieved.

In truth, the native community's concerns about the negative image of Jews created by the immigrant influx were not unfounded. Agitation against the perceived problems caused by the arrival of such large numbers of immigrants fostered an attitude of anti-alienism in the public imagination. Initially, attention was focused on the influence that the immigrants were perceived to have exerted on the job market, allowing 'sweating' conditions to emerge. Investigations into these allegations by various parliamentary committees found little substance to these claims, noting that sweating also emerged in trades in which immigrants did not figure prominently. As the 1890s progressed and the century turned, the focus of anti-alienism shifted to complaints related to housing issues. The immigrants were accused of causing rents to increase, overcrowding and unsanitary conditions. By March 1902, a Royal Commission was appointed to examine the alien question and their report was submitted in August 1903. Whilst it was agreed that a total prohibition on alien immigration was unnecessary, the report suggested that certain restrictions should be introduced in order to regulate the arrival of immigrants more carefully. The report advocated the advantages of preventing the entry of immigrants deemed to be 'undesirable', either as a result of their propensity to crime or their inability to provide for themselves, which could be expected to result in them becoming a welfare burden. An Aliens Bill followed in 1904, legislating the suggested reforms, and although this was delayed and slightly altered, it was passed in August 1905. Its impact was immediate; Lipman estimated that in the years 1906–14 an average of between 4,000–5,000 Jewish immigrants settled in Britain each year, a figure which represented about half the number of immigrants who came to Britain in the peak year of 1905 and about two-thirds of the annual average in the years 1891–1904.[66]

The outbreak of the First World War brought immigration to a complete halt. Consequently, the community became more settled in this period; the reduction in subsequent immigration enabled it to adjust to its circumstances without being continually strengthened in its eastern European identity by the arrival of more immigrants. It was noted above that in 1904, 74 per cent of marriage partners were immigrants, yet by 1934, 82 per cent were found to be native born.[67] Lipman has stated that

> From 1905 onwards immigration, though it did not cease altogether, was thus a restricted flow compared with the immigration of the previous quarter of a century. The task now was not so much the welcoming of new immigrants, but the absorption of the immigrants and their children and the building up of an integrated Anglo-Jewish community.[68]

In 1913, when a new chief rabbi was being elected for the community, the transformation which Anglo-Jewry had experienced over the preceding thirty years and the divisions that had been created were not remedied, but the Anglicization process to which the immigrants had been subject had begun to exert its influence. The opportunity now presented itself to create an Anglo-Jewry in which its constituent elements were brought together and preparations for the future could be implemented.

2

Joseph H. Hertz: The Formative Years

Joseph Herman Hertz acceded to the office of Chief Rabbi in 1913, aged 40. Born in 1872, in Rebrin, a small village in the Austro-Hungarian Empire, now part of Slovakia, Hertz and his family left the European Continent for the United States in 1884.[1] His upbringing exposed Hertz to a world in which Orthodox Judaism avoided the strictness often associated with Hungarian Jewry. His father, a religious teacher, scribe and Hebrew poet, who published a collection of his poems in 1881, entitled *Avnei Shoham*, had studied in Eisenstadt at the modernized yeshiva established there by Esriel Hildesheimer[2] from whom he received his *semikhah*.[3] This yeshiva, somewhat radically for its time, included the study of secular subjects in its curriculum, to the disappointment of many in the Orthodox Hungarian rabbinate. This blending of Orthodox and modern thinking influenced Simon Hertz and was in turn to influence his son. As an obituary of Simon Hertz noted, '[h]is character was marked by deep piety, while he was distinguished for his wide interests in matters literary and scientific'.[4] It is unclear whether the rigidity of the Orthodox Judaism to be experienced in Hungary was a factor in his decision to move his family to New York. An important consideration was their experience of antisemitism there and the presence of relatives in New York who urged them to come.[5] In the United States, he worked as a *melamed* (teacher of elementary Torah) on the Lower East Side and oversaw the Jewish education of each of his three sons, of whom Joseph was the second. Economic concerns probably influenced his preference that none of his sons should become rabbis. His oldest son became a lawyer, the third son was a dentist, and he had hoped that Joseph would become an engineer.[6] However, following his education at public school and New York's City College, Joseph H. Hertz chose to further his Jewish education at the newly founded Jewish Theological Seminary (JTS). He was a member of the very first class trained at the JTS and in 1894 was to become its first rabbinical graduate.

The background to the formation of the JTS is to be detected in the Pittsburgh Platform that was set out at the Pittsburgh Conference in 1885.[7] American Jewry, in the early decades of the nineteenth century, sought to sustain a religious unity across the differing theological emphases expressed by its different communities. The Hebrew Union College (HUC) had been created in 1875, to train ministers for all the different American Jewish congregations. An interest in maintaining unity was sustained, despite the growing radicalisation of Reform theology, up until the Pittsburgh Conference. Isaac Mayer Wise, head of the HUC, had been chairman of the conference and although he argued that the curriculum of the College was not influenced by the Pittsburgh Platforms, his defence of the Conference's principles finally persuaded a number of Sephardi and central European Jews, who had come to form part of the native community of American Jewry, that the rabbinic training of their rabbis should not be allowed to remain in his hands. The JTS, or Jewish Theological Seminary Association as it had originally been constituted, was therefore established in 1887, as an alternative, more traditionalist, training institution. Sabato Morais, a Sephardi Jew, was the inspirational figure behind the foundation of this Seminary and his motives for establishing such an institution were explained by Hertz, who had been one of his students:

> All around him were rabbis who were fanatically advocating the tearing up of Jewish life by the roots; endeavouring to banish the Sabbath, the Hebrew language, and the Sefer Torah itself from the Synagogue. To such revolution in religion, Sabato Morais was the life-long and inveterate foe, as persistent and as unyielding as the rocks; proclaiming that the precepts of the Torah were high above the peradventure of inclination, the whim of the demagogue, or the fashion of the hour.[8]

Concern at the overwhelming success of Reform Judaism in America compelled Morais, along with others who were quick to join the cause, to seek a means for defending the traditional teachings and practices of Judaism.[9] In 1886, when the Charter for the Seminary was granted, the perceived role of the institute was clearly stated:

> The purposes of this Association being the preservation in America of the knowledge and practice of historical Judaism, as ordained in the Law of Moses and expounded by the prophets and Sages of Israel in Biblical and Talmudical writings.[10]

It is important to understand that, notwithstanding its traditionalist agenda, the JTS had not been created with the intention of simply becoming an American yeshiva. The perception appears to have been that those who would seek to be defenders of Traditional Judaism in America, champions for Orthodoxy fighting to undermine the validity of Reform Judaism in their country, would require a rather more rounded education and more worldly outlook on modernity than could be provided in the yeshiva world. In its effort to produce Jewish leaders who could defend Judaism in its modern American setting, the JTS insisted that its students pursue a secular university training in addition to their Jewish education. From 1891 this was facilitated through an affiliation with Columbia University. Nonetheless, the traditionalism of the institution was attested to in the writings of Hertz as he described the goals Morais set for his students and the inspiration he provided them as he sought to prepare them for their battle in defence of Traditional Judaism in the US.

> To the students of the Seminary, he [Morais] was a hero who had consecrated his days to a heroic battle for a holy and heroic cause. We were thrilled by the clear, clarion notes of his call to the Wars of the Lord; by his passionate and loyal stand that the Divine law was imperative, unchangeable, eternal. He made rigorous demands upon him who would come forward as defender of the Judaism of our Fathers – piety and scholarship, consistency and the courage to stand alone, if need be, in the fight against unrighteousness and un-Judaism.[11]

The fact that, under the leadership of Morais, the JTS had been designed as an institution that could defend Traditional Judaism was further confirmed by his attempt to name this new educational institute 'The Orthodox Seminary', a title which pointed to both his own theological position and his aspirations for the establishment. He had been dissuaded from adopting this title by Alexander Kohut, another important figure in the foundation of the Seminary, whose theology was closer to what would become known as the Conservative position.[12] The disagreement over the title of the Seminary pointed to a greater struggle that would fester in the institution for several years as the more Orthodox and more Conservative factions within the JTS fought for supremacy. Both sides were keen to defend a more traditionalist Jewish alternative to the HUC and the congregations served by its rabbis, but they did not always agree on how traditionalist their interpretation should be. Although it was agreed that the JTS should not be named the Orthodox Seminary, as long as Morais remained in charge he ensured that its theological position was Orthodox and not Conservative. Even after his death, in November 1897, it was the Orthodox faction of the JTS that remained in control as their position was defended by Henry Pereira Mendes, who was acting president, Bernard Drachman, Dean of the Seminary since 1889, and Joseph Blumenthal, president of the institute's board of trustees.[13]

With the leadership positions in the hands of these men, each firmly located in the Orthodox camp, the JTS took the lead in creating a union with other Orthodox groups in America establishing an alliance with the growing eastern European immigrant Jewish community. This coalition, by uniting the religious factions of both East and West European Jewry in America, could hope forcefully to defend Orthodox Judaism against the Reform movement. It was a union that was made possible by the theological position of the JTS at that time since '[t]he Orthodox willingly accepted the leadership of such known traditionalists as Mendes and Drachman ... Organizationally, Orthodoxy had everything to gain, and ideologically it had nothing to fear.'[14]

The Orthodox Jewish Congregational Union of America was officially formed in June 1898 by thirteen committee members, of whom eleven hailed from the JTS, including Hertz. However, by 1902 a split had emerged within the Orthodox Union, between the eastern European Jews and the supporters of the Seminary, as the numerical dominance of the former group led the Union to embrace their attitudes. Differences regarding the use of Yiddish, the place of decorum in a synagogue, and the disposition towards integration by Orthodox Jews in the surrounding non-Jewish culture all became insurmountable obstacles to unity. The constituency of the JTS began to flounder; the Orthodox direction of the leading members of the faculty came to be viewed as untenable as American Orthodoxy came to be dominated by eastern rather than central European attitudes. The death, in 1901, of Joseph Blumenthal had already further weakened the Orthodox position in the JTS, and the failure to secure a laity for the Seminary, through union with the East-Europeans, strengthened the hand of those who wished to move the institution in a different theological direction. The search for a long-term replacement for Sabato Morais, someone other than Henry Pereira Mendes, now became more urgent. Those who questioned the theological position of Mendes and Drachman 'sought a scholar to be the natural leader of the *entire* Historical School, a man who would unite all its factions rather than embrace its traditionalist side'.[15]

It was against this background that Solomon Schechter was brought to the Seminary from Cambridge, England. Furthermore, his presidency of the institution had been laid down as a condition of the financial support which the Seminary was to receive from Reform sources that intervened to offer their help to revitalise the JTS. Leading members of Temple Emanu-El were conscious of the fact that their form of Judaism could not appeal to the immigrants, yet they wished to Americanize them and wean them away from their eastern European practice of Judaism.[16] They came to believe that the best method for achieving this was through the strengthening of a Conservative Judaism that could provide the immigrants with a halfway house in the Americanization of their religiosity. Thus, under the leadership of Schechter, Conservative Judaism emerged as a fully-fledged movement, on the theological left of Orthodoxy and to the right of Reform, centred around the JTS, which provided its theological focus. Both Mendes and Drachman came to sever their ties with the Seminary as its theology clearly drifted in a new direction.

Joseph Herman Hertz was educated at the JTS whilst it was still dominated by the traditionalists. Both he and his older brother, Emanuel, joined six other students when classes began at the Seminary in January 1887. The reasons behind Hertz's choice of this new seminary for his rabbinic training are unclear. It may be relevant that amongst the Seminary's founders and faculty there were a number of Hungarian rabbis: Moses Maisner, Gustave Lieberman, Alexander Kohut and Aaron Wise. As Wise was a contemporary of Hertz's father at the Eisenstadt yeshiva it is possible that, despite his preference for his son to avoid the rabbinate as a career, it was Simon Hertz who identified the JTS as an appropriate rabbinical training ground for Joseph. Regardless however of the motivations that led him to the JTS, in his later ministerial activities it becomes apparent how Hertz was inspired by his teacher Morais' call to fight the 'Wars of the Lord'. The institution's goal in those earlier years, of defending a Judaism that was steadfast to its Torah whilst remaining tenable in a modern society like the United States, was wholeheartedly adopted by Hertz. In 1894, receiving his doctorate from Columbia University, in addition to his ordination from the Seminary, Hertz became the first JTS trained rabbi.[17]

Although the JTS at that time had perceived a need for secularly-educated traditionalist rabbis, there were, as yet, few congregations to whom such rabbis could minister. Hertz went straight to an appointment at the Adath Jeschurun Congregation in Syracuse, New York State, but he was only to stay there for four years before leaving not only Syracuse, but also the US itself, for the African continent. The Syracuse congregation had been created in 1870, and by 1878 they had built their own synagogue. This had been constructed with a separate ladies' balcony to facilitate separation of the sexes during services, as was required in Orthodox Judaism, and also contained a *mikveh* – ritual bath – in the basement. Before Hertz's appointment to its pulpit the community had been served by a *chazzan* and a *shammes* (beadle). They had decided to appoint themselves a rabbi 'not so much for the usual duties of an Orthodox rabbi (as guardian and interpreter of Jewish law), but to have a lecturer, a preacher of sermons in English'.[18] Their assumption appears to have been that an English-preaching rabbi would not be rigorously Orthodox, for the community were veering away from some traditional practices. The ladies balcony had been made redundant shortly before Hertz arrived in Syracuse, when mixed seating in pews was introduced.[19] Bernard Drachman, one of Hertz's teachers at the JTS who had accompanied him to his installation service, had identified mixed seating as one of those practices that no rabbi who was a 'sincere adherent of Traditional Judaism' could concede.[20] Consequently, Hertz's ministry to this community appeared to be compromised from the outset; their new rabbi's traditionalist interpretation of Jewish law did not correspond with that of the community. He found himself in an awkward position and it could be argued that it was his training at the Jewish Theological Seminary that had created this problem.

The JTS had aimed at, and succeeded in, producing a rabbi in whom the beliefs and practices of traditional Judaism were combined with a secular education and an open mind to the modern world. However, it was the eastern European immigrants who had established the greatest number of Orthodox synagogues that could offer traditionalist rabbis a pulpit in America. These communities invariably sought a Yiddish-speaking *rav* traditionally trained in the old school. To these communities Hertz's rabbinical training would have been suspect.[21] On the other hand, there were only a small number of communities which sought an English-speaking preacher who had been trained in a more Orthodox environment than the Hebrew Union College and they still did not expect to encounter a staunch defender of traditional Judaism.[22] Hertz's training at the JTS had produced a leader with no viable role in either of these communities; yet these were the two types of communities that dominated the synagogal scene to be found to the religious right of Reform. The Jewish Theological Seminary, as neither a reformist institution nor a traditional yeshiva in its eastern European sense, had sought to train American rabbis who fitted somewhere between these two religious poles. This had been viewed as the necessary and expedient ideal in the religious circumstances to be encountered in the American Jewish scene. Hertz's early rabbinic experiences brought this logic into question, perhaps demonstrating the pertinence of the eventual shifting of theology that occurred in the JTS.

Hertz's decision to leave both Syracuse and America might have been influenced by the realization that this was the only tenable option open to him if he wished to maintain his Orthodoxy whilst ministering to a community. The Witwatersrand Old Hebrew Congregation in Johannesburg, South Africa presented him with an altogether different environment.

A Jewish presence was to be found in Johannesburg from the time that the city began to be developed in 1886, as Jews joined many other fortune-seekers attracted to the local goldfields. Formal services were held for the High Holidays that year and by 1887, the Jewish population in the city was estimated at one hundred individuals organized around the Witwatersrand Goldfields Jewish Association. In November 1887, the members of this Association had agreed to collect funds to build the community's first synagogue – the Witwatersrand Hebrew Congregation. By the time Hertz arrived in the city, in September 1898, there were three established Orthodox synagogues. The original synagogue, to which Hertz was to minister, had re-named itself the Witwatersrand Old Hebrew Congregation, to designate its seniority following a secession in 1891 which had led to the creation of the Johannesburg Hebrew Congregation. In addition, 1893 had seen the establishment of the Johannesburg Orthodox Hebrew Congregation, created by eastern European immigrants who looked upon the other two synagogues in much the same disparaging way that the eastern European immigrants in London viewed the synagogal institutions of the United Synagogue. An estimate of the Jewish population of Johannesburg in 1899, the year after Hertz commenced his ministry, calculated that there were 10,000–12,000 Jews in the city.[23] Whilst the earliest settlers had been of mostly English or German origin, the community had grown considerably through the immigration of eastern European Jews, mostly of Lithuanian origin. In a study of the Transvaal community at the end of the nineteenth century Dora Sowden noted:

> The English and German Jews, the first to come, took the lead in forming congregational and communal associations and for many years made their presence felt as the dominating social element. It was an ascendancy they lost after the South African War ...
>
> ... the *Chevra Kadisha* [burial society] reflected something of the character of the Jewish community as a whole. Like most of the early organisations, it was started by the 'aristocratic' elements, the English and German Jews who were used to western decorum and were conscious of social superiority. With the influx of east European Jews, causes of friction arose both as to personnel and procedure. The newcomers cared nothing for 'manners'. They accused the powers in command of dictatorship.[24]

Significantly, Sowden argues that the growing unity, which was to emerge in the Johannesburg Jewish community, was greatly influenced by the arrival of Hertz.

> As the century neared its close, an increasing cohesiveness could be observed within the Jewish community ... Two men who had a notable effect in promoting this increased cohesiveness of the

Jewish community were the Rev. J.H. Hertz and the Rev. David
Wasserzug. Dr Hertz ... spent some years in South Africa at a
very critical time ... he achieved two things: he became the
virtual head of all the congregations and he took the lead as
spokesman for the community. His dynamic personality and
forceful oratory were an educating and stimulating force to the
community at large.[25]

It is clearly inferred that Hertz was a natural leader. However, his
leadership and oratory were to lead to his expulsion from South Africa
during the Anglo-Boer War. The President, Paul Kruger, expelled him
in 1899 for his outspoken views on the civil disabilities imposed by the
Boers on Jews and Catholics – part of the so-called *uitlanders*.[26] In both
the first and second stages of his ministry in South Africa, he publicly
demonstrated his belief that religion need not be separated from
politics. His political activities in this period helped illustrate his
conviction that Jewish religious life could be engaged in all spheres,
including modern, secular life. Hertz here confirmed his qualities as
an obvious leader who would not shy away from conflict, even when
that conflict could have been viewed as outside his remit as a communal rabbi. He did not confine his role to supervision of the religious
life of his particular community. Rather, particularly through his
forceful preaching, he appealed to a larger audience both within the
Jewish community and outside of it to a non-Jewish audience.

Although expelled by the Boers, Hertz was able to return to
Johannesburg in 1901 when it came under British rule and it was
during this second, more prolonged, period in the city that he
succeeded in exerting a most important influence on Jewish life in the
Transvaal. He became involved in a number of activities that were to
remain of importance in his ministries. The two key areas were
community organization and religious education. He created a Jewish
orphanage in South Africa and, demonstrating his prioritization of
Jewish education, founded the first Talmud Torah school. Moreover,
from 1906 to 1908 he was professor of Philosophy at the Transvaal
University College. Perhaps more significantly still, it is Hertz who
was credited with providing the impetus for the creation of a Board of
Deputies for Transvaal, which he hoped would help further unify the
community.

The creation of such a representative and unified body could not
hope to enjoy whole-hearted support from the divided community
that was to be found in Johannesburg at the time. Hertz fought to
counter the opposition which the formation of the Board faced; he
argued that communal unity, between the westernised and eastern
European populations of the area, was an ideal which should be

championed since, if it were effected, it would undoubtedly enhance communal representation.

The Zionists were vigorous opponents of the creation of a Board of Deputies, fearing that non-Zionists might obtain power through such a board. They tried to argue that the Zionist Federation, which was already in place, provided perfectly adequate communal representation. Hertz, despite his role as vice-president of the Zionist Federation of Johannesburg, argued that, notwithstanding the many communal functions the Zionist Federation did perform, it was insufficient; it could never be fully representative of the Jewish community as long as members who could not accept Zionist principles remained.[27] Hertz had no intention of undermining the role of the Zionists. He was always to remain a great supporter of Zionism. Furthermore, the Zionist Federation had itself been instrumental in beginning the move towards greater unity in the divided Johannesburg community:

> Both Hertz and Wasserzug helped to stimulate the movement … The formation of Zionist committees perhaps more than anything showed how the forces of unification had been working to integrate the various immigrant groups into the fabric of a community.[28]

Nonetheless, it was Hertz's contention that full representation was required if the Johannesburg community wished to truly mend the divisions which it experienced across social and religious lines. In addition to his attempts to cajole the Zionists into supporting the Board, Hertz also endeavoured to win over the support of the eastern European immigrants. His main address at the communal meeting convened in April 1903 was followed with a speech in Yiddish, through which he ensured that the immigrants fully understood the proposal.[29] Although the resultant Board of Deputies of the Transvaal and Natal experienced difficulties in its earlier years of existence, by 1911 the Board was able to assert that 'the whole of Johannesburg and the West Rand are now fully represented'.[30]

By the time Hertz left South Africa, he had therefore ensured that the mechanisms were in place for the creation of communal harmony. In 1912 a national South African Board of Deputies was formed, uniting all the Jewish communities of South Africa under one common representative body. His experiences of this community, divided between a West-European establishment and an East-European majority, would be of considerable importance when he came to minister to the communities of Anglo-Jewish Orthodoxy. Indeed, his success in creating this improved communal harmony in South Africa provided a stepping stone to his attainment of the post of the British Chief Rabbinate.

Notwithstanding his interest and involvement in South African life, Hertz did begin to look further afield for new ministerial appointments.[31] In 1906, his interest in the religious life of the United Synagogue in London was already demonstrated when he applied for the newly vacant post at the New West End Synagogue. This attempt to move to London failed, yet his perception that a London pulpit could be suitable is notable since, following his experiences in Syracuse, Hertz would have realized that his future rabbinical appointments required more careful consideration.[32] As Hertz's interest in London amounted to nothing at this juncture, he began to examine other opportunities. In 1911, despite the earlier reservations he might have entertained about ministering to an American congregation, he was ready to leave Johannesburg and was persuaded to return to New York to take up the ministry of the Orach Chayyim Synagogue.

The very first clause of the constitution of the Congregation Orach Chayyim stipulates that '*Davening* must follow the *minhag* [custom] of the Frankfurt Shul'. This reference relates to the custom of religious worship established by Samson Raphael Hirsch in the *Israelitische Religionsgesellschaft* synagogue in Frankfurt, where he served as Rabbi from 1851.[33] The Orach Chayim's mention of this *minhag* indicated its support of a modernist approach to traditional Judaism, along the lines of the Orthodoxy promoted by Hirsch in Germany. In the light of his rabbinical training, some understanding of Hertz's theological position has been gained and parallels may certainly be drawn here between his theology and the theological programme developed in the Frankfurt shul. The move to a synagogue which advocated a Hirschian approach to Judaism may have reflected his realization that this was the theology closest to his own. It was congregations with this Frankfurt *minhag* which, differing from the other two prototypes of non-Reform synagogues, may have provided a platform for Orthodox thinkers like Hertz.

3

The Anglo-Jewish Establishment and the Office of the Chief Rabbinate

Only four months after his appointment to the ministry of New York's Orach Chayyim Synagogue in January 1912, Hertz travelled to England for a three-month visit during which time he preached at various London and provincial synagogues. As he later explained, some English friends had persuaded him to stop off in London, on his journey from Johannesburg to New York, to consider an application for the vacant Chief Rabbinate.[1] At that time he met with Lord Rothschild, president of the United Synagogue, and Lord Swaythling, president of the Federation, for talks which led to a formal invitation for him to return to England for a preaching tour, which would enable his candidacy to be better assessed. Upon his arrival in England a centre-page spread in the *Jewish Chronicle*, coinciding with the second convening of the Chief Rabbinate Conference, carried a prominent picture of him noting the seriousness of his candidacy for the 'Chief Rabbinate of the United Hebrew Congregations of the British Empire'.[2] Regardless, therefore, of the apparent theological compatibility between Hertz and the Orach Chayyim congregation in New York, the British Chief Rabbinate, for which he was being courted by the Anglo-Jewish establishment, held out an appeal to him which he countenanced even as he was preparing to assume his new position in the United States.

Prima facie, the Anglo-Jewish establishment's choice of a new chief rabbi could have been expected to focus upon the need to unify the two disparate, native and immigrant elements that made up the Anglo-Jewish community in 1913. Certainly, concern for communal unity had been part and parcel of Anglo-Jewish history for many years. As Cecil Roth has noted: '[o]ne fault for which Anglo-Jewry cannot be reproached is a lack of appreciation of the unity and inter-responsibility of Jewry: the principle that "all Israel are brethren"'.[3] The reaction to the emergence of the West London Synagogue of British Jews in 1842 demonstrated the existence of this inherent temperament in the community to avoid disunity, encouraged by Anglo-Jewry's status as a voluntary community and its sense of kinsmanship. Serious religious schism between the seceding reformers and the established communities, both Ashkenazi and Sephardi, was avoided. It remains a matter of dispute whether a formal *cherem* – edict of religious excommunication – was issued against the members of the West London Synagogue; in any case, the ban was rescinded within seven years.[4] Of greater relevance was the manner in which relationships remained intact between members of the Reform synagogue and the established communities throughout even this short period, not least since there were a number of family ties across the two groups.[5] A still more significant demonstration of the community's instinct to avoid schism occurred just three years later when the lay leaders of Anglo-Jewish Orthodoxy came to appoint a new chief rabbi in 1845, following the death of Solomon Hirschell. During their deliberations they removed the authority to issue a *cherem* from the powers of the Chief Rabbi. With the aid of hindsight, the Anglo-Jewish authorities came to decide that they did not wish to retain this powerful tool of schism in the armoury of their chief rabbis. During the election debates of 1912 Lord Rothschild reiterated this point, asserting, at the first Chief Rabbinate Conference, that the decision to prevent a chief rabbi from having the tool of the *cherem* at his disposal was a most important principle. The office of Chief Rabbi was to be viewed as a unifying force, not a potential cause of communal division.

It is, however, too simplistic to extend the principles of Jewish fellowship that helped the native community sustain unity in the 1840s to the more complex interest in preserving unity in an Anglo-Jewry expanded by the large immigrant population. The decision by the Anglo-Jewish establishment, in 1913, to appoint a chief rabbi who might sustain the viability of that office by continuing to provide the community with its representative voice was influenced by more practical considerations. As we have already seen, the influences of the Victorian age represent one cogent factor in the development of the Anglo-Jewish community and one that is not to be underestimated. The creation of hierarchical structures for the community, along similar lines to those found in the Church of England, fostered the inclination to create a religious leader for British Jewry who could in some ways be comparable to the Archbishop of Canterbury. Roth has noted that the Anglo-Jewish experience of emancipation was

> in accordance with the English genius of building up a doctrine from practical details, as opposed to the continental fashion of imposing a general principle without working out its implications.[6]

Anglo-Jewry experienced a *de facto* emancipation before this was recognized *de jure*, in contrast to what had occurred, for example, in France in the 1791 Decree of the National Assembly, whereby the Jews of France were offered full emancipation in one stroke. This absence of an emancipation based on principles inscribed in law heightened the community's eagerness to demonstrate their worthiness for the emancipation they nonetheless were able to enjoy in practice in their socio-economic activities. Engaging in the host society, whilst seeking to maintain their religious identity intact, members of the Anglo-Jewish community were keen to establish their credentials as English gentlemen and women whose religious differences presented no barrier to engagement and interaction with members of the host society. It was in endeavouring to demonstrate this suitability that they looked around them for models of true Englishness and identified the Church of England as a suitable paradigm. As Michael Goulston has, persuasively, argued in his study of the development of the Anglo-Jewish rabbinate, for Anglo-Jewry:

> The image of the English gentleman, the bourgeois ethic, and the hierarchical nature of institutions, including the church, were all factors with which the Jew, wishing to be English, had to reckon … Casting around for behaviour patterns and institutional models, they found the established Church of England an adequate example. The vertical and centralized authority structure of the community, from Parliament to the Board of Deputies and through them to the Jewish ecclesiastical authorities, bears a strong resemblance to the English ecclesiastical structure …
>
> The United Synagogue as 'the church', the rabbinate as the 'clergy' and, by implication if not writ, the Chief Rabbi as someone akin to an Archbishop, may have produced an acceptable image to the outside world.[7]

Significantly, Anglo-Jewry did not experience numerous conversions to the Church of England from its upper classes. Jews remained adherents of their religion. Instead of converting they simply adapted the structures of their religious institutions. They endeavoured to make them appear more presentable, more English, and in that way justify both their sustained Jewishness and demonstrate their worthiness as Englishmen. Stephen Sharot has explained that:

> the upper-class Jew's acculturation to the life-style of the 'gentleman', which was an essential prerequisite for membership in the English upper class, did not involve accepting the religious beliefs or imitating the religious practices of the Church of England. In the sphere of religion the English upper class was tolerant and pluralistic … There was Jewish acculturation in the religious sphere, but it was only in the form, as opposed to the content.[8]

The transformation of the Anglo-Jewish rabbinate into mirrors of the Anglican pastor demonstrates one adaptation that occurred in Anglo-Jewry. The role of the Anglo-Jewish rabbinate did not correspond to that of the traditional rabbi. English-trained rabbinical students did not earn the title of rabbi; they were ministers, trained to preach rather than engage in religious decision-making. As A.H. Jessel was reported to have noted at a United Synagogue council meeting, United Synagogue ministers had no need of rabbinical diplomas since they were not called upon by their congregants to answer questions of Jewish law.[9] Indeed A.A. Green, Minister of Hampstead Synagogue, had admitted in an interview with the *Jewish Chronicle* that there was only one occasion when he had been asked to exercise a traditional rabbinical function and provide a halakhic ruling (according to Jewish law) regarding the *kashrut* of a fowl brought to him. As he recalled, he had declared the animal *trefa* (unfit according to Jewish law); the congregant then decided to present it to the Bet Din for their halakhic ruling and they promptly declared it kosher.[10]

Such an emasculation of the role of the Anglo-Jewish rabbi ensured that power in religious matters was more firmly focused in the hands of the Chief Rabbi. He was the only minister designated by the title of rabbi and religious decisions affecting each of the synagogues under his control were his sole prerogative. In 1897 a furore was created in Anglo-Jewry when Hermann Gollancz, minister of the Bayswater Synagogue (1892–1923), went to Galicia to receive rabbinical ordination.[11] Upon his return to England he argued for his right to be known by the title of rabbi. Hermann Adler, Chief Rabbi at the time, opposed this. As Geoffrey Alderman has explained:

> In eastern Europe every Jewish community had its own rabbi. Hermann Adler regarded the whole of the British Empire as one community, presided over by one rabbi – namely himself.[12]

This attitude also extended to the officers of the Bet Din, whose role it was to superintend halakhic decision-making on a day-to-day basis. Although the Bet Din was also under the overall control of the Chief Rabbi, it was served by dayanim who, as a result of their greater religious learning, might have been expected to enjoy greater authority in religious matters than United Synagogue ministers, such as A.A. Green. However, the official English title ascribed to a dayan was 'Ecclesiastical Assessor to the Chief Rabbi', amply demonstrating their inferior relationship to the Chief Rabbi and further reinforcing his supreme authority in the religious sphere.

The British Parliament's Marriage Registration Act of 1836 had already inadvertently enhanced the authority of the Chief Rabbi as the religious leader and representative of the Anglo-Jewish community. During the two Adler Chief Rabbinates this designation of their role, as the religious authority for the community, was taken to heart. As has already been noted, shortly after assuming his post in 1845, Nathan Marcus Adler carried out a survey of the individuals and communities under his control in Britain. His *Laws and Regulations* of 1847 clearly set out his perception of the role of Chief Rabbi, a perception that assumed total religious control for his office.

> The duty of superintending the synagogue as far as religious observances are concerned, devolves on the Chief Rabbi when present; in his absence, on the Dayan; in the absence of the Dayan, on the Minister; in the absence of the Minister, on the Reader, provided these latter officers be authorised for that purpose by the Chief Rabbi and their respective Congregations.[13]

The establishment of the United Synagogue in 1870 further enhanced the authority of the Chief Rabbinate. Under Adler's son this total superintendence of religious matters by the Chief Rabbi came to be clearly acknowledged, at least within the confines of the United Synagogue. In 1894 during a United Synagogue council meeting, regarding the use of musical instruments in synagogue services, the Chairman stated that it was not the place of the Council to make decisions on religious matters. This was viewed as the prerogative of the Chief Rabbi alone. When it was suggested that other rabbis might also be consulted on this matter, the Chairman rebutted such a notion by asserting 'for us, the authority of the Chief Rabbi is supreme'.[14]

Even the emergence of the Federation of Synagogues as a distinct synagogal body, catering specifically for members of the immigrant community in Anglo-Jewry, was not intended to weaken the authority of the Chief Rabbi. Indeed Samuel Montagu, president of the Federation, was instrumental in bringing the Machzike Hadath within the confines of the Federation and thereby also under the authority of the Chief Rabbi. Moreover, the Chief Rabbi's right to allegiance from the Federation was maintained even after its leadership complained at their allocation of a derisory number of votes in the Chief Rabbinate elections of 1890.

Hermann Adler, during his Chief Rabbinate, lent heavily on the Anglican Church model which underpinned his role. Hence he asserted that '[t]he visitation of Provincial Synagogues and Schools is exclusively the function and duty of the Chief Rabbi, as is the visitation of a diocese by its Bishop'.[15] His perception of such parallels was heightened by his religious dress, which was completed with clerical collar and gaiters. Chaim Bermant, comically, observed that when the Chief

Rabbi was called to represent the Anglo-Jewish community on State occasions and sat on a podium beside the Archbishop of Canterbury and the Cardinal of Westminster: 'with his black garb, his gaiters, the insignia of the Order like a pectoral cross on his chest, it could be difficult to tell the Rabbi from the Bishops'.[16]

Whilst the Church of England model of ecclesiastical, hierarchical structures provided a framework for the lay leadership of Anglo-Jewry, this was reinforced by the lay leaders' experiences of exercising authority in both family and business matters. Aubrey Newman has noted how religious organization in Anglo-Jewry was greatly eased by the fact that the lay leadership was

> in the hands of people who had certain basic common assumptions about what they and their associates wanted in their religious organisations, and, above all, in the hands of people accustomed to making decisions in family and commercial concerns without having those decisions come under the scrutiny of many others.[17]

It will become apparent that this applied most paradigmatically once Robert Waley Cohen became involved in the lay leadership of the United Synagogue and assumed an autocratic attitude to his decision-making.[18] Examining his business background it becomes evident that Waley Cohen, appointed vice-president of the United Synagogue in 1918 and president in 1942, approached his lay leadership duties with a similar attitude to the one upon which he had been weaned at the Shell Oil Company, where he worked from 1901 to 1928. At Shell, he had enjoyed the exercise of considerable autocratic powers without being required to refer decisions to a committee of directors. Moving to the United Africa Company, following his retirement from Shell, he encountered a different management ethic to which he was unable to adapt. He was forced to resign in 1931 for his failure to accept the Board's edict that 'no member of the Committee in the course of his interviews with the Managing Directors or the staff shall give instructions to them otherwise than through the Committee'.[19] In his governance of the United Synagogue, Waley Cohen felt no compunction to alter his autocratic approach to leadership. As Newman has recorded:

> In many ways he [Waley Cohen] was the last of the Grand Dukes of Anglo-Jewry, not merely in the way in which he belonged to the sacred Cousinhood … but in the way in which time and time again he persisted in his own way, dominating – almost domineering – over discussions and meetings.[20]

The Anglo-Jewish establishment's choice of a chief rabbi in 1913, and their perception of his role, was also influenced by another factor. As has already been noted, the massive growth of the immigrant Jewish population had bred fear amongst the native Anglo-Jewish community. Geoffrey Alderman adeptly captured the Anglo-Jewish sentiment:

> This great influx dismayed and at times terrified the Anglo-Jewish leadership ... these foreign Jews drew attention to themselves, and brought political controversy in their wake, so that the public mind became focused upon Jews as foreigners and a cause for concern at the very time at which the established Jewry was trying its hardest to blend itself, chameleon-like into its non-Jewish environment ... The immigrants reminded the British Jews of their lowly and foreign origins; worse still they reminded the Gentiles. British Jewry wished to be thought of as modern; the immigrants gave, it was argued, the impression of primitivism, or at least of medievalism. The established community wished to stress its qualities as British citizens who happened to profess Judaism; the manners, customs, mores, and even politics of the immigrants all skewed the overall character of British Jewry in a quite opposite direction. As a result, the safety and standing of the community already here was felt to be in jeopardy.[21]

The established Anglo-Jewish community feared that they would become tarnished by association with the immigrants. It was this fear that led them to adopt a policy of Anglicization of the immigrants. Attempts to bring them within the fold of the native community, reduce their differences in appearance, and teach them English all represented a first stage in the lay leadership's plan to reduce the perceived threat to their own existence by minimizing the un-Englishness of the immigrants.

A second stage to this plan was the recognition that, so long as a chief rabbi could purport to be providing the immigrant community with representation, the lay leadership of Anglo-Jewish Orthodoxy hoped that they might prevent the immigrants from asserting their own, distinct voice. In this way, the Jewish establishment could preserve their notion of unity in Anglo-Jewry; the perception of the Chief Rabbi as the acknowledged representative of all English Jews could be sustained. Yet, perhaps most significantly for them, a careful appointment should ensure that the representative voice of Anglo-Jewry would continue to be dominated by the opinions of the native community.

One clear example of the nature of this fervour to maintain control over the affairs of the community and ensure that it was the voice of the establishment which was licensed to dominate, was Anglo-Jewish reactions to the growth of Zionism in Britain. David Cesarani has argued that Zionism grew in Anglo-Jewry not out of fervent nationalist aspirations for a Jewish homeland, but rather as a result of the potential it provided those outside the established leadership to gain a voice in the community.[22] Although Zionism did enjoy considerable support amongst the immigrant community, many in the native community sought publicly to dissociate themselves from this nationalist movement. A letter appeared in *The Times* in 1917 expressing Anglo-Jewish opposition to the establishment of a Jewish State. The letter was signed by David Alexander, in his capacity as president of the Board of the Deputies, and Claude Montefiore, in his capacity as president of the Anglo-Jewish Association. The implication was that this was *the* Anglo-Jewish position in relation to the question of Zionism, coming as it did from these two leading communal bodies dealing with temporal aspects of the community, respectively on the national and international scenes. Furthermore, the League of British Jews, formed only a week after the publication of the Balfour Declaration, provided an additional vehicle for the Anglo-Jewish establishment's presentation of their own perception of the 'Anglo-Jewish opinion', distinct from the pro-Zionist sentiment expressed by the majority immigrant community.[23] Robert Henriques framed the archetypal question of the native community regarding the question of Zionism and its place within Anglo-Jewry. Noting the rising stock of Chaim Weizmann in non-Jewish circles, Henriques recalled Weizmann's assertion that Zionist ideals were supported by a majority of Anglo-Jewry and asked with incredulity: 'Was Anglo-Jewry now to be re-defined as the numerical majority of Jews living in Britain, of foreign origins …?'[24]

Just as the lay leaders of the native community sought to prevent divergent opinions from being voiced in the political realm, allowing only certain Anglo-Jewish figures to speak in the name of the community, regardless of majority opinion, they also attempted to prevent the religious attitudes of the eastern European immigrants from gaining accurate representation. By appointing a chief rabbi whom they could present as a representative of the disparate elements of the community, they sought to retain the allegiance of the immigrants to the office of Chief Rabbi. In this way, they could succeed in preserving their own conceptions of the Chief Rabbi, as the religious figurehead of the whole community. Moreover, they could prevent, or at the very least reduce, the expression of 'foreign' attitudes in the religious realm. The assumption that Anglo-Jewry's choice of a chief rabbi would focus on the importance of re-creating unity in a disparate community proves to be correct. However, this choice was not influenced merely by an inherent sense of religious fellowship amongst the lay leadership of Anglo-Jewry. In their courting of Hertz they might have been attempting to elect a chief rabbi who could possibly succeed in unifying the community, yet their impulse to effect such unity was motivated by less noble considerations.

4

A Chief Rabbi for 'East and West'

A few months before he died, Hermann Adler, Chief Rabbi between 1891 and 1911, had written a letter that was to be opened after his death; it contained his advice on the priorities that should be taken into account when the lay leadership came to consider appointing his successor. Printed in the *Jewish Chronicle*, it declared his firm belief that someone had to be chosen 'who will be equally acceptable to the East and to the West, the native and immigrant'.[1]

On 14 January 1912, the Chief Rabbinate Conference met for the first time to discuss the appointment of a new chief rabbi. If we examine the advice offered by the United Synagogue president on this occasion, we discover a rather different sentiment regarding the qualifications that the lay leadership of Anglo-Jewish Orthodoxy deemed essential for a chief rabbi. Lord Rothschild, in his opening Presidential Address, whilst acknowledging the importance of religious learning, firmly asserted his opinion that the new Chief Rabbi must be 'acquainted with English life, English laws and able to speak English'. According to the *Jewish Chronicle* report of this meeting, Lord Rothschild

> enforced this argument by adjuring the meeting that the circumstances of Anglo-Jewry demand that its Ecclesiastical representative shall be fervid in his Judaism of course but fervid too in his English predilections. And it was this nice balance of loyalty to Judaism and loyalty to the land of their birth or adoption which Lord Rothschild commended strenuously to the community at large.[2]

Rothschild's inclination to appoint a chief rabbi suitably acquainted with English life, language and mores derived from those very influences, identified in the previous chapter, as pivotal to the native Jews' perception of the office of Chief Rabbi; it was hoped the religious leader would fill a role somewhat akin to an archbishop. His reference to 'the circumstances of Anglo-Jewry' represented Rothschild's attempt to convince the immigrant community of the validity of this inclination. In referring to Anglo-Jewry's circumstances, Rothschild sought to redirect the attention of the immigrants onto the role that the Chief

Rabbi played in representing the 'Anglo-Jewish opinion' on official matters such as the Aliens Bills, which directly affected the immigrant Jewish population. In this way, he hoped to switch the attention of the immigrant Jewish population away from their focus on the rabbinic learning of a leading rabbi onto issues of Englishness.

In its coverage of the election process leading up to the appointment of a new chief rabbi, the *Jewish Chronicle* repeatedly expressed its concern at this decision by the lay leadership only to take into consideration rabbis who had some form of English connection. Both in editorial comments and in numerous articles composed by 'Mentor' in a column entitled 'In the Communal Armchair', the *Jewish Chronicle* bemoaned the narrowness of the criteria applied in the search for a new chief rabbi.[3] In one column, 'Mentor' questioned how the first quality sought in a new chief rabbi could be his Britishness, rather than the nature of his Jewishness. Was this not, he suggested, quite clearly the wrong way around?[4] Albert Jessel, commenting after the elections on the work of the Selection Committee, claimed that the field of candidates for the post had been expanded into Europe and America, but without success.[5] Regardless of whether or not this was true, the fact remains that the lay leadership of Anglo-Jewry had clearly placed considerable importance on the new Chief Rabbi having some English connection.

Hermann Adler, despite his failings as a chief rabbi who could appeal to the immigrant community, had still managed to recognize by the end of his life that the pattern which he and his father had established for the British Chief Rabbinate during the Victorian age could not be continued. At this new juncture in the history of Anglo-Jewish Orthodoxy, the divisions which existed in the community – divisions that were transparently demonstrated by the differing emphases which the lay leadership and immigrant community each sought to place on, respectively, either the cultural or rabbinic standing of a new chief rabbi – had led to this glaring need to find a candidate who could appeal to both ends of the religious spectrum.

Although they were not officially consulted by the Chief Rabbinate Conference, the immigrant perspective was stated unequivocally by a deputation from the Association for Furthering Traditional Judaism in Great Britain, who approached the Sub-Committee of the Chief Rabbinate Conference in April 1912 claiming to represent 'several thousand members'. They began by questioning the very notion that there was a need for any chief rabbi in the country, suggesting that the position, which was established by defining its role over and above that of other rabbis, invariably led to the undermining of Orthodox Judaism by weakening the status of individual rabbis. They conceded, however, that 'for the sake of peace in the community', they would be willing to withhold their objections, but insisted that this support could only be granted

> on the conditions that the Chief Rabbi to be elected should be a man of great piety, strict orthodoxy, and live in strict accordance with the injunctions of our religious code (Shulchan Aruch) from which he must not deviate either to the right or to the left. He must be a great Talmudic scholar, and then we will honour him in accordance with his deeds and merits.[6]

We find here, lucidly demonstrated, the distance that existed between the opinions of the lay leadership and the immigrant community of Anglo-Jewish Orthodoxy on the subject of the appointment of a new chief rabbi. The attitude that was evinced by the native community, as represented by the lay leadership at the first Chief Rabbinate Conference, failed to recognize that the future viability of the British Chief Rabbinate, as an institution per se, rested in the hands of those who would make the new appointment. As had been noted in the *Jewish Chronicle*, the office of Chief Rabbi had become, if it had not been created as, the key leadership position in the Anglo-Jewish community: 'It has come to be associated with a quasi-social and quasi-political leadership of our brethren in the United Kingdom.'[7] If the lay establishment insisted on focusing on those aspects of the role of chief rabbi which were of greatest significance to them – an eloquent speaker, a university-trained rabbi who could hold his own with other religious leaders in England, a dignified representative of a supposedly dignified community – they would be foisting a religious leader on the Anglo-Jewish community who represented the values and concerns of only a minority of that community. They would have utterly failed to recognize that the opinions of East End Jews had to be taken into account. Whilst there were many purposes to be served by ensuring that a new chief rabbi could continue to perform his role as a respectable figurehead for the community, it was imperative to the sustained viability of the post that the new appointment would avoid alienating the immigrant community and could, in fact, provide them too with official representation. Without this, the institution would become the representative of such a small proportion of Anglo-Jewry that the title 'Chief Rabbi' would become a misnomer. As has already been noted, the institution of the British Chief Rabbinate is, indeed, peculiar to England. For eastern European immigrants, a chief rabbi was either a rabbinical leader imposed on a Jewish community by the government, or a *rav* whose Jewish learning had earned him the respect of his community. If the immigrant community in England was to accept the authority of a chief rabbi, it was his traditional learning rather than his

English standing which would secure their support for his position.

Two other candidates eventually joined Hertz on a shortlist for the position of chief rabbi.[8] They were Moses Hyamson, a member of the London Bet Din, and Bernard Drachman, who had been a former teacher of Hertz in America.[9] Significantly, by the time this shortlist of candidates had been agreed, an editorial in the *Jewish Chronicle* acknowledged that, notwithstanding its concern that the election process should have been broadened to include rabbis who were unacquainted with English life

> in all the months that have gone by ... there has not been one [candidate] definitely known to be available, and whose *renomee* was so overmastering as to command anything approaching a universal demand that he should be appointed.[10]

The rabbis on the shortlist therefore appeared to be the most suitable candidates.

Hyamson had been promoted to the London Bet Din in 1902, at a time when Hermann Adler's Chief Rabbinate had come under increasing attack from the immigrant elements of Anglo-Jewry. The decision to appoint Hyamson and Asher Feldman, two foreign-born Jews, to the Bet Din has been viewed as an attempt, at that time, to try to placate the immigrant community. However, strong opposition was voiced against this move at a protest meeting held on 1 March, in London's East End. At this meeting the immigrants decried 'the action of the United Synagogue in attempting to elect as Dayanim, men in whom the East End has, and can have, no confidence whatsoever'.[11] Each of the new dayanim, though born in eastern Europe, had been educated in England, studying at the University of London and receiving their rabbinical training at Jews' College. As such, they did not enjoy the support of the immigrant community. Consequently, it can be reasoned that when Hyamson's candidacy for the British Chief Rabbinate came to be considered, his inability to secure the respect of East End Jewry as a dayan impaired his chances of securing the appointment as the appropriate Chief Rabbi for the community that had emerged by this time.

This assumption was confirmed by the report of Lord Swaythling, president of the Federation, on the attitude of members of his institution to the different candidates. Although the Federation had excluded itself, or been excluded, from the elections,[12] its greater knowledge of East End opinion had been sought and received and the Selection Committee acknowledged the influence of this report in their deliberations. The Federation had suggested that Hyamson could not hope to enjoy the support of the immigrant community.

Moreover, from the report received by the *Jewish Chronicle* on the deliberations of the Selection Committee, it becomes clear that it was not only the Federation's assessment of the lack of support that Hyamson would enjoy that had persuaded the Selection Committee against supporting his appointment. The suggestion that Hyamson was unsuitable as the candidate who might be, in Adler's words, 'equally acceptable to the East and to the West' had been backed up by 'every East End worker with whom we came into association'.[13]

Whilst Hyamson might have appeared an unacceptable candidate in the eyes of East End Jewry, a rumour emerged that the candidacy of Bernard Drachman was being frustrated by a perception among some members of the native community that he was, perhaps, 'too' Orthodox. In his autobiography, Drachman recalls his receipt of a letter from Leopold Greenberg, editor of the *Jewish Chronicle*, informing him of the existence of this opposition to his candidacy from some important members of the community. The letter offered him the opportunity to respond. Drachman stated that he preferred to avoid 'becoming the object of a public controversy',[14] but Greenberg nonetheless went ahead and roundly criticized the existence of such a sentiment. He expressed particular concern that this perception of Drachman's Orthodoxy as too strict was emanating from 'men high in the hierarchy of the United Synagogue ... and certain of our Ministers'.[15] The eagerness with which A.H. Jessel, in his summary of the activities of the Selection Committee, attempted retrospectively to quash the rumour that it was this greater orthodoxy which ruled out Drachman, implies that this might, indeed, have been the crucial factor in Drachman's inability to secure the post.[16] Moreover, this was the explanation which Drachman was himself led to believe had been the cause of his failure.[17]

By the time of the actual elections, aside from the concern that Drachman was too Orthodox to be acceptable to West End Jewry, his candidacy was further weakened by his refusal to partake in any formal contest for the position of Chief Rabbi. As the *Jewish Chronicle* recorded:

> Dr Drachman has made it a condition of his candidature that he shall not be run in a competition. Hence the choice left to the Selection Committee, if Dr Drachman is to be included at all, necessarily compels it to put forward Dr Drachman as the only candidate.[18]

Drachman appears to have believed that a formal contest for the position of Chief Rabbi would undermine the prestige that was appropriate to the post. He was not prepared to assume the office under these circumstances. He therefore forced the Selection Committee either to appoint him without recourse to a contested election, or to remove his name altogether from consideration. He was not alone in opposing an election. The *Jewish Chronicle* had led the way in voicing opposition to the notion of holding formal elections for the Chief Rabbinate. Comments in one editorial perfectly captured the concern:

> Suffice it to say that nothing that could be devised could be so calculated to demean the office itself and to paralyse for years to come the energy and activity of whoever might become Chief Rabbi, as a contested election.[19]

There were a number of reasons for this opposition. For one thing, it was suggested that the first years of Nathan Marcus Adler's Chief Rabbinate had been marred by his need to try and overcome the communal divisions that had emerged during the electioneering tactics of the contest that had preceded his appointment. In contrast, when Hermann Adler had been voted into the position, since his election had been unanimous, he had benefited considerably from the absence of any such acrimony.[20] However, a second and perhaps more significant objection to a formal election derived from the manner in which votes had been allocated for these elections.

It was the Council of the United Synagogue that decided upon the allocation of votes, at a meeting held on 13 May 1912, and it was their decision to appropriate 314 of the approximately 431 votes available to their own institution. For one thing, this meant that the Provinces were most unfairly under-represented. For example, whilst the Jewish community of Leeds was granted one vote and all of Manchester Jewry received just seven, the United Synagogue in Hampstead was allocated thirty-five votes. However, it was the Federation of Synagogues which was most aggrieved with this division of the votes. Its estimated membership of 6,500 was to receive only twenty-eight votes in contrast to the 314 allocated to the 5,412 members of the United Synagogue. The lay leadership of the Federation had already seceded from the Chief Rabbinate Conference, suspecting in advance that the Conference would refuse to allocate votes in relation to membership numbers, choosing instead to distribute votes in accordance with financial contributions to the office of Chief Rabbi. The derisory number of votes finally allocated to the Federation confirmed their worst expectations.[21] The Federation suggested that it would now simply have to 'trust' that the appointment of the new Chief Rabbi would be acceptable to them. However, as the *Jewish Chronicle* noted, if just one candidate could have been presented to the Conference the

issue of voting would have become redundant. This would have
enabled the Federation to remain involved in the election process and
would have guaranteed their support for the new Chief Rabbi, rather
than leaving it up to the Federation to grant their support after the
event.

In the final analysis, the Selection Committee, in January 1913, chose
against presenting just one name for election, preferring to forward
the names of both Hyamson and Hertz to the Electoral College. It
seems incredible that this was, in fact, the second time that the names
of these two candidates had been forwarded to the Chief Rabbinate
Conference by the Selection Committee. This decision had already
been made once before, in June 1912. On that occasion the Editorial of
the *Jewish Chronicle* had been led to suggest that despite the clear
merits of Hertz's candidacy, if the election of the Chief Rabbi was
reduced to a contest between these two candidates, it was assumed
that the influence of electioneering hustle would lead to Hyamson's
appointment.[22] It was argued that the question of Hyamson's ability to
fulfil the criteria of being equally acceptable to East and West, native
and immigrant Jews, would cease to be relevant if the election boiled
down to a competition for votes. The decision to postpone the election
at that earlier stage derived from the belated interest of Drachman in
the post. It was decided that he should be given an opportunity to
undertake a preaching tour, similar to that performed by Hertz, before
a final decision was made. If he failed to take up the invitation to
travel to England then the election would proceed between Hertz and
Hyamson. The awareness on the part of the Selection Committee that
there had been complaints regarding the narrowness of the search for
the new Chief Rabbi, and the desirability of avoiding an election, if at
all possible, encouraged them to delay the election process just in case
Drachman had proved suitable.

Prior to the Selection Committee's 1913 announcement of their decision, 'Mentor', in the Communal Armchair, noted that Drachman's
candidacy was coming under increasingly careful consideration. It
was suggested that Drachman had come to be viewed as the compromise candidate. The names of Hertz and Hyamson had been floating
around for so long that the mere existence of an alternative enhanced
the appeal of Drachman's candidacy. The article issued a warning
against this:

> If selection from the three selected is to be made for preference
> there can be little doubt that Dr Hertz's energy, his mentality, his
> wide knowledge of affairs, and his strong Jewish spirit, would
> instantly commend him … the suggestion that those who favour
> not Dr Hyamson should divert their preference to Dr Drachman

makes that learned Rabbi the compromise candidate. If he lacks some of the mental activity, the energy, the force, the 'go,' that characterises Dr Hertz, he is also free from the imperfections which are painfully apparent as outstanding features of Dr Hyamson.

Mentor rejected such compromise, unless it was certain to produce the utmost harmony in the community.

> Averse as I am from anything in the nature of canvassing it would be unbecoming to mention which of the three should be run as the single candidate, if it came to 'taking all risks with both hands'. But I will go so far as to say that it should be neither Dr Hyamson nor Dr Drachman.[23]

When the Selection Committee made their announcement a positive development did emerge, from what had otherwise proven to be an unnecessary six-month delay. Even whilst ensuring that an election would occur, the Selection Committee, finally influenced by the opinion of East End Jewry, had been persuaded to attach their 'strong recommendation' to Hertz's candidacy. An editorial in the *Jewish Chronicle* suggested that Hyamson had been retained as a candidate by the Selection Committee only out of considerations of fairness. To exclude him from the deliberations at this late stage, after two years of electioneering during which he had served admirably as acting Chief Rabbi (alongside Asher Feldman with whom he shared the task), had been viewed as a decision that 'would, to say the least, have been altogether arbitrary'.[24] Nevertheless, the *Jewish Chronicle* argued that the most preferable course of action would have been for Hyamson to withdraw his candidature, in the light of the committee's strong recommendation and thus secure unanimity for Hertz's election.

Hyamson did not follow the advice of the *Jewish Chronicle* and sustained his challenge. In the eventual outcome though, despite the concern over the consequences of a formal contest, the results of the vote, held in February 1913, were deemed to have granted Hertz a victory that was close to unanimous. He received 298 votes to Hyamson's thirty-nine. More importantly, he achieved a majority even without the United Synagogue monopoly over the voting process.[25] Hertz had succeeded in emerging as the best candidate for the difficult job at hand. Unsurprisingly, the majority he achieved in the voting was heralded as a great advantage in his eventual exercise of authority as Chief Rabbi.

Whilst some of the reasons for the failure of the candidacies of Hyamson and Drachman have been made clear, it remains to be seen what made Hertz appear to be the best choice for the British Chief Rabbinate. Hermann Adler's warning that his replacement had to be someone who could appeal to both West and East End Jewry is certainly central. It was precisely those contradictory elements in Hertz's rabbinic character, the traditionalism and modernity that had made his ministry to the Syracuse Community so problematic, which were tailor-made for the Anglo-Jewish Orthodoxy that he was to serve.

The lay leadership of the native community dominated the elections of the new Chief Rabbi, an establishment whose concern for Orthodoxy was buried beneath a desire for a chief rabbi who could, as the Adlers had done, present a suitably educated and refined public image to reflect favourably on the community he represented. In truth, it was the emphasis, placed by Rothschild, on securing a chief rabbi 'acquainted with English life', which ensured that Hertz could figure amongst the leading candidates for the British Chief Rabbinate. Through his ministry in South Africa he had developed a reputation as a great preacher – his Friday night sermons attracted large audiences of both Jews and non-Jews. During his three-month visit to England the previous year he had demonstrated the power of his oratory, and various editions of the *Jewish Chronicle* recorded the positive impression he left on his listeners. Indeed, in a special report on one of Hertz's sermons delivered at the Bayswater Synagogue – Hermann Adler's pulpit before he assumed the Chief Rabbinate – a most favourable comparison was drawn between the two rabbis. Despite the pervading high esteem with which Hermann Adler was characterized by the *Jewish Chronicle*, Hertz's extempore delivery and the breadth of knowledge demonstrated in his sermon were most positively contrasted to Adler's rigid use of a written text for his sermons and the impression that he had always exhausted his knowledge of a subject.[26]

In addition to Hertz's obvious preaching skills, his outspoken support for the policies of the British Empire in South Africa (which following the Anglo-Boer War then formed part of the British Empire) had established his credentials as a Chief Rabbi who should not offend the non-Jewish authorities of Britain. Indeed, he had received a favourable report from the British High Commissioner for southern Africa, Lord Milner, which ensured that his candidacy was most carefully considered.[27] Aubrey Newman, gaining access to the diary notes of Saemy Japhet, a member of the United Synagogue subcommittee that was to appoint the new Chief Rabbi, has demonstrated the importance of Lord Milner's support. The diary states:

> it happened that Lord Milner, in the course of a conversation, mentioned to Lord Rothschild that Dr Hertz, also an aspirant [for

the vacant Chief Rabbinate], was a most desirable candidate. Lord Milner reported that during the Boer War Dr Hertz, then at Johannesburg, was openly pro-British. He had suffered for his convictions. This was sufficient for Lord Rothschild. He declared the campaign at an end, and proclaimed Dr Hertz as the sole candidate of the United Synagogue.[28]

Throughout the election process for the new Chief Rabbi the lay leadership, largely insensitive to Adler's warnings, sought to impose the priorities of the establishment onto the wider community. Rothschild appeared unaware of other suitable qualities that Hertz possessed.[29] Yet, notwithstanding Rothschild's lack of interest in other factors that equipped Hertz for the British Chief Rabbinate, the substantial majority which Hertz received in the elections might have been influenced by the recognition, from other parties, of his all-round suitability for the post. Whilst Hertz did possess those characteristics that were likely to garner the support of the lay leadership of the United Synagogue, his background, rabbinical training and own theo-logical position had created a complex character who was also able to appeal to the immigrant community. His unerring attachment to Orthodox Judaism, an attachment that had made his ministry to the Adath Jeschurun Community in Syracuse impractical, ensured that he was a viable candidate for the lay leadership to present to the so-called 'foreign' element of Anglo-Jewish Orthodoxy.

From the very beginning, in his cable to the Anglo-Jewish press accepting his new position, Hertz acknowledged the dual roles that he had been elected to fulfil. He declared:

> I am deeply conscious of the vast and sacred responsibility which the office of Chief Rabbi imposes upon its incumbent …
>
> … my life and my strength shall be consecrated to the uphold-ing and maintaining of the sway of Torah over our lives and the sanctification of the Divine Name, both within and without the ranks of Anglo-Jewry.[30]

5

The Progressive Conservative Theology of Joseph H. Hertz

While Hertz's ministerial background had pointed to his suitability as a Chief Rabbi for the particular circumstances of his election, it was his theological approach to Judaism that made him the ideal religious leader of the rival factions in Anglo-Jewish Orthodoxy throughout much of his Chief Rabbinate.

He described his theological approach to Judaism as 'progressive conservative'. The theological juxtaposition of opposing elements, which was to make him so suitable a Chief Rabbi for the Anglo-Jewry to be encountered in 1913, is thus clear even in the title he ascribed to his religious thought. By his own definition, this theology of Judaism was to be understood in the following terms:

> Progressive conservatism – the synthesis of the best citizenship and the broadest humanitarianism, with the warmth and colour, the depth and discipline of the olden Jewish life.[1]

It will become clear that the interpretation Hertz made of 'the olden Jewish life' emphasized 'discipline' in a manner that was entirely Orthodox. This facilitated his ministry to the immigrant community. His openness to what he termed here 'the best citizenship and the broadest humanitarianism' enabled him to address most secular studies, ensuring that the native community of Anglo-Jewry was able to find him acceptable as their Chief Rabbi. However, the most important idea upon which to concentrate is his concept of synthesis. The term synthesis, in Hertz's theology, suggests a rigorous attempt to fuse two separate elements into one complex, yet viable, whole.

He explained that in his understanding of 'the olden Jewish life':

> By Judaism, we mean first of all the web of fast and festival, precept, symbol and ceremony that is the foundation of the Jewish Way of Life. That Way of Life has come down to us from our fathers of old. It is rooted in the Hebrew Scriptures, and the inheritance of Israel as the depository and guardian of the truths held by it for mankind. It has been nurtured by the instruction of God-enlightened prophets and seers, sages and saints.[2]

This was an interpretation of Judaism, its origin, its development, and its practices, which was in accordance with traditional Jewish teachings. Furthermore, Hertz maintained a traditionalism in his approach to key Jewish beliefs. During the Chanukah festival of 1925, he began a series of sermons, entitled *The New Paths*, directed against the Liberal movement in Anglo-Jewry. In this particular area of religious reform, he certainly refused to act as a unifying figure. Noting the appeal that the Hellenistic world held for Jews in the Maccabean period, to which the Chanukah story related, he observed:

> It is not difficult to see that we too are witnesses of a fundamentally similar spiritual conflict in Anglo-Jewry to-day. This clash between the forces that cherish our Jewish heritage and those that would break away into religious adventures recalling the aberrations in Maccabean times, is an undoubted fact. This fact must be openly faced.

An insight into Hertz's character can be gleaned from his description of what he presented as the best method for dealing with this issue:

> And, as ever, the first defensive step against this new Hellenism is neither to mock nor denounce nor even to lament it, but to *understand* it; that is, to consider it in the light of history, and fully realise its fatal consequences to Jewry and Judaism.[3]

Pointing to the Maccabees' decision to reject Hellenic wisdom, Hertz argued that these defenders of the temple had recognized that Hellenistic thought was not something which could be synthesized with Judaism. As he sought to reinterpret these events into a lesson for his own time, he maintained that, unlike many other Jews of the period, the Maccabees had recognized that Jewish thought had to hold primacy. Synthesis was only possible where conflict between the essential terms of Judaism was absent. For Hertz, the crucial element in Judaism's participation in non-Jewish spheres of knowledge was the understanding that synthesis was not always possible. Jewish thought always required human reason to be circumscribed by the Revealed Law of God. Notwithstanding this belief, an indispensable aspect of his theology remained the conviction that the attempt at synthesis should never be disregarded wherever it might retain the potential to be successful.

Hertz most lucidly defined his understanding of this concept in his opening address to the 1935 Conference of Anglo-Jewish Preachers. That year the 800th anniversary of the birth of Maimonides was celebrated.[4] In eulogizing this great thinker, Hertz argued that

Maimonides had provided the archetype of the correct method for effecting a synthesis between Jewish knowledge and human wisdom. In elucidating the theological methods of Maimonides, Hertz also took the opportunity to argue for the orthodoxy and correctness of his own progressive conservatism, which similarly sought an appropriate synthesis between the Jewish and non-Jewish worlds. He insisted that the lasting value of Maimonides lay in the fact that '[h]e approached the problems of God, man, and the universe with Jewish eyes'.[5] He did not merely express 'a double Amen to everything taught by Aristotle'.[6] Here we identify the crucial element of Hertz's theology; namely, that any Jewish approaches to human wisdom must always retain the revealed word of God as the basic standard of judgement. He stated:

> The voice of Maimonides resounds to us across the ages … to have the courage to *negate* whatever philosophical and pseudo-religious concepts are incompatible with our Judaism, even though these concepts be idols of the day in the market-place of contemporary philosophy. Judaism as a system of religious thought, as a *Welt-* and *Lebensanschauung*, is something far other than merely an echo of the philosophical whims or theological shibboleths of the passing hour.[7]

It is imperative to understand just how integral this notion was in the theology of Hertz, since it entirely coloured his approach to non-Jewish spheres of knowledge and the art of synthesis. In a much earlier stage of his rabbinic career, indeed his first formal study within the realms of Jewish scholarship, entitled 'Bachya and "The Duties of the Heart"', it was this point that formed a central part of his thesis.[8] In this paper, written in 1898, he demonstrated Bachya's use of non-Jewish sources in his composition of the *Duties of the Heart*, a combination of Neo-Platonism, Neo-Pythagoreanism and the ideas of various Mohammedan sects. Hertz vigorously argued that this apparent lack of originality in Bachya's writings actually demonstrated the potential for Jews to effect a synthesis between traditional Jewish teachings and elements of the surrounding cultures with which they interact. He suggested that in his use of non-Jewish sources

> Bachya … was always a chooser, knowing what to reject … in every respect [he] rises vastly superior to his sources. At most he takes from them vapour – but he turns it to water, pure and limpid, quickening to the thirsty soul.[9]

Hertz presented this as an essential Jewish faculty: the ability to choose what can and cannot be synthesized with Jewish ideals.

Although this approach to the Jewish attainment of non-Jewish wisdom retains a strict and orthodox attitude towards Jewish ideals, it also succeeds in maintaining an open disposition to the attainment of human wisdom and an education in non-Jewish subjects. Furthermore, and significantly, for Hertz it was precisely by effecting the synthesis of these two fields that one arrived at an Orthodox Judaism.

His perception that attempts at synthesis must always be tested against Jewish teachings led him to place a tremendous emphasis on Jewish education. He argued that with a thorough Jewish education it could become apparent that Judaism was able to synthesize many ideals of modernity into its own theology. Moreover, a thorough religious education would also enable students to perceive that Judaism itself had often laid the foundation for the ideals advocated in the western world. In his *Translation and Commentary on the Pentateuch*, Hertz referred to a process of 'cross-fertilisation'[10] between Judaism and other cultures. This two-way process had helped the Jewish religion to both endure and contribute in its passage through time and various different civilizations. The theology underpinning Hertz's progressive conservative Judaism was strong enough to interact with other cultures, synthesize aspects of those cultures, and also impart its own truths to the non-Jewish world. He believed that it was merely ignorance of, and estrangement from, the religious heritage of Judaism that led Jewish youth to reject its birthright. Education demonstrated that Judaism retained a viable theology and remained a vital religion. Armed with this perception of the vitality of Judaism, non-Jewish spheres of knowledge could be approached with the confidence that enables the attempt at synthesis to be made without undermining Judaism.

Hertz defined his theological approach further through the notion of 'positive historical Judaism'. This was to enable him to reinforce his emphasis on the attainment of both Jewish and secular knowledge. Positive historical Judaism is a concept built upon two principles. The notion of religion as a positive phenomenon identifies its legalistic aspect: its posited laws. Hence he referred to 'the positive, historical Judaism of our fathers, with its sanctification of everyday existence through symbol and immemorial rite; with its Thou shalts and Thou shalt nots'.[11] The association of this positivism to an identification of the historic nature of Judaism, as a religion that spanned the ages, demonstrated the value of these practices:

> Positive, historical Judaism ... is a religious civilisation, steeped in holiness and aglow with a passion for righteousness; and has been the discipline and inspiration of a hundred generations in Israel.[12]

Hertz acknowledged that the origins of this concept of positive historical Judaism could first be identified in the work of nineteenth-century German thinkers such as Leopold Zunz and Zechariah Frankel. He commended them for providing the student of positive historical Judaism with 'a new consciousness that filled his soul with sacred pride in the eternal values entrusted to his care'.[13] Jews, when they had become aware of their history, were provided with the tools to identify the historic location of Judaism in the story of human civilization, informing the student of the influences to which the religion was subject and which it had exerted on its surroundings. This notion of positive historical Judaism provided Hertz with a justification for an actual insistence on a rounded education, in both Jewish and secular studies. In this way, a student could be equipped with sufficient knowledge to identify commendable and dubious aspects of non-Jewish culture that could exert, or have exerted, an influence on Judaism.

Hertz explicitly proclaimed his belief that 'there is no such thing as starting with a clean slate in law'.[14] He argued that

> Jewish Law resembles 'an ever-flowing river'. It is not merely a book but it may be said to be a moving equilibrium of all the living forces in a Jewish community – ritual and oral, domestic and economic.[15]

It becomes abundantly clear that for Hertz's theology to be practicable it is necessary to ensure that Jews obtain an understanding of those 'living forces' that can influence Jewish Law. Wherever there is ignorance of these, Judaism's ability to synthesize an Orthodox theology and practice with modern citizenship will prove forbidding. At the same time, provided that the correct education is in place, his progressive conservative theology affirms the possibility for interaction with non-Jewish sources of wisdom and the scope for synthesis. Hertz objected so vehemently to Liberal Judaism because it had failed to maintain what he viewed as the essential values of Judaism. He was not opposed to synthesis per se, but stated that it had to be based on an understanding of Judaism that would ensure that the religion's interaction did not result in its corruption. He placed great emphasis on the revelation at Sinai as a basis of this theology. This lay at the heart of his progressive conservative theology and it was also an essential factor in his success as a Chief Rabbi who could minister to two distinct groups within Anglo-Jewish Orthodoxy.

The value Hertz attached to the work of men like Frankel focused primarily on their contribution to religious education. Hertz considered the establishment of Frankel's Jewish Theological Seminary in Breslau to be '[n]othing less than epoch-making in Jewish spiritual history'.[16] The potential that the new 'scientific' methods of learning provided for Jews to experience self-respect outweighed all other considerations; this included questions regarding the orthodoxy of these thinkers. It ensured that '[t]he Jew henceforth viewed things Jewish under Jewish categories of thought'.[17] In Hertz's opinion Frankel and Zunz had worked in 'an "orphaned" and "impoverished" generation, ... there was a flight from Judaism, certainly a flight from the Judaism of history. Infatuation with everything Christian became a veritable mania.' For Hertz the greatest triumph of positive historical Judaism was therefore the fact that it ensured that '[t]he charlatanism and self-contempt of the post-Mendelssohnian era were definitely exorcised'. The education provided by the positive historical approach to Judaism was intended by Hertz to arm Jewish ministers, and in turn their students, with the confidence in Judaism that would ensure that it was sustained.

The role of education as the cornerstone of Hertz's theology has already been identified. He identified four key areas as pivotal to that education: Jewish religion, its principles, beliefs and practices; the Hebrew language; Scripture; and Jewish history. Combined together this religious education was to serve a three-fold aim in preserving Orthodox Judaism. Primarily, it secured a thorough grounding in the basic tenets of Judaism, which was designed to ensure that any attempt at effecting a synthesis remained compatible with Orthodox Judaism. Knowledge of the essential elements of the religion prevented synthesis from undermining that religion. In addition, it imparted a perception of Judaism as a religion in which Jews could maintain a pride. By identifying the contribution it had made to other civilizations it would become possible for Jews to perceive the value attributed to their religion by others. This removed a source of Jewish self-contempt, ending the perception of Judaism as an inferior source of morality. Moreover, it demonstrated that syntheses have occurred in the history of Judaism and represent a valuable endeavour that need not be feared. Overall, the effects of religious education were to combine to serve a fourth and final role: the attainment of general confidence in Jews' comprehension of their Judaism. Once Jews were instilled with knowledge and understanding about their religion they were in the best position to sustain it, defending it against external or internal attacks with assurance. They could also attain the confidence that would empower them to engage personally in interaction. Education in Jewish history demonstrated that it had occurred in the past: the general confidence that a rounded religious education created should ensure that interaction could occur in the present and future. Confidence safeguarded Jews from entertaining fear, either concerning their understanding of their Judaism or regarding their interaction with modernity.

The importance of carefully choosing what was and was not compatible with Judaism had been portrayed by Hertz as an essential faculty of the Jewish personality. However, the essential prerequisite of the task of synthesis is confidence, particularly in the value of modernity. Hertz lived in what was surely one of the most tragic centuries experienced by the Jewish people, yet he never relinquished his belief in the positive value of synthesis and the potential for Jews to derive value from a non-Jewish source of wisdom and truth. This confidence, which is integral to a progressive conservative theology, evolves out of the assuredness provided by an appropriate religious education. Throughout his Chief Rabbinate, Hertz issued a warning to the Anglo-Jewish authorities regarding the importance of religious education and the provision of Jewish schools. At a celebration to mark twenty-five years in office, he once again took the opportunity to reiterate the value he placed on religious education, a value derived from the confidence that it could impart to its students.

> Be it noted that it is only by understanding its past that any people can maintain its identity, and become the architect of its future. Israel is no exception to this rule.[18]

Confidence, in one's understanding of Judaism and its moral value, removed the potential for fear from a Jew's encounter with the non-Jewish values of modernity and facilitated control in the destiny of the Jewish future.

The character of Hertz himself exuded tremendous confidence and may provide the best example of the benefits of the education that he lauded throughout his rabbinic career. It certainly provides the final key for a complete understanding of the factors that led the Chief Rabbi to place religious education at the centre of his theological system. The confidence imparted by education emerges as the bedrock under-pinning Hertz's own theology and activities as Chief Rabbi.

Hertz gained renown for his confident nature. He earned a reputation as a man who held a strong belief in certain principles and was always prepared to fight for them vigorously. This had first been evident in South Africa when he spoke out against the Boer attitude to the uitlanders. By the time he left Johannesburg 'Hertz had already earned for himself the title of the "Fighting Parson"'.[19] Upon arriving in England as Chief Rabbi, Hertz unfailingly fought to secure his authority as the religious head of all Anglo-Jewry, defending his religious position against attack even when, as we shall see, those attacks were directed against him by the lay leaders of the community. Following his death the *Jewish Chronicle* declared that he had earned himself the undisputed title of 'Jewry's Fighter-Scholar'.[20] He powered through opposition to assert his own opinions. An infamous tale emerged recounting the suggestion, made to the Chief Rabbi by an Anglo-Jewish minister, that it might be worth considering the use of peaceful means for resolving arguments. He retorted that he always used peaceful means, but only once all other methods had failed.[21]

The confidence Hertz exhibited in defending his religious authority derived from a self-belief in the principles he propounded. This self-belief emerged out of his conviction that these principles were correct, a certainty he obtained from the assurance he had in his own religious education. Hertz believed that his religious education had equipped him with a complete knowledge of Judaism that enabled him fully to understand the religion. This knowledge and the self-belief it bred facilitated his construction of a theological system for Judaism whose principles he was empowered to defend out of his confidence that they were correct. Confidence enabled him both to promote his progressive conservative theology of Judaism and was integral to his exertion of the authority of his office. It ensured that Hertz need feel no compunction to shy away from using his religious authority to advocate his theology. He refused to be cowered into any subversion of his principles by external authorities. As such, he was capable of providing Anglo-Jewry with the forceful leadership figurehead they required.

Hertz characterized this confidence as an essential element in the makeup of all religious leaders. In an address on the role of the religious guide and preacher he questioned whether Anglo-Jewry had grasped this point: 'do we realise how essential, systematic and comprehensive Jewish knowledge is to success in our sacred calling?'[22] Once Jewish leaders were inspired with confidence in the ideas that they propounded, they were provided with the essential tool with which to defend their theology. As he had argued earlier in his Chief Rabbinate: 'only scholarship will enable us to justify our progressive conservatism'.[23]

Significantly, it was Hertz's contention that there was a biblical precedent for his focus on the importance of religious education in general, and more particularly an historical understanding of Judaism. He pointed to the text of Deuteronomy 32:7, stating

> 'Remember the days of old, consider the *changes* of many generations', is the farewell admonition of the Lawgiver. Note that the exhortation to consider and understand the changes from one cycle to another, is parallel to 'remember the days of old', and is as vitally instructive.[24]

His translation of this Hebrew verse, in truth, is tendentious. The emphasis was his own yet the Hebrew word translated as 'changes' is translated elsewhere, including his own translation of the Pentateuch, as 'years', this being the accepted meaning of the term *sh'not*. In his commentary on this verse in his *Pentateuch*, he refers readers to his essay, at the end of the book of Deuteronomy, on 'The Hallowing of History'. There, he argues that the Jewish People were the first to recognize the value of history as a divine revelation across time and 'as a guide to the generations of men'. Hertz stated that it was of vital importance for modern historians of the Jewish people

> to explain the position of the Jews in the national history of the countries where they dwelt ... In this way alone can we in time hope to understand the 'cross-fertilisation' of Jewish and non-Jewish ideas and influences in literature, folklore and life.[25]

In Hertz's understanding, there is an inextricable link between historical knowledge and the potential for, or existence of, syntheses. This explains how the passage of 'years' across the generations could be reinterpreted by Hertz, to designate 'changes'. In the particular address in which he cited this section of the verse, Hertz was exhorting the Anglo-Jewish ministry to step up their efforts to 'reach the hearts and souls of our young and old'. He called upon them to inspire their communities with self-respect in their Judaism, since this was to underlie the understanding of both history and the scope for change in the Jewish religion.

6

Progressive Conservative Judaism: In Anglo-Jewry

Although the lay leadership of Anglo-Jewry might have had little intention of truly providing the immigrant community with religious representation, there remained a glaring need for a chief rabbi who could, in fact, appeal to both East and West End Jewry. The appointment of Hertz to the British Chief Rabbinate provided the potential for a resolution of the disunity that existed within the community. Indeed, following his installation into the office, the *Jewish Chronicle* expressed its hope that this new Chief Rabbi

> may yet build a golden bridge which will unite the dissatisfied with the satisfied, whilst sacrificing nothing that either holds essential ... the sympathies of the estranged may be revived, and, linked with the ardour of the Traditionalists, may bring a new life to Judaism in these isles.[1]

Hertz was himself keenly aware of the importance in fact, rather than merely in theory, of representation for all elements of a Jewish community. During his ministry at the Witwatersrand Old Hebrew Congregation in Johannesburg, this future Chief Rabbi had already displayed an enthusiasm to procure a voice for all the different communal elements. He viewed this as the only means of securing an authority and legitimacy for the community's representative voice that could enable it to purport, genuinely, to be speaking for all the Jews in the Transvaal. In the context of Anglo-Jewry, it was not simply his understanding of the importance of representation that made Hertz's election to the Chief Rabbinate a critical appointment at that time. As has already been suggested, his progressive conservative theology was ideally suited to a community divided between a West-European established minority and an East-European immigrant majority, whether that community was located in Johannesburg or Great Britain. Progressive conservative Judaism built a bridge between Orthodoxy and modernity. It sought a synthesis between traditional Jewish practices and beliefs and 'the best citizenship and the broadest humanitarianism'.

The 'East End Jews', upon arriving in England, had been alarmed at the Anglicized forms of Judaism that characterized the United Synagogue. They saw an Anglo-Jewish ministry and Chief Rabbi dressed in clerical garb, with what the immigrants perceived to be a distorted understanding of the role of the rabbinate in traditional Orthodox communities. They wondered how they could possibly offer this native community their allegiance; they also wondered why they should allow the community's Chief Rabbi to speak on their behalf as their religious representative. It is not that the Orthodoxy of either of the Adlers could be questioned. The problem was that the Adlers had themselves become part of the establishment. They too were enmeshed in the attempt to demonstrate the Englishness of the Anglo-Jewish community and thus justify their titles as Englishmen. In the new era that was dawning, a chief rabbi who could claim allegiance from the immigrant community, as well as the native community, was required.

From the very first sermon Hertz delivered as Chief Rabbi of the United Hebrew Congregations of the British Empire, upon the occasion of his installation into the office, he stressed his perception of the importance of moderation as a vital factor in his ministry to a divided community. He based this sermon around the closing comments of the first verse in the Mishnah *Avot*: 'Be ye moderate in judgement; raise up many disciples; and make ye a fence to the Torah.' His elucidation, in this sermon, of the three points raised in the verse is most instructive of his entire programme for Anglo-Jewry throughout his tenure as Chief Rabbi. Explaining the first clause of this verse, Hertz detailed the importance he placed on the practice of moderation and issued the following caution:

> To all parties alike comes this warning for moderation in judgement. The revolutionaries need it. Theirs is the cry of 'New lamps for old'. But there is no inherent, sacramental virtue in change as change. The new is not always the true ... And, ye men of older years and views, be moderate in judgement. 'New occasions teach new duties', and new conditions require new methods ... Let us, therefore, whether we be traditionalists or revolutionaries, first of all disenthral ourselves, on the one hand, from masterly inactivity or from methods obsolete even in Russia; and, on the other, from the spell of new remedies which have proved pathetically futile, and worse than futile, in Germany and America – and we shall save our young for the future. For our children's sake, therefore, be ye deliberate, moderate, charitable in judgement.[2]

Only through the practice of moderation, between the religious poles characterized in Anglo-Jewish Orthodoxy by the immigrant and native communities, could the Chief Rabbi hope to construct the bridge that was required in Anglo-Jewry.

If just one epithet was sought to describe the main activity of Hertz's Chief Rabbinate to the Anglo-Jewish community, the most apt might be 'mediator'. Anglo-Jewry was in need of a mediatory figure, a bridge-builder, someone who could effect a unity among the greatest possible proportion of its members. It was through this mediation that he could effectively provide Anglo-Jewry with its representative voice and a religious figurehead who could viably be seen to be presenting the religious opinion of the community. Hertz's theology of progressive conservative Judaism facilitated this mediation and enabled him to serve Anglo-Jewry profitably. It prevented him from advocating either a reform or fundamentalist defence of Traditional Judaism. Seeking to represent a majority he fought for the validity of the middle ground that could encompass both immigrant and native Jews.

We have already seen that, during his Chief Rabbinate, Hertz engaged in a vociferous attack on Liberal Judaism. In his pulpit addresses on *The New Paths* Hertz more fully explained his progressive conservative approach to the life of a religious people. He had already pointed to this approach in his Installation sermon when he discussed the importance of creating a 'fence to the Torah'. He identified observance of the traditional practices of Judaism as the pivotal factor in Judaism's survival through its encounter with civilizations across the ages.

> For well we know that, when the framework of the ancient Law falls away, when the immemorial rites, customs, and ceremonies go, we are left without God in our lives. We may – for a time – remain an ethical, but we are no longer a religious people.[3]

Hertz viewed the undermining of religious observance as a first stage in the eventual undermining of religion per se. The observance of prescribed practices came to be threatened once the notion that those laws had been revealed was questioned. He argued that the examination of the revelatory nature of laws eventually led to the questioning of the revelatory nature of morality. Once Jews presumed that they could determine, by their own human endeavour, what was and was not moral in Jewish teaching, they undermined the very future of the Jewish religion. This was the basis of his attack on Liberal Judaism in *The New Paths*. He claimed that its failure to maintain the 'fence to the Torah', that is, its questioning of Jewish observances, derived from its undermining of revelation which thus eroded the whole structure of Judaism.

As we have seen, revelation acted as the defining criterion in the attempt to create a synthesis between Judaism and principles of human wisdom that derived from non-Jewish sources. Hertz's denunciation of Liberal Judaism was an attack on that movement's dismantling of the revelatory framework that could enable Jews to interact with the non-Jewish world. He argued that Liberal Judaism, in seeking to practice morality without reference to Judaism's revelation of moral laws, removed the one aspect of those practices that could ensure that they would remain compelling. He insisted that it was not truly possible to discern a lasting morality without the aid of revelation. It was the contention of Hertz that, although it might be possible to remain an ethical person without a divine imperative, there is no basis for sustaining ethical principles outside the religious context in which these moral laws are presented as religious laws. The removal of the revelatory element of Judaism ultimately ensured that the religion could not be sustainable as a lasting moral phenomenon. Moreover, it created a Judaism that would lack the tools which Hertz believed were necessary to enable it to progress into the modern world and, where possible, effect synthesis and nonetheless retain a viable Jewish identity that could be perpetuated down the generations.

The potential for synthesis was also undermined, however, by those to the religious right of Hertz's theological position. In seeking to mediate between extremes and demonstrate the possibility for harmony in Anglo-Jewish Orthodoxy, Hertz was also critical of those who sought to defend a fundamentalist traditionalism. The second clause of the verse from *Avot*, around which he constructed his Installation sermon, referred to the imperative to 'raise up many disciples'. As he explained, this reference to the education of Jewish youth was to be perceived as the means for preserving all Jewries. He presented religious education as a cornerstone of his entire theological system. As was noted in the previous chapter, religious education was to provide the knowledge of Judaism, its thought, beliefs, practices, history and development, which would enable Jews to approach non-Jewish spheres of knowledge armed with an understanding of Jewish essentials. In particular, education was integral to the understanding of positive historical Judaism. This knowledge ensured firstly, that Jews could identify the value of their religion, identifying the contribution it had made to other cultures, thereby preserving a confident perception of their religion that could prevent it from losing its primacy in the mind of the Jew. Secondly, by learning the history of Judaism it became clear that the practice of synthesis had been a feature of earlier generations when interaction with the ideas of the surrounding non-Jewish culture had been permitted. Thirdly, it prevented Judaism from being weakened through its interaction with alternative sources of wisdom, guaranteeing that synthesis only proceeded where it was compatible with those essential values of Judaism that the religious education had shown to be axiomatic. Religious education was pivotal for Hertz, both in securing Judaism's ability to interact with non-Jewish spheres of knowledge which existed outside Judaism, and also in preventing the emergence of extremist interpretations of Judaism that undermined moderation within Judaism. As he explained in this sermon:

> Our religious education must be broadened and deepened! We suffer from partial, fragmentary views of Judaism and of the Jewish world-conception … It is only when once more we see Judaism in its totality that, instead, we will bless and render thanks to our Maker for the happiness of our portion, for the beauty and glory of our heritage.[4]

Through attaining a complete understanding of the Jewish 'heritage' the potential for synthesis was learned. In a later essay, on the subject of the Garden of Eden, Hertz most clearly elucidated his opposition to a fundamentalist traditionalism which obscured this ability of the Jewish religion to effect synthesis through its interactions with the modern world. Contrasting the Christian notion of the Fall of Man with the Jewish perception of human life, he affirmed his belief that

> Judaism clings to the idea of Progress. The Golden Age of Humanity is not in the past, but in the future (Isaiah 2 and 11); and all the children of men are destined to help in the establishment of that Kingdom of God on earth.[5]

Education demonstrated the existence of theological development through the history of Judaism, identifying the capacity for progress through time. Hertz rejected the idea that it was only the past that had a lesson to provide to the present and future of Judaism. He refused to accept that the old traditions and practices were to be sustained simply because of their old age. Yet, nor were they to be discarded simply because of their origin in antiquity. Indeed, this was the explanation for the value that he ascribed to revelation in the life of a religious people. The derivation of a tradition or religious practice from the 'word of God' secured a lasting value for that teaching. This value was to be accepted neither because of its age nor because of the ability to discern that value by human thought alone. Hertz therefore rejected both a fundamentalist traditionalism and excessive reform in favour of the balance achieved by a fully educated Jewish youth's striving for moderation.

For Hertz it was inappropriate to seek to shelter Judaism from non-Jewish sources of wisdom; to undermine the potential for synthesis that has helped and indeed may continue to help the Jewish religion and its people progress from one age into another and gain a greater understanding of their Judaism. Similarly, he viewed it as just as inappropriate to seek to distance Judaism from the value of revelation and religious practice in the misguided belief that human wisdom alone could lead to morality. The attempt to mediate between each of these two extremes, advocating religious moderation, provided the basis of his Chief Rabbinate.

Hertz perceived that his progressive conservative theology of Judaism was, in fact, tailor-made for the Anglo-Jewish Orthodoxy which he hoped would emerge from its experience of polarization between East and West. It is perhaps this perception that is of greatest significance in an attempt to understand his activities as Chief Rabbi. Following the cessation of hostilities at the end of the First World War, Anglo-Jewry had established the Jewish War Memorial Fund to honour the Jewish dead. This was intended to be an educational trust that could secure the future of 'Traditional Judaism'. Hertz defined this Traditional Judaism as

> the life consecrated by Jewish religious observance … in indissoluble union with the best thought and culture of the age, and with utmost loyalty to King and Country.[6]

He argued that:

> This is a working description of Traditional Judaism, the Judaism of a Saadyah, a Maimonides, a Manasseh ben Israel, a Moses Montefiore, or a Nathan Marcus Adler. What is more, it may fairly be called the ANGLO-JEWISH position in theology.[7]

It was the contention of Hertz that a theological line could be drawn connecting the Judaism of Maimonides to the Judaism which he advocated for Anglo-Jewish Orthodoxy. In the Judaism of each, the implementation of a positive historical approach was central. As he explained at the 1932 Conference of Anglo-Jewish Preachers:

> Nothing can be of greater importance than to examine our religious position in the light of the assured results of modern research, or of the thought that has stood the test of time. In this we are merely following the example of Saadyah, Maimonides and Crescas.[8]

In examining why Hertz thought his theology was so appropriate to the Anglo-Jewish Orthodoxy to which he was ministering, it is necessary to return to our understanding of the nature of the community at that time. The passage of the 1905 Aliens Act had resulted in a steady fall in immigration from eastern Europe so that by 1913, when Hertz assumed the office of Chief Rabbi, the composition of the community had become more stable. Following the end of the First World War, the period of his Chief Rabbinate was to encompass the era in which the immigrant Jews emerged, geographically beyond the East End, socially into the middle classes and into leadership positions, and religiously into the United Synagogue.

In East End Jewry's geographic expansion into the suburbs the Federation, which had originally provided the immigrants with many of its synagogues, lacked the financial means to provide the new places of worship that came to be needed. Consequently, it was often the United Synagogue, with its greater financial liquidity, which established the new suburban synagogues that the immigrants joined.[9] The 1920s and 1930s also saw the immigrants and their children gaining greater access to positions of authority in the community or gaining the confidence to assert their opinions by forming their own political organizations. In 1928, the Federation elected Morry Davis as president, following the removal of Louis Montagu from office. Geoffrey Alderman has suggested that Davis' appointment signalled an important shift:

> The rise to power of Morry Davis within and through the Federation bore witness to the self-confidence and assertiveness of the immigrants and their children. The establishment was put on notice, so to speak, that its unfettered discretion to order the affairs of British Jewry was at an end. Issues which the establishment would rather have kept off the communal agenda were firmly secured there by the actions of the new power-brokers.[10]

Although immigrants failed to gain ascendancy in the Board of Deputies and the United Synagogue Council until the late 1930s, the growth of Zionism, in particular, afforded them leadership opportunities.[11] The B'nai B'rith and the Zionist Federation, as well as Jewish trade unions and friendly societies, helped the immigrant community express its distinctive voice and might also be seen to have aided them in their transition into confident members of Anglo-Jewish society. The immigrants and their children had taken part in, and been transformed by, the Anglicization process which had been created for them by the established leadership. The adult English classes, specially created clubs and societies, and Jewish schools, such as the Jewish Free

School, designed to effect a cultural and social assimilation alongside a linguistic assimilation, had each served to transform the East End community.

Hertz, through his theological programme, endeavoured to help this new section of the Anglo-Jewish community engage in the religious life of Anglo-Jewish Orthodoxy. His theology of progressive conservative Judaism, applied in this context, provided the means for the Chief Rabbi to attempt to prepare this new generation for their encounter with the English world and its non-Jewish sources of wisdom. Their environment was no longer the introverted East-European ghetto. The Anglo-Jewish authorities had deliberately sought to Anglicize the immigrants, hoping in that way to remove the perceived threat caused by their foreignness. Subsequently, the immigrants and their children had imbibed a sense of Englishness; Hertz was concerned to ensure that their Judaism would remain intact, vital and proud.

As will become still more apparent later, Hertz fought a two-way battle through his Chief Rabbinate. He sought to preserve the traditional thought and practices of Judaism from an onslaught by those to his religious left. He attacked Liberal Judaism and also attacked attempts to bring a more spiritist approach to the practice of Orthodox Judaism, an approach that placed far less emphasis on religious observance than Hertz was willing to concede. Meanwhile, he also fought to defend Orthodox Judaism's interaction with non-Jewish cultures and spheres of human wisdom. He rejected an insular Judaism which those to his religious right were willing to promote. Hertz sought to draw a connecting line between the theology of Maimonides and the 'Anglo-Jewish position', since the thought of Maimonides provided the Chief Rabbi with a basis for his own progressive conservative theology of Judaism. Maimonides' *Guide to the Perplexed* reflected the possibility that existed within Judaism for an interaction between Jewish and non-Jewish cultures. Yet, crucially, the *Guide* also demonstrated the difficulties that can emerge when such interaction occurs. The effecting of a synthesis, as we have seen, was not something that Hertz believed could be achieved without care or without the appropriate Jewish education. Although he advocated interaction with non-Jewish sources of wisdom there was an obvious need to prepare Anglo-Jewish youth for its encounter with the English world. It was this preparation, based upon a progressive conservative theology of Judaism, which could enable the new generation to mediate between the positions that existed on the religious right-wing of Hertz's theological position and amongst those who maintained a spiritist approach to Orthodoxy or were on the left wing of the community. In this way, Hertz's theology sought to build the required bridge between the religious poles that had been represented by the positions of the native and immigrant communities around 1913. Through the building of a bridge a greater harmony could be effected within the community which could enable Hertz to speak with an authoritative voice as the religious figurehead of 'the Anglo-Jewish position'.

7

Joseph H. Hertz, Chief Rabbi of the United Hebrew Congregations of the British Empire

There is considerable irony in the fact that the appointment of Hertz to the British Chief Rabbinate had been intended to preserve the dominance of the lay establishment over the immigrant majority. The attempt to retain control in the community by, firstly, subduing the voice of the immigrant community and, secondly, preserving the Chief Rabbinate as a viable official representative of Anglo-Jewry, was to be achieved by appointing a chief rabbi who could, at least nominally, be presented to the immigrant community as an acceptable representative. As such, a very different character to either of the Adlers was to be appointed. Yet in so doing, the leaders of the native community elected a chief rabbi who, as it would turn out, had a rather different perception of his role to that entertained either by the Adlers or, indeed, by the lay leaders.

As Hertz understood his position, the Chief Rabbi was expected to oversee all the religious matters of the Anglo-Jewish community. His confidence in both his religious principles and his authority ensured that he was more than willing to assert this control. However, there was a considerable divergence of opinion on religious matters between the Chief Rabbi and Sir Robert Waley Cohen. The United Synagogue vice-president believed that the Chief Rabbi should adhere to the advice offered to him by the lay leadership, yet as Aubrey Newman noted:

> whereas the Adlers had been willing to accept domination by the Rothschilds, Joseph Hertz was determined to be no Adler to a man who was himself not a nineteenth-century Rothschild.[1]

In 1940, the Chief Rabbi and United Synagogue introduced a campaign to strengthen Judaism in Anglo-Jewry. The burdens of war were undermining religious observance; provision of adequate supplies of kosher food was difficult, it was not always possible to maintain regular synagogue services, and evacuation posed a threat to the religious education of Jewish children. Moreover, there was a perception that just as the Second World War was making England into 'the bulwark

of human liberty for the whole of mankind',[2] Anglo-Jewry had been
thrust to the forefront of attempts to defend the future of Judaism. The
persecution of Jews on the European continent passed on a greater
responsibility to the Jews of England as guardians of their faith.
However, there was disagreement concerning the form that such a
campaign should take. The differences in opinion which characterized
the relationship between Hertz and Waley Cohen through much of the
Chief Rabbi's tenure were precisely captured in this debate, regarding
the best methods for revitalizing Judaism in England at that particular
time. Waley Cohen, notwithstanding his senior role within the United
Synagogue, championed a spiritist approach to Orthodox Judaism in
which emphasis was placed on religious ideas rather than specific
practices. The sermon Hertz delivered to inaugurate the campaign
expressed his own conception of the nature of Judaism and was utilized
to attack Waley Cohen, at least implicitly, by expressing the Chief
Rabbi's opposition to the very position advocated by the United
Synagogue vice-president.

> [T]his is not 'A Recall to Religion' but 'A Recall to the Synagogue'.
> The difference is profound … our Recall is not to some nebulous
> something, allegedly spiritual that opposes itself to nothing in
> particular, nor is it to some modernist religious vagary from
> overseas; it is a 'recall to the Synagogue', *i.e.* to the positive,
> historical Judaism of our fathers, with its sanctification of every-
> day existence through symbol and immemorial rite; with its Thou
> shalts and Thou shalt nots, and its absolute demand of justice,
> piety and purity in life; with its priest-people consecrated to the
> humanisation of man through its teachings of Righteousness and
> Holiness.[3]

Hertz was determined that it was his opinion that should be promoted
on this occasion. It was clear to him that this was a religious issue in
which lay interference was misplaced. The formation of this campaign, discussed at a United Synagogue Conference held the previous
month, had already provided him with the opportunity to try to
impress upon Waley Cohen his belief that the office of Chief Rabbi
empowered him to exercise religious authority over the community.

> The architects of the United Synagogue, Sir Anthony Rothschild
> and Lionel Louis Cohen, provided it with a Constitution that
> permits no ecclesiastical interference in matters of finance; and, at
> the same time, these great-hearted Jewish gentlemen had a horror
> of lay interference in religious law. They therefore placed the
> entire religious administration and educational supervision under

the control of the Chief Rabbi; and, of course, his remained the religious leadership and public representation of the community.[4]

This was not the first time that Hertz had voiced these opinions on the appropriate divisions of power in Anglo-Jewry. At the 1927 Conference of Anglo-Jewish Preachers he expressed concern at lay attempts to interfere with the authority of religious leaders in the community.

> [L]eadership has almost everywhere to-day been wrested from the Jewish minister by the lay element … who … desire the clergy to surrender their independence and perform the functions delegated to them as the controlled servants of the lay element, and as the paid interpreters of the aspirations or prejudices of that lay element.[5]

Hertz acknowledged that the functions of his office precluded responsibility for temporal matters that affected the community. He was willing to acknowledge his lack of expertise in affairs related to this sphere and consequently refrained from interfering. However, he expected reciprocity from the lay leadership, trusting that they would restrain themselves from interfering in religious matters that fell into the spiritual sphere in which he believed he held the monopoly of expertise. Hertz was intent on providing religious leadership for Anglo-Jewry as he saw fit; he was unwilling to accede to the agenda set by the native community and its lay leadership.

The sharp differences of opinion and resulting conflicts which characterized the relationship between the Chief Rabbi and Robert Waley Cohen demonstrated that Hertz's request to be granted the sole religious authority, which he believed his office was due, went largely unheeded. The fundamental problem was that each held differing conceptions about the extent of their own authority. Since they also disagreed about the nature of the Judaism that they wished to promote there was considerable scope for discord. Waley Cohen's biographer noted that the 'theme which had never been far from the centre of his mind [was] how to redress the balance inside the community by revivifying the spiritual side of Judaism'.[6] He was willing to interfere in religious matters because he entertained his own vision of how best to promote Judaism in Anglo-Jewry. When Hertz engaged in his attack on Liberal Judaism, in *The New Paths*, Waley Cohen sought to intervene and temper the comments of the Chief Rabbi. The changes he appended to the draft of a sermon which Hertz had forwarded to him were rejected by the Chief Rabbi with the comment that '[t]he words as re-drafted by you sound apologetic. This would of course misrepresent my attitude.'[7] The truth was that Waley Cohen was more than willing to misrepresent the Chief Rabbi's attitude, in order to replace it with his own opinions that removed what he perceived as Hertz's excessive focus on the importance of religious practices. Yet, as Hertz explained in a letter written in response to a different attempt by Waley Cohen to exert his authority over that of the Chief Rabbi:

> the Chief Rabbi is the moral teacher and guide of the Community, and not the bondman of any one individual of the community. Threats and invective are of no avail to divert me from any course of action which I deem is dictated to me by conscience, self-respect or considerations for the welfare of Judaism and the Jewish People.[8]

Aubrey Newman has stated that the battles between Waley Cohen and the Chief Rabbi 'show what happens when one side is responsible for "spiritual" and the other for "temporal" matters without a careful definition of the two terms'.[9] In truth, the problem extended beyond this. Robert Henriques, Waley Cohen's biographer, suggested that the frequent differences of opinion between Sir Robert and Hertz could partially be explained by what Henriques perceived to be the Chief Rabbi's vanity.

> Possibly Bob never quite understood how offensive his letters seemed to a man who was older than himself and who, *while obviously of lesser stature*, considered that his office made him more eminent.[10] [my emphasis]

Henriques reflects Waley Cohen's own belief that the Chief Rabbi should be the 'bondman' or 'controlled servant' of the lay leadership of the native community. Although Hertz had been led to believe that his office armed him with stature and authority, Waley Cohen's attitude to him demonstrated the perspective of the lay leaders who had appointed him to his office. They assumed that, notwithstanding the title of the office and their own propaganda about the authoritative nature of the role, no Chief Rabbi would consider asserting his power over them. It was not, as Newman suggests, simply that the extent of their respective spheres of authority had been poorly defined, but rather that previously there had been deemed to be no need for any such definition. Subsequently, when Henriques came to interpret the relationship between Hertz and Waley Cohen he interpreted the Chief Rabbi's conceptions about his role as the result of vanity and presumptions above his station. There was no conception that Hertz might simply have acted in response to what he had been told about the nature of the office of Chief Rabbi. Upon his appointment to the Chief Rabbinate, at his installation ceremony, Lord Rothschild had handed him a *Sefer Torah* and declared 'Dr Hertz, I give the Torah into your keeping'.[11] Hertz himself noted that there were

> distinct rights and prerogatives of the Chief Rabbi as laid down in the Deed of Foundation of the United Synagogue and re-affirmed in the Resolutions of the Chief Rabbinate Election Conference. I may add that the first Lord Rothschild, the President of that Conference, as well as of the United Synagogue, enclosed those documents in his Letter to me announcing my election and indicating to me the rights and duties consequent thereon.[12]

Nonetheless, Waley Cohen sought to maintain the reality of the situation as it had been under the Adlers, despite the changed circumstances that existed in the later period.

The full title of Hertz's office was Chief Rabbi of the United Hebrew Congregations of the British Empire. Taking this title at face value, Hertz was eager to perform the first journey to the Dominions ever undertaken by a chief rabbi, to visit each of the communities under his religious authority. Moreover, since the Chief Rabbinate was portrayed as the figurehead of the Jewish community, comparable in some ways to the Archbishop of Canterbury, Hertz thought it would be appropriate to visit the King before his departure on this tour. He had been led to believe that, just as the Archbishop of Canterbury was the representative to the King of adherents of the Anglican Church, the Chief Rabbi represented the Jews of the Empire. In a letter to Waley Cohen, Hertz therefore suggested that he should meet with the King in order to receive a Royal message which he could pass on to the communities he would visit during his trip. Waley Cohen was quick to oppose such a suggestion, which appeared to him to demonstrate what he believed was the Chief Rabbi's inappropriately inflated perception of his prestige. However, this can be viewed as another example of Hertz believing the propaganda associated with his office and therefore coming into conflict with the opinions of the lay leadership.

Not only had he clearly expressed his refusal to accept the role of 'paid interpreter' to the lay leadership, Hertz's personality prevented him from accepting such a position. Certain activities during his Chief Rabbinate, such as his visit to the Jewish communities of the British Empire, enabled him to secure an authority and prestige for his office that established his position without recourse to any power that Robert Waley Cohen was willing to concede to him.

Hertz's own experiences in one of the Empire's Jewish communities heightened his awareness of the needs of congregations in the

Dominions and the advantages that could be provided by a visit from the Chief Rabbi. In March 1920, the United Synagogue Council had agreed to the tour and extended a formal invitation to Hertz to proceed with the trip. He departed on 8 October for Cape Town and his journey then took him 'to forty-two different communities on three continents … extending over eleven months, and covering more than 40,000 miles'.[13] Its impact on the communities visited was greater than even Hertz might have imagined. Recounting the details of this 'First Pastoral Tour' to the Jewish Historical Society of England, he recalled the official welcomes made in his honour in each of the different cities. There were formal civic receptions held by Mayors, receptions with Cabinet ministers, Justices, heads of churches and Principals of academic bodies. Governors-General and State Governors were also involved. Upon his arrival in Johannesburg:

> The Mayor and Councillors and the leading members of the Jewish and non-Jewish community awaited us at the railway station. The crowds that thronged the station could not be kept back by the barricades that had been erected in anticipation, or even by the special cordon of police. The large mass that cheered our arrival and followed us, preceded by the Boy Scouts and Band, is a scene that will not easily be forgotten. All traffic was stopped on the route to our hotel.[14]

He recalled that the welcome he received from non-Jewish audiences in New Zealand exceeded all expectations. 'I became the text of sermons and pulpit addresses; and my Bible Lecture, the theme of Church synodal resolutions, exhorting the faithful not to miss it.'[15] Hertz returned to England with a reputation as a Jewish leader that was now recognized worldwide. He had left a positive and lasting impression on everyone he met.

Between 1924 and 1931 Hertz's reputation was further enhanced by his activities in what he entitled *The Battle for the Sabbath at Geneva*. This involved Hertz in vigorous attempts to prevent the acceptance of a proposal for calendar reform that had been submitted to the League of Nations. The proposal recommended the creation of a 364-day calendar to improve economic efficiency by creating a year that could be divided into four equal quarters.[16] The uncontrollable 365th day of the solar year was to become a so-called 'blank-day' at the end of the year. Subsequently the days of the week of the following year would be altered and 'the religious, as distinct from the secular, Sabbath would move to a different week-day each year'.[17] Hertz's initial attempts to respond to this proposal and combat it led to a request from the Conference of American Liberal Rabbis that he represent them too in expressing Jewish opposition to the calendar reforms. The Rabbinical Authorities of the Conservative and Orthodox Jews in America also approached him and asked him to provide them with representation as well. He noted that 'I was thus in a position to inform the League that the Jews in America, Orthodox and Liberals alike, were in absolute agreement with their European brethren on this question'.[18] Although the proposal was dismissed in 1925, lobbying for its adoption continued and in October 1931 a meeting of delegates to the League of Nations was reconvened. On that occasion, when Hertz addressed the Conference he stated that 'I have been deputed to transmit World Jewry's Resolutions of Protest to this Conference'.[19] He noted the potential effects of calendar reform on both observant and non-observant Jews. Orthodox Jews would experience financial difficulties as a result of this floating Sabbath that would result in a closure of their businesses on a different day of the week each year. Hertz also argued that it would affect non-Orthodox observance of this fundamental institution of Jewish life. Moreover, he presented the rejection of this proposal as an issue of religious liberty.

In his activities in this *Battle*, Hertz put aside the theological differences that divided the different factions of World Jewry to whom he provided representation. His primary objective was to ensure that they could be united in a battle in which they shared a common concern. This importance that Hertz placed on Jewish unity, regardless of religious divisions, was also elucidated in a letter to the President of the Reform Hebrew Union College in Cincinnati, Ohio, on its Jubilee in October 1925. Whilst affirming his opposition to religious reform Hertz suggested that:

> perhaps as important as the issues that divide us, are the things that should bind us; and, especially, that common action in defence against dangers from within and without – whether in local or in pan-Jewish problems – has become a vital necessity for the Jew of to-day and to-morrow.[20]

Hertz's perception, that his role as Chief Rabbi had established him as a representative figure for Jewry in England, the Empire and beyond, enabled him to shift his focus onto the importance of religious unity rather than religious principle if he deemed it appropriate. This was demonstrated in England by his willingness to participate in certain communal affairs of the Reform community in Anglo-Jewry.[21] In an address to the West London Synagogue in 1934 he acknowledged that:

> I feel that my presence here requires some words in explanation. It is certainly not due to the fact that I dismiss the religious issues

that led to the formation of this Synagogue ninety-four years ago as of trifling importance. I am the last person in the world to minimise the significance of religious difference in Jewry.[22]

The conceptions about his office, which had motivated Hertz to engage in a Pastoral Tour in order to visit the communities represented by the Chief Rabbi across the Empire, similarly motivated him to call upon Reform synagogues in Anglo-Jewry. If he was Chief Rabbi to all the Jewish communities in the Empire, he was also Chief Rabbi to all the Jewish communities in Anglo-Jewry. As a constituent part of Anglo-Jewry, Hertz believed that Reform communities were also to be provided with representation by his office.

Hertz's theological system and confidence in his authority each enhanced his chances of succeeding in the task of constructing the requisite bridge for Anglo-Jewry. The perception of the Chief Rabbi as a representative office, combined with his triumph in achieving authority and prestige for the office from sources that lay outside the control of the lay leadership of the native community, were additional factors of importance in his successes.

If in no other way, Hertz's mediatory achievements in Anglo-Jewry may be demonstrated through statistical evidence that points to the period covered by his Chief Rabbinate as a period in which the centre exerted itself over the extremes of its religious left and right wings.[23] It must be acknowledged that the data is incomplete; comprehensive studies of religious affiliation in the period that preceded Hertz's Chief Rabbinate do not exist. However, the Anglo-Jewish community in the earlier period was in a transitional stage altered in almost every facet of its make-up by the constant influx of immigrants. It was only after the reduction in immigration, caused by the introduction of the Alien's Acts and the outbreak of the First World War, that the identity of a more homogenous Anglo-Jewish community began to re-emerge.[24] Consequently, although in the absence of comparative statistical evidence from the earlier period it is not possible to state conclusively that Hertz's Chief Rabbinate was alone responsible for strengthening the religious centre, in truth, such data, if it did exist, would not in and of itself provide an especially useful comparator.

Between 1921 and 1948 statistics show that 96.8 per cent of Jewish marriages that occurred in synagogues were performed in synagogues classified as 'Central Orthodox', which encompasses the United Synagogue and Federation. The percentage of marriages performed during this period in synagogues that are classified as 'right-wing Orthodox', such as those affiliated to the Union of Orthodox Hebrew Congregations (UOHC), was just 0.3 per cent. The figure for Reform synagogue marriages was 1.7 per cent and 1.5 per cent for Liberals. By 1965 these figures had altered considerably. The 'Central Orthodox' sector's share had fallen to 74.6 per cent, whilst the 'right-wing Orthodox' total had risen to 2.5 per cent. The Reform number had grown to 11.1 per cent and Liberal marriages accounted for 8 per cent. By 1975 the 'right-wing Orthodox' figure had risen further to 6 per cent and Progressive synagogues performed 22 per cent of marriages. The Central Orthodox share had dropped to 70 per cent.[25]

Beyond these particular figures, pointing to a strengthening of the right and left wings of Anglo-Jewry at the expense of the religious centre, there are two additional points of significance. Central Orthodoxy's weakening grip over the Anglo-Jewish community was even worse than might be inferred from the figures for synagogue marriages. Not only has the percentage of marriages performed in Central Orthodox synagogues fallen, the actual number of marriages occurring within the community has dropped, in line with the population decline experienced by Anglo-Jewry. Consequently

> the real numerical decline by the 1970s had reduced the actual number of synagogue marriages in this group to around a third (1,000 a year) of the annual total of the decade 1938–47.[26]

In addition, the synagogue growth that occurred in the community in the period following Hertz's death was disproportionately in favour of the right wing. Between 1947 and 1970 the number of synagogues classified as 'right-wing Orthodox' rose by 27 per cent of total synagogue growth in London, despite this group representing just 2.6 per cent of the total London Jewish population, and 3.28 per cent of the Orthodox community in the capital.

The religious polarization between immigrants and natives that had existed at the beginning of Hertz's Chief Rabbinate had been alleviated during his tenure of the office. His confident exertion of authority and an eagerness to provide real representation for Anglo-Jewry, in line with his understanding of the nature of his role as Chief Rabbi, enabled him to succeed in strengthening the centre of Anglo-Jewish Orthodoxy, acting as a mediator and thus increasing the unity of the community. Following his death, in the absence of his unifying and moderating force, the possibility for polarization resurfaced. This would not divide the community solely according to origin, so much as by attitude to religious practice.

8

Forces of Polarization

Robert Waley Cohen represented a focal point for the forces that sought to shift Anglo-Jewish Orthodoxy away from its emphasis on specific religious practice to a more generalized concern for religious spirituality that we have labelled 'spiritist Orthodoxy'. The battles that occurred between the Chief Rabbi and Waley Cohen were undoubtedly influenced by this fact, in addition to the personality clash that characterized their relationship. As we have seen, the 1940 campaign for the Recall to the Synagogue most clearly demonstrated Hertz's continuous efforts to defend his progressive conservative Judaism and counter Waley Cohen's attempts to downgrade the importance of religious observance.

Soon after the mass immigrations of the 1880s had commenced, Orthodox factions on the religious right wing of the community had begun their agitations in the opposite direction to the one that Robert Waley Cohen was later to adopt, urging Anglo-Jewry to be more stringent in its observance of religious laws. These forces on the right wing continued in existence throughout Hertz's Chief Rabbinate and in his defence of a mediatory position for the Anglo-Jewish community he fought to counter their religious stance. He opposed the profundity of their exclusion of the modern world just as he opposed the extent of inclusivity advocated by those who maintained a spiritist approach to Orthodoxy.

His objection to the theological position of the right wing was lucidly illustrated in 1926 in his response to attempts by the ultra-Orthodox community in Gateshead to establish a yeshiva. This independent community, founded in the north-east of England in 1887, across the River Tyne from the established community of Newcastle, had invited Rabbi Abraham Sacharov to come to England and serve as their Rosh Yeshiva. Hertz intervened and persuaded the Home Secretary, Sir William Joynson-Hicks, to refuse entry to the appointed rabbi. When asked by the *Jewish Chronicle* for an explanation of this decision he was reported to have defended his actions by pointing to the fact that

> there are many Rabbis of foreign origin now in England who could well fill the position, and who, as Dr Hertz put it, 'are

walking about with their hands in their pockets starving'. In such circumstances he did not feel justified in facilitating the arrival in the country of yet another rabbi from abroad.[1]

In truth, his objections stemmed from his reluctance to support the creation of a bastion of ultra-Orthodoxy that would train and produce independent rabbis who would question his authority. Assessments of Hertz's Chief Rabbinate often focus on the issue of authority as one of his central areas of concern.[2] Hertz's disapproval of independent communities, such as Gateshead, or the Adath Yisroel synagogue in London, may therefore be portrayed as a result of their refusal to accept his authority. Bernard Homa has suggested that the Chief Rabbi's authority over certification of marriage secretaries for syna- gogues was used as a means of securing allegiance for the office of Chief Rabbi from communities that were otherwise independent. It was only after the Adath Yisroel threatened to take the Chief Rabbi to court for refusing to certify them that Hertz was forced to relent and register them in 1919, six years after they had first applied for permission to appoint a Marriage Secretary. He refused to register the Gateshead community until 1935 and then only did so simultaneously with the registration of the Liberal Synagogue. However, his dis- approval of their insular theology, rather than issues solely of authority, may be identified as an influential factor in his various efforts to undermine the position of the Gateshead community and its attempts to develop into the pre-eminent European yeshiva that it was later to become. The religious authority of the Chief Rabbinate was an issue of concern to Hertz since it was that which enabled him to promote his own theology, the theology that he felt to be appropriate for Anglo- Jewish Orthodoxy.

The Union of Orthodox Hebrew Congregations (UOHC) was to play one of the key roles in representing, defending and promoting right-wing opinion in Anglo-Jewish Orthodoxy. The Adath Yisroel synagogue referred to above was the leading institution behind its establishment. The Adath Yisroel had emerged out of the Machzike Hadath, the group responsible for undermining Hermann Adler's claims to ultimate religious authority in 1891 when they insisted on the right to supervise their own *shechitah*. As has already been noted, when the Machzike Hadath had finally reached a compromise with the Chief Rabbi, in 1905, the western and central European section of the community, influenced by their background in the *Austritts- gemeinde* of Germany and Austria, chose to secede. In 1909 they invited Victor Schonfeld, a Hungarian-born rabbi who had been serving the Montefiore Verein synagogue in Vienna, to become their *rav*, and in 1911 they constituted themselves as the Adath Yisroel Kehilla, a name associated with Hirschian communities, and built a new synagogue in Highbury in 1913. Schonfeld was later to explain that, 'The Adath Yisroel ... was founded purposely in order to be independent of the Lay and Clerical Authorities of the United Synagogue'.[3] It was under his leadership that the challenge had been mounted against the authority of Hertz and his right to withhold certification for a marriage secretary. It was also Schonfeld who led the way in the establishment of the UOHC, or United Orthodox Jewish Congregations as they had originally named themselves, which was intended to preserve the independence of the Adath and any other communities that chose to join. They acquired their own burial ground in 1924 and were officially formed as a distinct synagogal movement in 1926. Notwithstanding the western and central European origins of this movement and the consequent influence of a Hirschian theology on many of its members, it has been suggested that '[h]ere it was not so much Hirsch's *Torah im Derekh Eretz* which mattered – it was the philosophy of *Austritt*'.[4]

Within just a few years the UOHC was flexing its muscles in the community. In 1928 the British Government had passed an Act detailing legislation for the slaughter of animals in Scotland. This act recognized the Chief Rabbi as the sole licensing authority for Scottish *shochetim*. Rabbis of both the Federation and the UOHC convened a rabbinic conference on 12 January 1930 to protest against the precedent that was set by this position. They were joined by the Spanish and Portuguese congregation in their fight to prevent the extension of such a state of affairs to England and Wales.[5] Hertz viewed the UOHC as the leading group behind this public attack on the authority of the Chief Rabbinate.[6] Through our understanding of his perception of the importance of the role of his office it becomes clear how problematic this situation was to Hertz. Nonetheless the agitators succeeded in persuading Parliament to alter the Slaughter of Animals Act in England when it was passed in 1933. In contrast to the situation in Scotland, a Rabbinical Commission was created to act as the licensing authority for *shechitah*. This was to be led by the Chief Rabbi, but also included a deputy chairman from the Spanish and Portuguese community, three rabbis appointed by the United Synagogue, two Federation appointed rabbis, one rabbi representing the UOHC, and two rabbis selected by the President of the Board of Deputies to represent provincial Jewry.

The impetus of the UOHC, confirmed by 1933, came to be strengthened considerably further by the rise to power of Hitler in Germany, which subsequently caused an influx of Continental European refugees to arrive in England. By 1939 some 55,000 Jews had entered England from the extended empire of the German Reich.[7] These figures were not particularly consequential when contrasted to the number of

immigrants that had entered the country between 1882 and 1911. As
Aubrey Newman has noted however, their impact was 'qualitative
rather than quantitative'.[8] The religious affiliation of these refugees
could broadly be divided between the progressive and the right-wing
Orthodox communities. They therefore helped strengthen the outer
wings of Anglo-Jewry rather than contributing significantly to the
centre. The theology of the United Synagogue was either deemed too
stringent or too lax, so the newcomers tended to join existing Reform,
Liberal or UOHC affiliated congregations and thus bolster those
communities. In addition, they were also responsible for establishing a
number of new synagogues.

In their history of the development of Reform Judaism in Britain,
Jonathan Romain and Anne Kershen argue that '[i]t is highly unlikely
that the future Reform movement could have developed in the way it
did without the rabbinic support that it was able to call on as a result
of Hitler'.[9] The immigrants included amongst their number no less
than thirty-five Reform rabbis. The West London Synagogue subsequently appointed three new assistant ministers and also employed
several of the refugee rabbis as teachers. Synagogues in need of
ministers could obtain one from this source and the growth of small,
new congregations was greatly assisted by the presence of rabbis willing to assist and serve embryonic Reform communities. The human
and intellectual resources which Reform adherents and rabbis from
the German Reich provided to the movement in England significantly
helped the creation of a Reform Bet Din and a Rabbinical Seminary,
which was later to become the Leo Baeck College. An independent
Reform congregation was also created almost exclusively by refugees
from the Third Reich. The Belsize Square Synagogue held its first
Friday night service in March 1939, reproducing the format that had
become accepted by *Liberale* Jews in Germany. The immigrants responsible for establishing the Belsize Square Synagogue were unwilling to
compromise their German practices to conform to the standards of
progressive institutions in Britain. Their preference was therefore to
found an independent community that could preserve the traditions
of German *Liberale* Judaism. Although they initially affiliated to the
Union of Liberal and Progressive Synagogues (ULPS), believing that
Liberal Judaism in England would be the same as their *Liberale*
German Judaism, they quickly realized that they were distinct. They
maintained their own prayerbooks and services, conducted religious
classes in German until 1952, and generally sought to preserve their
German cultural traditions rather than adapt to the practices of progressive English Jews.[10]

Another almost exclusively German community established by
refugees was the Golders Green Beth Hamedrash, founded in 1934

by Eliyahu Munk (1900–78). However, the background of these members was predominantly the *Austrittsgemeinde* of the major Orthodox communities of Germany. Munk was himself the son of Ezra Munk (1867–1940), who had succeeded Esriel Hildesheimer as rabbi of the Adass Jisroel congregation in Berlin and who had also been rabbi of the Koenigsberg congregation when it had seceded from the general community. The Golders Green community adhered to a strictly secessionist Hirschian theology. The Hendon Adath Yisroel Congregation, founded in September 1939, was another synagogue established by central European refugees who were keen to maintain a stricter level of Orthodox observance than they found in the United Synagogue. A publication commemorating their first twenty years of existence further explained that 'a number of orthodox Jewish families living in the Borough of Hendon were anxious to provide a more intensive Jewish education for their children than that available locally'.[11] Rabbi Joseph Dunner (b.1906), who arrived in Britain from Koenigsberg in 1938, was responsible for establishing another refugee minyan in England in Westcliff, Essex. He was later to take over the pulpit of the Adath Yisroel Synagogue and assume the leadership of the Bet Din of the UOHC.[12] The refugees also provided 'an unexpected boost' to Gateshead's yeshiva:

> By 1939 the *Yeshiva* with 100 boys was working to capacity and now developed a senior group drawn from the more advanced refugee students. A number of very able people came to Gateshead as adults and between them helped to turn this small provincial centre into a formidable educational complex.[13]

Significantly, the Orthodox refugees were also able to exert an influence on the mainstream of Anglo-Jewish Orthodoxy, despite their different theological approach, through the appointment of their rabbis to certain vacant communal positions more closely associated to the United Synagogue. Aubrey Newman noted:

> One of the basic difficulties which had always faced the United Synagogue was that of recruitment to the ministry. Many of those who had been able to secure entry visas into Great Britain had been rabbis, and in the absence of a sufficient number of 'native-born' recruits to the ministry and to Jewish religious teaching these refugees filled a vital need. This was particularly true of the Beth Din, where the problems of finding scholars with the requisite experience had always been manifest.[14]

In Manchester, Alexander Altmann, arriving from Berlin in 1938, became communal Rabbi and *Av Bet Din* (head of the rabbinical court).

Meanwhile, the London Bet Din was reinforced by the appointments of Isidor Grunfeld and Julius Jakobovits. The former had arrived in England from Bavaria in 1933. He had been appointed to the pulpit of the Finsbury Park Synagogue in 1936 and became a dayan in 1939. The latter had been a dayan in Berlin before his arrival in Britain and was appointed to a similar position in the London Bet Din in 1945, remaining in the post until his death in 1947.

Perhaps one of the most important appointments to the London Bet Din was made in 1935, when a rabbi of eastern rather than central European origin was made dayan. Yekhezkiel Abramsky had been brought to England from the USSR in 1932 to serve as *rav* of the Machzike Hadath. Born in Lithuania, he had studied at several of the major Talmudical centres of learning in eastern Europe, which helped establish his credentials as a leading *halakhist* (decision-maker of Jewish law). He had served as rabbi in Smolevitch and Slutzk before being imprisoned by the Soviet government in 1930 when he had intended to leave the USSR to assume leadership of the Petach Tikvah community in Israel.[15] His appointment as rabbi of the Machzike Hadath congregation had helped secure his release and his son, Professor Chimen Abramsky, recalls that his father's arrival in Britain was deemed to be of such consequence that it was noted in the English National Press at the time. Yekhezkiel Abramsky was to serve as a focal point for efforts by those on the right wing of Anglo-Jewish Orthodoxy to improve observance in the community. He immediately set to work on tightening the *shechitah* laws and it was on his authority that the Bet Din finally agreed to ban the sale of hindquarter meat altogether, a move that had been sought since the Machzike Hadath had turned their attention to the practices surrounding the slaughter and preparation of kosher meat in Britain.[16] In an interview following his appointment, questioned about his goals on assuming the post of dayan, he stated: 'My aim is to strengthen Yiddishkeit both in the practice and knowledge of Judaism.'[17]

Robert Henriques, reflecting the opinions of the lay leadership of the native community in Anglo-Jewry, expressed grave concern at the theological direction that the community appeared to be taking in this period. He argued that Hertz 'derived new power by an extraordinary and (literally) unholy alliance [with] the ultra-orthodox religious Jews who placed ritual observance above all other considerations'.[18] In August 1935, a month after Abramsky's appointment to the Bet Din, the *Jewish Chronicle* complained that a handful of Orthodox extremists were 'hijacking' religious control in the country'.[19] Once again Henriques captures the sentiment of the native community when he suggested that:

> In Britain there was arrayed against Bob, as against nearly all
> British Jews of his [spiritist] tradition and background, an alliance
> of alien dogma, custom and superstition which had never before
> been any part of Judaism except in dark corners deep inside the
> ghettoes of Eastern Europe.[20]

Henriques contended that it was the influence which this section of the
community were able to exert on Hertz which ensured that Waley
Cohen's attempts to promote a spiritist approach to Orthodox observance could not succeed. Concern was heightened by the fact that this
source of influence was located outside the United Synagogue. Its
theology bore little relation to mainstream Anglo-Jewish Orthodoxy;
moreover, it proponents cared little for the established institutions of
the community.

The perception grew that the religious leadership of the community
was swinging to the religious right with the Chief Rabbi being swept
along with it. This viewpoint was exacerbated by the marriage of
Hertz's daughter to the son of Victor Schonfeld.[21] Solomon Schonfeld,
alongside Yekhezkiel Abramsky, was a pivotal figure in the rightward
shift that affected Anglo-Jewish Orthodoxy. Victor Schonfeld had died
prematurely in 1930, aged 49. His son, only 18 at the time, was sent
abroad to study and gain his rabbinical diploma so that he could
assume his father's mantle on his return.[22] In 1933 Solomon Schonfeld
was appointed rav of the Adath Yisroel and head of the UOHC. He
also assumed his father's leadership of the Jewish Secondary Schools
Movement (JSSM) whose first school had been established in Finsbury
Park just a few months before Victor Schonfeld's death. Over the
years, the schools of the JSSM would exert a considerable influence on
the strengthening of an independent Orthodox Judaism in England.
The idea that such a man could exert an influence on the Chief Rabbi
was most worrying to members of the native community, especially
Robert Waley Cohen. In 1939 Solomon Schonfeld had persuaded
Hertz to establish the Chief Rabbi's Religious Emergency Council
to lead British attempts at rescuing Jews from Nazi Europe. As the
executive director of this organization he used the Chief Rabbi's
association with it as a method for opening important political doors,
which helped him rescue thousands of adults and children. Yet his use
of the power linked to the Chief Rabbi's office further influenced the
perception that Schonfeld and Hertz were working together very
closely, heightening concerns that Hertz was being affected by his son-
in-law's religious position. This concern was intensified still more by
a comment that Hertz had himself made to Dayan Lazarus, who
reported the Chief Rabbi's lament that since the death of his wife
'he had no one to fall back on at all, and he had therefore made

Dr Schonfeld his right hand man in everything'.[23] This created a false impression of the situation.

In a private meeting with Neville Laski, in June 1941, Hertz had explicitly been asked if his son-in-law might have become 'the power behind the throne'. The Chief Rabbi emphatically denied this allegation.[24] In a letter to Robert Waley Cohen, in May 1942, he had stated that: 'The idea that I am "giving ear" to unwise counsel or that I am guided by anyone in my dealings and correspondence ... is quite illusory'.[25] Hertz left Schonfeld to run the Chief Rabbi's Religious Emergency Council. Hertz was not involved in its daily activities and did not therefore work closely with his son-in-law in this area. Schonfeld made use of the authority and influence attached to the Chief Rabbi's office, which compounded the assumption that the two worked together. However, this was not the case and Hertz immediately intervened to correct the Home Office when they mistakenly assumed that Schonfeld held the position of 'Deputy Chief Rabbi'. He was not inclined to allow Schonfeld to obtain authority in his own right in the eyes of the Home Office.[26] This position has also been acknowledged in a biographical account of Schonfeld's activities during the war, which explained that:

> This rescue organisation, nominally under the auspices of the Chief Rabbi was really the organ for Rabbi Schonfeld's manifold activities. Rabbi Schonfeld continued to perform his work single-handedly, but when he approached government agencies with requests for additional entry permits or turned to individuals for financial and other practical assistance, he would be able now to cite as his authority the Chief Rabbi of the British Empire.[27]

As for his reliance on Schonfeld as his 'right hand man', Bernard Homa has documented the Chief Rabbi's reliance on his help to secure an Orthodox appointment to the position of Senior Chaplain in 1943, when Robert Waley Cohen had decided to appoint a Liberal minister to the post. Homa was a member of the Jewish War Services Committee whose advice was followed by the War Office in the appointment of chaplains. When Mark Gollop, the incumbent in the office, had become ill Waley Cohen, as chairman of the Committee, had made an appointment without consulting any of the other members, let alone the Chief Rabbi. Hertz had been required to convene a special meeting to prevent Waley Cohen's appointment from being confirmed and to select Israel Brodie for the role instead. Homa has recorded his receipt of a letter from Hertz thanking him for his support in this matter and asserting that he 'could not have done anything without your co-operation'.[28] As numerous letters between Hertz and Waley

Cohen testify, and as the mild furore surrounding the *Recall to the Synagogue* movement demonstrated, the war period saw a considerable growth in attempts by those on the spiritist wing of Anglo-Jewish Orthodoxy to exert their influence on the community. Hertz did turn for support to those on the right wing of the community, such as Homa, or indeed Schonfeld, to ensure that the movements being made by those who maintained a spiritist approach to Orthodoxy could be counterbalanced. This did not mean that his own theological position altered. His balancing acts were designed to preserve the strength of the centre, as the theological position he advocated in his sermons on the *Recall to the Synagogue* perfectly demonstrated. He continued to herald the same 'positive, historical Judaism of our fathers' that he had advocated on the occasion of his installation to the office of Chief Rabbi.

The background to the appointment of Abramsky to the London Bet Din would appear to lend weight to this argument. Geoffrey Alderman has stated that this selection had been achieved through the influence of Hertz, who 'overcame the objections of the United Synagogue in insisting on the appointment'.[29] Since the new dayan was to play such an influential role in increasing the strictness of Jewish observance in the Anglo-Jewish community, the support which he is perceived to have received from Hertz has often been viewed as a clear example of the transformation which occurred in the Chief Rabbi's theological position. However, the personal recollections of Chimen Abramsky raise questions about this assumption. As he recalls the events surrounding his father's selection for the post, Waley Cohen was the leading figure in persuading Yekhezkiel Abramsky to accept the role. The United Synagogue archives further support this view, recording the manner in which Waley Cohen pursued Abramsky to accept the post. An interesting insight into the forces at work in the selection of the new dayan can be derived from a curious juxtaposition of ideas in comments made by Robert Waley Cohen at a meeting of the Honorary Officers of the United Synagogue and representatives of the Federation of Synagogues, convened in May 1935. Waley Cohen stated at this meeting:

> We have got to ask him [Abramsky] to accept the authority of the Chief Rabbi. He told me that he had agreed to do that. He is very well-known in Jerusalem. I think he is a man of world-wide position.[30]

As an Honorary Officer of the United Synagogue Waley Cohen felt obliged, on at least one level, to uphold the authority of the Chief Rabbi. However, the personal conflicts that often fuelled his relationship with

Hertz persuaded Waley Cohen of the advantages of appointing someone to the Bet Din who would have the authority to stand up to Hertz:
someone with a worldwide position.[31]

Although it had been the Chief Rabbi who, in 1934, mentioned the
name of Abramsky, amongst others such as Isaac Herzog – then of
Dublin, soon to be appointed Chief Rabbi of Palestine – and Sails
Daiches of Edinburgh, as a possible replacement for the retiring
Dayan Hillman, it was Waley Cohen who pursued him to accept the
post. In February 1935, at a meeting of the Honorary Officers, the
minutes note that Robert Waley Cohen had insisted that he still felt
Abramsky was the best candidate and should keenly be pursued even
though the rabbi had pulled himself out of consideration in July the
previous year.[32] Offered the post for a second time in June 1935, certain
contractual discussions ensued in which Waley Cohen again demonstrated his desire, through the appointment of Abramsky, to undermine Hertz's religious authority. In a letter to Sir Isidore Salmon, his
fellow vice-president, Waley Cohen stated his opposition to the inclusion of a clause in Abramsky's contract requiring him 'to perform any
duties which in the opinion of the Chief Rabbi properly apply to the
office of Dayan'. He claimed that this opposed

> what it has always been a vital principle of the United Synagogue
> not to do, namely, vest in the Chief Rabbi the allocation of
> duties instead of finally in the Honorary Officers of the United
> Synagogue.[33]

Waley Cohen was fighting for the authority he believed to be the
rightful preserve of the Honorary Officers and more particularly
himself. By undermining the religious authority of the Chief Rabbi
he hoped to be in a better position to wield more authority in his
own right.

Objections to the appointment were raised in the *Jewish Chronicle*.
There was concern that a man who could not speak or write English
properly and who was not viewed as capable of working with the
disaffected amongst Anglo-Jewish youth was being appointed to the
Bet Din. The New Year edition of the paper focused on this point in its
review of developments that had occurred in the community in the
previous year. It was suggested that

> Though there was general recognition of the scholarship and
> ability of the new Dayan, regret was expressed in several quarters
> that the opportunity of the vacancy had not been seized for the
> purpose of appointing an English-speaking Dayan.[34]

The disappointment at the selection of an eastern European rabbi reflected concern at the new dayan's stringent Orthodoxy. Since Waley Cohen sought to promote a less strict version of the moderate Orthodoxy championed by Hertz, his selection of Abramsky, conscious of his credentials, could appear contradictory. However his battle to undermine the authority of the Chief Rabbi appears to have overtaken his ability to consider the broader implications of this appointment. Notwithstanding his interest in preserving the outward perception of the authority of the Chief Rabbi, Waley Cohen had already demonstrated his own reluctance to give the Chief Rabbi free rein. By appointing Abramsky, he appears to have hoped that Hertz's use of the power of his office could be curtailed from another direction. Hertz appeared conscious of the effects Abramsky's appointment would have on his own position. As Chimen Abramsky recalls, when Hertz heard of the intended appointment and deliberated on his lack of consultation in the matter he sought to intervene and assert his authority over such appointments, as was his prerogative according to Adler's *Laws and Regulations*. However, Dayan Abramsky responded by threatening the Chief Rabbi with a public resignation from the Bet Din to expose Hertz's attempts to assert his authority, and the Chief Rabbi consequently backed down. In this matter Hertz had been made powerless and Chimen Abramsky confirms the notion that the appointment of his father signalled a transition in the authority of the Chief Rabbinate.

However, any success that Waley Cohen was able to achieve in terms of the diminution of Hertz's powers was counterbalanced by the influence that Abramsky would come to exert over the community through the Bet Din. Nonetheless, at the time of his appointment, it should be understood that the deliberations of the Bet Din were hardly 'world-shattering'.[35] Hertz was quite happy to leave the Bet Din to go about their business without his interference. As Isaac Levy noted 'There weren't the same problems then ... They were responsible for arbitration and conversion. He could leave them to it.' In truth, it is possible to argue that it was not until after the Second World War, following the decimation of the leading communities of eastern European Jewry, that the activities of the London Bet Din came to grow in significance. From this point onwards the Bet Din assumed an authority all of its own, whose growing influence we shall have further reason to examine below. Until this time, there were other religious authorities that exerted a far greater influence on religious decision-making in the Jewish world. It could be conjectured that at the time of Abramsky's appointment, Waley Cohen entertained no fears that the decisions passed by the London Bet Din would impede the direction in which he wished to take the United Synagogue and

Anglo-Jewry; he had no conception of the authoritative role which the London Bet Din would come to assert in post-Shoah Europe. He also failed to predict the influence that the burgeoning right-wing Orthodox community would exert on Anglo-Jewry, once strengthened by the immigration of refugees from Nazi Europe.

Nonetheless, the appointment of Abramsky did increase the profile of the London Bet Din and it also slowly increased the respect that was given to it by synagogues of the UOHC, the Federation and Yeshiva Etz Chaim. The association of such a widely respected halakhic luminary as Abramsky bolstered the belief that the London Bet Din might deserve respect, despite its affiliations to the United Synagogue. Subsequently elements on the right wing of the community gradually increased their interest in the religious life of mainstream Orthodoxy in Anglo-Jewry.[36]

Ultimately though, the selection of Abramsky as a member of the London Bet Din did not signal the rightward shift in the theological position of the Chief Rabbi that at the time was perceived to have occurred. On the contrary, it marked out Hertz still more evidently as the mediator between the spiritist and right-wing interpretations of Anglo-Jewish Orthodoxy that were becoming increasingly vocal in the community. Even within the mainstream of the community, ignoring the fortification that was occurring in the UOHC and in the progressive sections of Anglo-Jewry, in the London Bet Din, designated as the Court of the Chief Rabbi, the mediatory position defended by Hertz was being marginalized. Yet he maintained his support of a progressive conservative approach to Judaism and in 1940 was still able to argue that the United Synagogue with its mediatory theological position was 'an Institution that stands for the Golden Mean in Judaism'.[37]

The growth and strengthening of the right wing in Anglo-Jewish Orthodoxy nonetheless had occurred in this period. The changes that were occurring in the Reform movement took place outside the mainstream. They had an impact within that movement but this did not truly encroach on United Synagogue Jews at that time. The concern was therefore fostered that all the elements for a theological transformation of the community towards its right wing were in place. It was this, rather than any real transformation in Hertz's theology, which heightened the fears of those who were in favour of a spiritist approach to Orthodoxy.

Aubrey Newman has noted that in this period it was alleged that

> the honorary officers of the United Synagogue were doing all they could to sabotage any attempts made by the Chief Rabbi to induce a religious revival and that instead they were trying to sweep away all distinctions among Orthodox, Reform and Liberal Jews.[38]

Waley Cohen, leading the honorary offices and representing the spiritist wing of Anglo-Jewish Orthodoxy, engaged in counter-attacking measures designed to suppress any rightward swing that was occurring in the community. Moreover, he sought through his actions to subvert the new alliance that Hertz was perceived to have established with the right wing. The appointment of a Liberal minister to the position of temporary Senior Chaplain was one such example. With the help of Lily Montagu, he mooted the creation of a General Jewish Religion Committee that was to have transferred discussion of religious issues away from the domain of the Board of Deputies to a new committee, representative of all sections of the Anglo-Jewish community.[39] The selection of Norman Bentwich and Lily Montagu as co-chairmen of an Education Committee established by the United Synagogue Council during the Second World War was another clear indication of Waley Cohen's attempts to bring the United Synagogue into closer alignment with the progressives.[40] Since Hertz had continually made clear how pivotal religious education was in his religious programme for Anglo-Jewry, the fact that Waley Cohen could have chosen this field as a battleground for his retaliations against the Chief Rabbi is particularly significant. Waley Cohen's decision to form new alignments with the progressives reflected his concern that the right-wing elements that were growing in strength and influence in the community would never be assimilated under the umbrella of the United Synagogue. He realized that their engagements in the mainstream were intended to drive Anglo-Jewish Orthodoxy further to the right. Indeed, when issuing a statement commenting on the United Synagogue's appointment of Abramsky, to the London Bet Din, the UOHC had asserted:

> It is to be hoped that the new Dayan, whose appointment was doubtlessly due in no small measure to the representations made by so called 'militant orthodoxy', will do his utmost to bridge the gap that still exists. … [It is now] more than ever necessary for the Union to maintain a watching brief for Orthodoxy, and to continue to set the pace for the many improvements that have yet to be made … and the Union will not rest content until all this has been satisfactorily achieved.[41]

From personal recollections, Chimen Abramsky has corroborated this notion that Waley Cohen sought to create further rapprochement with the non-Orthodox as a counter-balance. It was this that subsequently pushed Hertz into alliances with the right-wing Orthodox to create his own counter-balance, because he simply could not accept Waley Cohen's activities and the spiritist attitudes that were his motivation.

Barry Kosmin, in his study 'Localism and pluralism in British Jewry', has affirmed that the period covered by Hertz's Chief Rabbinate represented Anglo-Jewry's 'golden age of homogeneity, unity and communal bliss'.[42] Nonetheless, Hertz's time in office also oversaw the period in which the extremes on the spiritist and right wings of Anglo-Jewish Orthodoxy were strengthened. Perhaps one of the greatest tragedies in the history of the theological development of the community is the fact that Hertz experienced declining health and eventually succumbed to his illnesses at a time when the need for strong yet mediatory leadership had clearly re-emerged. Towards the end of his Chief Rabbinate Hertz's ability to fight in defence of a mediatory position waned. He was caught in the centre of a battle over the future theological direction of the community. He maintained his moderate theological position but slowly lost the strength required to secure its success. Meanwhile, those representing the battle on the spiritist and right wings of the community outlived the Chief Rabbi and looked forward eagerly to their forthcoming opportunity to exert a greater influence on Anglo-Jewish Orthodoxy than Hertz had been willing to concede.

9

'Papal Infallibility': The Election of a New Chief Rabbi

Early on the morning of Monday, 14 January 1946, Hertz passed away. Commenting on his tenure as Chief Rabbi of the United Hebrew Congregations of the British Empire, the Editorial of the *Jewish Chronicle* stated that he

> did more than preserve a tradition; [he] exemplified, as never before, the vital functions of the Chief Rabbinate and its absolute indispensability to the welfare of Jewry in Great Britain and the Empire. It would be the crassest folly, therefore, to contemplate abolishing this precious office, or reducing its power, however difficult the task may prove once more to fill it. *For the community, as a whole, it represents the chief, if not the only, unifying power in British Jewry.* To non-Jews it is the symbol of that unity, and the direction to which they more and more turn for the expression of Jewish views and wishes. *To eliminate or in any way reduce it, therefore, would be to invite disunity and confusion* ... and to throw away an invaluable instrument of progress.[1] [my emphasis]

When he had assumed his post in 1913 the Anglo-Jewish community was in a precarious position. The flow of eastern European immigrants had effectively halted, but these newcomers were now beginning their attempts to settle into a community that was deeply divided between native and immigrant, between East and West. Hertz was to act as mediator for these two communities, preventing either group from asserting their dominance. He sought to create communal harmony by defending a moderate theological position that rejected both the exclusivity and insularity of the eastern European ghetto as well as the spiritist stance of native Anglo-Jews, who often evaluated their Judaism from the perspective of British, rather than Jewish, values. He experienced considerable success in this task as a result of the confidence he held in his theological system for Judaism and his perception of its pertinence for Anglo-Jewry, two key factors which enabled him to make full use of the authority of his office. His death, however, occurred at a time when the potential for religious polarization, which he had alleviated through much of his Chief Rabbinate, re-emerged. This fact, and the state of the post-war world of January 1946, both heightened the urgency for the community to have a strong leader in place at their head. In his memorial address on the occasion of Hertz's death, Abramsky, notwithstanding the theological differences that he and the Chief Rabbi had experienced, readily acknowledged the value of Hertz's leadership.

> Our Rabbis tell us that on the death of Abaye the bridge across the Tigris collapsed. A bridge serves to unite opposite shores; and so Abaye had united the opposing groups and conflicting parties of his time. Likewise Dr Hertz's personality was the bridge which served to unite different Jewish communities and bodies in this country and the Dominions into one common Jewish loyalty.[2]

The clear imperative in the circumstances of 1946 was to identify and appoint a strong Chief Rabbi, in a similar mould to Hertz, in order to give Anglo-Jewry a leader who could, once again, fulfil the role that Hertz had fulfilled upon his election. Furthermore, it was essential to make this appointment as rapidly as possible in order to re-impose a leadership structure for the community that could prevent either the right wing or spiritist sections of Anglo-Jewish Orthodoxy from asserting their positions. In the absence of leadership the religious position of the community would be allowed to drift as the different forces dictated. Nonetheless, procrastination was to dominate the election proceedings. It was to take over two years for a new chief rabbi to be elected and for a considerable time the United Synagogue, under Robert Waley Cohen's continued presidency, was to shroud all debate on the new appointment in secrecy.

Following almost a year of inactivity since the death of Hertz, the *Jewish Chronicle* expressed the concerns of the community when it condemned the lack of progress that had been made in the selection process for a new chief rabbi. The United Synagogue had not even proceeded so far as to create the electoral body that would make the appointment. The letters column in the *Jewish Chronicle* frequently reflected the communal anxiety at this prolonged absence of religious leadership and the continued failure of the lay leadership to commence the drawn out processes through which a new chief rabbi would be appointed.[3] An editorial noted how

> the unfortunate impression has got about that there are some who would not welcome the advent of *a commanding and religious authority* whose interpretations might not seem to support their own views on Jewish tradition.[4] [my emphasis]

Significantly, Aubrey Newman's study of the history of the United Synagogue uncovered memoranda from council meetings that suggest that there *was* a concern that the appointment of a new chief rabbi should avoid the perceived pitfalls of Hertz's chief rabbinate. References to the previous '[l]ack of Co-operative spirit' and '[t]endency to papal infallibility' found their way into these documents, reflecting the fears of the Honorary Officers of the United Synagogue.[5] Regardless of the community's need for a strong unifying voice in the office of Chief Rabbi, the United Synagogue, under the leadership of Robert Waley Cohen, clearly demonstrated its reticence to appoint such a rabbi.

Not until March 1947 did a meeting of the United Synagogue Council carry a resolution to convene a Chief Rabbinate Conference at which all the representative bodies could meet. The election process was finally set in motion when the Conference first met on 9 November 1947, almost two years after the death of Hertz.[6] Waley Cohen's interest in exerting an influence over proceedings was evident from his opening address to this conference, when he took the opportunity to assert that: 'The qualities and qualifications required of the Chief Rabbi are of a very high order. He must be, above all, a man deeply imbued with a truly spiritual outlook.'[7]

From the outset, the concern to try and exert a greater control over the activities of a new chief rabbi was laid before the Conference as a key concern. The first significant change to the Chief Rabbinate was the introduction of a retirement age of 70. In addition there was a clause stipulating that 'arrangements would have to be made for the termination of the appointment' if there was any deterioration in the health of a chief rabbi that extended beyond twelve months.[8] Before delegates had even met to discuss the new appointment the United Synagogue, at another council meeting in June of that year, had also mooted the idea of instituting a Lay Advisory council that could assist the new Chief Rabbi in his decision-making. The first business on the agenda of the June Council meeting had been the re-election of Robert Waley Cohen to the presidency of the United Synagogue. Under his leadership this idea of an Advisory council had evolved, which could ensure liaison between the Chief Rabbi and the laity. At the Chief Rabbinate Conference he tried to present the creation of such a consultative council as a means for the laity to work in cooperation with the Chief Rabbinate. In reality, it was designed to protect the concerns of the laity, securing a channel for them that could guarantee that they would be able to voice their opinions to a future incumbent of the office.

There were 123 delegates in attendance at the first Chief Rabbinate Conference. These were made up of forty-four representatives from the United Synagogue, ten from the Federation, some sixty-one from the Provinces, and eight from the Dominions.[9] As had occurred at the Chief Rabbinate Conference of 1912, the first activity was the appointment of a committee that would decide the duties, privileges and conditions of the office. It was this committee that was to consider the creation of a Lay Advisory council. In addition, they were to deliberate on the nature of the relationship that would exist between the new Chief Rabbi and the congregations to which he would minister, and were also to consider the emoluments of the office, the functionaries attached to it, and the resources through which these would be funded. By February the committee had concluded that they were unanimously in favour of the creation of a 'Consultative and Advisory Committee for the Chief Rabbi'. This would supervise any proposed absence of the Chief Rabbi from the United Kingdom, his pastoral visitations, and 'Any public pronouncement proposed to be made on behalf of, or in relation to, the Jewish Community by the Chief Rabbi either in his own name or in association with other Jewish bodies'.[10] Perhaps unsurprisingly, it was Robert Waley Cohen who submitted the committee's favourable report on the introduction of this council. The committee he chaired also sought to make use of this new council to resolve another problem area that had concerned the honorary officers of the United Synagogue during Hertz's tenure as Chief Rabbi. The manner in which Solomon Schonfeld had made use of the office of the Chief Rabbi led to an additional condition being attached to the position on this occasion: any delegation of the Chief Rabbi's duties was to be prevented unless the prior agreement of the Consultative and Advisory Committee was received. It was laid down that:

> The name or title of the Chief Rabbi shall not be associated with any appeal for funds, etc., unless the Consultative & Advisory Committee is satisfied ... Nor shall the name or title of the Chief Rabbi be embodied in the name or style of any organisation or charity.

Although this council had been designed by Robert Waley Cohen as a mechanism for limiting some of the powers of a new chief rabbi, in public, at the February meeting of delegates from the Chief Rabbinate Conference, the United Synagogue President spoke out in favour of preserving the authority of the Chief Rabbi's office. He protested vigorously against a suggestion that the influence and authority of the Chief Rabbi's Bet Din should be increased, thereby reducing the future Chief Rabbi's autonomous decision-making powers in the halakhic sphere. Representatives from the Federation were absent from the February meeting of the Conference, awaiting a response to their proposal that the powers of the dayanim of the Bet Din be altered to allow halakhic decisions to be made by majority voting. They insisted that the Chief Rabbi should not be allowed to exercise a veto over a decision of the Bet Din if he was in the minority. The exercise of such 'unfettered' authority was viewed as an unacceptable feature of the office of Chief Rabbi and its removal was presented as a proviso of the Federation's participation in the elections and as a condition of their support for the future appointment.

In the absence of Federation delegates a vote on the recommendations of the Committee appointed in November, including their support for the implementation of a Lay Advisory council, was postponed in the hope that reconciliation would quickly be achieved.[11] However, the Federation's suggestion that the Chief Rabbi's powers of veto be removed represented an attempt to exert their influence on the powers to be exercised by the new Chief Rabbi, and Waley Cohen fought against this.

Prima facie any attempt to reject this plea by the Federation would seem to represent a desire to preserve the authority of the Chief Rabbinate. Indeed Waley Cohen sought to undermine this proposal by appealing to the written constitution of the United Synagogue, which established the 'unfettered religious authority' of the Chief Rabbi over that institution. In his statement to the Conference, he asked: 'Should they [the United Synagogue] substitute the majority of the Beth Din for the authority of the Chief Rabbi as he had stood for 120 years?'[12] He appeared to be unwilling to allow persons outside these institutions to exert an influence on the established practices of the community.

However Waley Cohen's entire approach to the appointment of this new Chief Rabbi was not aimed at the preservation of the authority of the office, as was now threatened by the Federation. As both the United Synagogue memoranda and his lobbying for the creation of a Lay Advisory Council demonstrated, the United Synagogue President was keen to prevent the new Chief Rabbi from exercising an unfettered authority. Nevertheless, even during Hertz's Chief Rabbinate, Waley Cohen had been attentive to the public image of a chief rabbi's authority. Despite his own frequent attempts to undermine Hertz, Waley Cohen always fought against attempts by others to undermine the prestige of the office. Once again, Robert Henriques captured the situation perfectly when he noted that

> Bob would tolerate no attacks on the Chief Rabbi from anyone except himself and his own immediate colleagues in the United Synagogue and War Memorial Executive ... Bob never failed to defend the Chief Rabbi against attacks.[13]

Waley Cohen opposed the Federation's overt attempt to reduce the powers of the Chief Rabbi. He wished to preserve the public image of an authoritative chief rabbi intact. Consequently, his own attempts to weaken the future Chief Rabbi's hold on authority had been more covert. He had ensured that a mechanism was in place to officially advise Hertz's successor on lay opinions; and he was intent on appointing a rabbi whose spirit for cooperation was highly developed.

Notwithstanding the public posturing of the United Synagogue, the influence Dayan Abramsky was able to exert over the selection process ensured that the position which had been advocated by the Federation, regarding the Chief Rabbi's right of veto, was in fact put into place. In March 1948, following the defeat of their proposal, the Federation affirmed their decision to exclude themselves from the elections for the new Chief Rabbi. Furthermore, they stated their intention not to recognize the authority of whichever chief rabbi did come to be appointed. However, according to the personal recollections of Chimen Abramsky, his father had insisted that a future chief rabbi must be willing to accept the Dayan's absolute and final authority over all halakhic decisions. Only a rabbi who was willing to subdue his personal halakhic opinions to the judgements of Abramsky would gain the approval of the Dayan and stand a chance of being appointed. A *Jewish Chronicle* editorial discussing the requirements of a new chief rabbi had stated that:

> First and foremost, his status in the field of Jewish learning must be unchallengeable. He must be a *Talmid Chacham* in the highest sense of that term. Not only must he possess the fullest Jewish religious knowledge but he must also be able to impart it ... The incumbent of the Chief Rabbinate must without question be capable of presiding over the *Bet Din*.[14]

It appears that the Bet Din did not share this opinion on the basic necessary qualifications for the office of chief rabbi. In practice, despite the defeat of the Federation's motion at the Chief Rabbinate Conference, it was to be the Bet Din that was to enjoy the final say in religious judgements. This was a decision that was to pave the way towards establishing far greater authority in the religious domain for the dayanim of the Bet Din at the expense of the religious authority of the Chief Rabbi.

According to Chimen Abramsky it was this issue that had served to weaken the candidacy of Alexander Altmann, one of the leading contenders for the vacant post of chief rabbi. Altmann had arrived in England from Berlin in 1938 and settled in Manchester. He was appointed Communal Rabbi there and was instrumental in opening an academic institute for higher Jewish education in Manchester.[15] Born in Hungary and with German associations, his Germanic accent is frequently cited as the explanation for his failure to secure the position of chief rabbi since it was thought to be both inappropriate and inopportune to appoint a German at that time, so soon after the Second World War.[16] However Chimen Abramsky has discredited this assumption, on the basis of his conversations with his father at the time. He argues that Altmann had refused to grant ultimate halakhic authority to Dayan Abramsky and it was this that thwarted his application. Altmann had not been willing to hand over these powers of the Chief Rabbinate because he entertained a confidence in his own abilities in religious decision-making, a confidence that was reminiscent of Hertz. Notwithstanding the concerns that certainly did exist regarding Altmann's German background, the eagerness to avoid appointing a chief rabbi who would confidently exert his authority was here demonstrated by those on both the spiritist and right wings of Anglo-Jewish Orthodoxy. The advantage of communal unity, which a confident and powerful chief rabbi could achieve for Anglo-Jewry, was apparently not considered sufficiently important to outweigh the perceived disadvantages that would accrue from such an appointment.

The concern to preserve public perceptions about the authority of the Chief Rabbi, evident in the actions of both Waley Cohen and Abramsky, provides the explanation for this information remaining obscured and the Federation being given no assurances that their attempt to secure a greater authority for the Bet Din had, in fact, been achieved. Abramsky had exhibited this concern before, during Hertz's Chief Rabbinate, when he had written to an acquaintance in Palestine seeking to ensure that the Chief Rabbi receive a suitable welcome when he visited the country in 1936 for the Passover festival.[17] He asked that an appropriate reception be laid on for the Chief Rabbi's arrival in the country with the requisite amount of grandeur to suit the occasion, and that meetings be arranged for him with leading rabbinic personalities. This interest in the hospitality that was to be organized for the Chief Rabbi reflected two things. Firstly, it demonstrated Abramsky's positive regard for the late Chief Rabbi, also illustrated by his comments in the memorial address for Hertz. Secondly, it pointed to the Dayan's awareness of the function of public image in the role of a chief rabbi. He recognized that a visit to Palestine by Hertz, even though it was a personal trip that had no official status, should be met with the pomp and ceremony that was befitting to the office. When the time came to appoint a new chief rabbi, Abramsky was aware that there was much to be gained from preserving the public perception of the Chief Rabbi as an authoritative, representative figurehead for the Anglo-Jewish community. Notwithstanding his personal regard for

Hertz, he was nonetheless keen to secure ultimate authority over the halakhic affairs of the community in order to improve religious observance, his stated aim on assuming the post.[18] So long as he attained this authority and the influence that went with it he was aware that it would be beneficial to allow the image of a new Chief Rabbi to remain untarnished.

It was the importance of public image that played a role in undermining the candidacy of two other main contenders for the office of chief rabbi. Louis Rabinowitz was a British-born rabbi who had ministered in a number of London synagogues and had served as a Jewish chaplain in the army during the Second World War. Like Hertz, he was rabbi in Johannesburg when he was being considered for appointment as chief rabbi, having moved there in 1945. In 1947, in a highly public protest against the activities of the British authorities in Palestine, he stood up in synagogue and tore off the army decorations he had earned during the war. This motivated the Anglo-Jewish establishment to remove him swiftly from their consideration for the Chief Rabbinate, keen to avoid appointing a man in whom the British authorities might take offence. Kopul Rosen was aged only 33 when he was being considered for the vacant post, and this relatively young age has often been given as the reason for his rejection as a candidate.[19] It was suggested that he would have another chance of being considered for the office at the next elections, making it easier to discount him from consideration on this occasion.[20] However, once again, the personal recollections of Professor Abramsky call into question this reading of events. He has argued that a key factor in Rosen's rejection as a candidate was his lack of a university doctorate. The native community's concern that its religious representative should present a favourable, educated image of the community remained as important a factor in the 1940s as it had been in previous elections. As an Editorial in the *Jewish Chronicle* had succinctly stated: '[I]t is essential that our religious leader should be able to meet the world of scholarship on equal terms'.[21]

The Anglo-Jewish establishment's concern for the public perception of the Chief Rabbi's power reflected its interest in establishing a religious figurehead for Anglo-Jewry, a leader who could provide them with representation alongside the Archbishop of Canterbury. Image was so important because, as we have already seen, the Chief Rabbinate enjoyed little formal power. Although the 1836 Marriage Registration Act and the creation of the United Synagogue had enhanced the powers of the Chief Rabbi, there was still no inherent authority in the office. Rather, the scope to provide leadership derived from the abilities of the individual incumbents of the Chief Rabbinate to demonstrate their suitability and thus demand authority for their office. Hence the vital characteristic of a chief rabbi would prove to be his personality. This peculiarity of the office was readily acknowledged:

> It did not derive any of its real authority and grandeur from man-made laws of the State or from official authority and sanction. Its power and influence depended entirely upon the character and achievements of the incumbent of the office, which means, in effect, that its authority was personal and intimate.[22]

As an obituary to Hertz these comments were fitting, yet the fragile nature of a chief rabbi's authority should have meant that concern for public image was less important than the appointment of a strong character, suitably empowered to exercise authority.

Recording the final proceedings of the Selection Committee that nominated the new Chief Rabbi, the *Jewish Chronicle* suggested that the authority of the office had actually been extended in these elections. Each of the provincial communities that had participated in the elections had agreed to accept the same 'unfettered religious authority' of the Chief Rabbi as was constitutionally required of the United Synagogue. Nonetheless, it seems quite apparent that the activities of both right wing and spiritist elements had ensured that this unfettered religious authority existed in name only. A weakened chief rabbinate had been created, which was now required to yield to the ideas of both the lay and religious leadership.

In the last letter written by Hertz before his death, a letter which was to remain unsent, the Chief Rabbi had asserted: 'My only object is to transmit to my successor the constitutional rights of my high office undimmed and undiminished.'[23] The events which followed his death suggest that the concern to avoid the appointment of a chief rabbi who might have 'tendencies to papal infallibility' ensured that in this most important task Hertz was unable to succeed.

10

Israel Brodie

It was not until the end of May 1948 that the Selection Committee finally reached its conclusions and decided to submit just a single name for election by the Chief Rabbinate Conference. Their preferred candidate and the unanimous choice of the Conference was Rabbi Dr Israel Brodie. Elected to the office of chief rabbi in the first week of June, he was installed in his new post on 28 June. According to the logic of previous election contests for a chief rabbi, his experience of an uncontested election should have secured an unambiguous authority for his tenure, especially when allied to the theoretical extension of his unfettered religious authority.

In Aubrey Newman's history of the United Synagogue, in what was no more than a passing comment, he had noted that,

> Sir Robert Waley Cohen was very much in favour of the appointment of Rabbi Israel Brodie ... At all events, at an informal meeting in September 1946, Sir Robert was reported as urging Rabbi Brodie's claims on his colleagues.[1]

Despite the procrastination that characterized the election contest, and notwithstanding the much-complained-about absence of discussions in the public arena, the evidence suggests that from as early as September 1946, within just a few months of Hertz's death, the United Synagogue President had already decided that he had found his man. The official and behind-the-scenes processes for identifying a rabbi who would not become a new Hertz, a chief rabbi who would follow the advice of others rather than rigidly adhering to his own confident principles, had proceeded. Abramsky had cast his eye over the main candidates in order to come to his own conclusions. Yet throughout this period Robert Waley Cohen appears to have been convinced that an ideal candidate had already been identified. He spent this time facilitating the implementation of a Lay Advisory Committee that could act as a second line of defence against a chief rabbi becoming over-enthusiastic in his exercise of religious authority. Overall, however, he spent the intervening period acting out the role of kingmaker, persuading his colleagues to follow his lead, in order to ensure that he achieved his desired aims.

It seems quite certain that Israel Brodie's background exerted a considerable influence in making him the preferred choice for the vacant chief rabbinate in the eyes of the Selection Committee and Waley Cohen. Brodie was an Englishman by birth, born in Newcastle in 1895. He was also a product of Jews' College. He had entered that institution in 1912, at which time he also affiliated with University College, London and he received his BA in 1915 in Hebrew, Syriac and Arabic. When he then proceeded to Balliol College, Oxford, on a scholarship the following year, his qualifications in the eyes of the lay leaders of the native community of Anglo-Jewry had been confirmed.

When the First World War interrupted his studies he served as an army chaplain from 1917 to 1919 before returning to Oxford, where he obtained a B.Litt. in 1921.[2] Apart from his activities as a chaplain, Brodie had already begun ministering to a community whilst he was in Oxford. Upon completion of his studies he acted as temporary minister both in his hometown, Newcastle, and also at the Hammersmith United Synagogue. He then became affiliated to the New West End Synagogue, performing social work in the East End under their auspices. In 1923, when the Rabbinical Diploma was conferred upon him, he immediately took up an appointment as Senior Minister to the Melbourne Hebrew Congregation in Australia.

His experiences in this distant part of the British Empire might have been perceived as a useful training for his future duties on behalf of Anglo-Jewry. He had been viewed as a central leadership figure for the Australian Jewish community during his time there and had also served as president of the Bet Din of Victoria.[3] Although he was involved in negotiations for the newly vacant ministerial post at the Hampstead Synagogue in London in 1929, he failed to secure the position and the Melbourne community persuaded him to stay with them rather than seek any other ministerial posts in Britain. Thus he was destined to remain in Australia for a total of fourteen years. He did not return to England until 1937, at which time he decided to commence research work in Oxford for a D.Phil., rather than take up another rabbinical post. After just one year at Oxford he was appointed to a lectureship at Jews' College, before war once again intervened in his academic career and he returned to army chaplaincy during the Second World War. Initially he entered the RAF to become its first Jewish chaplain. However in 1944, as was noted earlier, following the retirement of Mark Gollop, Brodie came to be appointed Senior Jewish Chaplain of the British Armed Forces.

These credentials clearly made Brodie a suitable chief rabbi in the eyes of a lay leadership whose concern for public image remained as vital as it had been in the 1840s. He was a British-born, Jews' College-trained, Oxford man, who had served his country and Anglo-Jewry, with credit, during the war. Furthermore, it has already become clear that Robert Waley Cohen perceived in Israel Brodie a chief rabbi who could be expected to be more amenable than had proved to be the case with Hertz.

Waley Cohen's perception would prove correct; moreover Abramsky was also quickly convinced that Brodie was a suitable candidate. As Chimen Abramsky recalls, Brodie had unequivocally relinquished authority over religious matters to Dayan Abramsky before being accepted by him as a viable contender for the Chief Rabbinate. Brodie had agreed that it was the Bet Din rather than the office of Chief Rabbi that would enjoy ultimate control over religious decision-making. Archival evidence suggests he would prove to be as submissive as had been hoped in this sphere. Correspondence between the office of Chief Rabbi and the Bet Din during Brodie's tenure demonstrates the extent to which he was willing to defer judgement to the dayanim. When a straightforward halakhic enquiry had been addressed to his office from the recently-widowed wife of Kopul Rosen, on behalf of the Jewish boarding school Carmel College, instead of providing a simple response the secretary to the Chief Rabbi followed what was evidently standard procedure: he forwarded the question to the Bet Din for their halakhic decision. This was then passed back to the secretary of the Chief Rabbi to enable him to reply to Mrs Rosen. There appears to have been no notion of Brodie responding to the relatively straight-forward question himself.[4] Despite his experiences as a dayan in Melbourne he was conscious of his inadequacies in contrast to the qualifications of the dayanim of the London Bet Din and therefore appeared unwilling to make his own decisions. His eagerness to avoid conflict with men whose experience he believed to be greater than his own would come to characterize his entire approach to the position of chief rabbi. Newman has noted that Brodie 'was determined not to see such events as had occurred earlier'.[5] His approach was perhaps captured best by John Shaftesley who suggested that, as Chief Rabbi, Brodie was 'A man who, it might be paraphrased, would only resort to war when all peaceful methods had failed'.[6]

The contrast between Hertz and Brodie, demonstrated by Shaftesley's characterization, was comprehensive. An insight into the reasons behind Brodie's success in securing appointment to the British Chief Rabbinate is thus attained. A gulf lay between the personalities of these two chief rabbis, a chasm which had to affect each man's exertion of the powers of their office since the authority of the role was so poorly defined otherwise: 'As is well known, the measure of the Chief Rabbi's power is not fixed, varying according to the ... personal prestige of the Chief Rabbi'.[7]

The significance of personality was fundamental to a chief rabbi's exercise of power. However an additional, crucial factor in Hertz's success as Chief Rabbi was the strength he gained from having a comprehensive, well-thought-out theological system. The confidence he derived from his theology empowered Hertz's Chief Rabbinate. His progressive conservative principles enabled him to defend the 'mediatory' theological stance for which he fought throughout his tenure. If an analysis of Brodie's theological statements could identify a similarly systematic and empowering theology, this might have been able to provide him with the tools to defend his own position. Regardless of the weakening in authority that his office had experienced, Brodie's eagerness to avoid conflict might have resulted in success in a more subtle way than Hertz had been able to achieve.

In the preface to a collection of Brodie's sermons and addresses, published after his first ten years in office, the new Chief Rabbi noted that through his utterances he had

> sought to convey the contribution which the revealed wisdom of Judaism, contained in the sacred Scriptures, tested and worked out in the historic experiences of a tried and patient people – 'familiar with afflictions and miraculous deliverances' – could make to the challenge of mighty issues facing all peoples in the aftermath of wars, catastrophes and revolution.[8]

An analysis of Israel Brodie's thought highlights the manner in which he viewed his Chief Rabbinate in the shadow of the Shoah and the fears that pervaded in a post-Shoah world concerned at the looming potential for a third and final atomic world war. In the Installation sermon he delivered upon being inducted into the position of 'Chief Rabbi of the United Hebrew Congregations of the British Commonwealth of Nations', Brodie expressed his concerns about the nature of the world in which he and the Anglo-Jewish community found themselves. He asserted his contention that their age was worse than all the others that had been experienced by Anglo-Jewry. Previous periods in the history of Anglo-Jewish Orthodoxy had, in Brodie's opinion, experienced a far greater stability than could be hoped for by his generation.

> Compared with our age, our predecessors lived and worked in days stable, steadfast and spacious. We and our fellow-citizens of other creeds are passing through a bewildering chapter of crises: economic, moral and spiritual.[9]

In response to these experiences, his assessment was that: 'The true leader in Israel has to renew and strengthen our religious and moral preparedness to meet the challenge of the hour'.[10] The feelings of bewilderment that underlined his approach to the modern world prevented him from perceiving a broader horizon that extended beyond the immediate challenges of the hour. In his role as a religious leader, he acknowledged that his focus was narrowed on the here and now, precluding any expansive or idealist vision. If one term was sought to define Brodie's approach to theology the most apposite might be 'reactive'. He responded to each of the circumstances he experienced whilst Chief Rabbi but displayed few hints of a proactive mindset for dealing with theological issues.

The fears of the age resonate throughout the theology of Israel Brodie. He viewed the world as critically sick: 'Morally, socially and economically the world is … on the danger list'.[11] Considering the period in which he ministered, it is perhaps not surprising that the Chief Rabbi took this view. Bewilderment at what had passed and a fear of what may lie ahead were the pervasive feelings and experiences of the age. However, rather than focusing merely on a method for dealing with current issues as and when they arise, it could be suggested that, ideally, the 'leader in Israel' should be exerting his influence to attempt to control the direction in which he believes they should be moving.

The theme which Brodie himself identified as the central idea of his Installation sermon revolved around the message he sought to derive from Proverbs 3:6, 'Acknowledge Him in all thy ways and He will direct thy steps aright'. He spoke of the importance of knowing God in order to know oneself. Indeed he also argued that nations were in need of the knowledge of God in order 'to avoid catastrophe'. He explicitly stated that this knowledge of God was not meant to be an intellectual or theological knowing. Rather, to be effective, knowledge of God involved an abiding awareness of the Divine presence exerting an influence 'as a real factor in our individual and social experience in human history and its interpretation'.[12] In truth, this too may be viewed as an idea that focused on the attempt to understand and interpret recent history and current experience, through reference to an inexplicable yet pervasive consciousness of the divine presence. The central message of his Installation sermon, a theme that he was placing at the heart of his Chief Rabbinate, was therefore unequivocally non-intellectual and an example of his 'reactive approach' to the theological problems that the despair of his age had thrown up.

Brodie's motives for placing knowledge of God's presence at the core of his message as a leader in Israel derived from his belief that an awareness of the divine should improve religiosity, which he hoped would improve morality. He believed that the world had experienced a moral implosion that had infected the human mind. Advances in technology, with both the benefits it offered and the greater fear of its effects that it had inculcated, had brought a spiritual and moral malaise to the new era that it had heralded.

> The discoveries of science and their technological application have in no small measure contributed to the creation of a dominating materialistic and de-personalising outlook which affects the basis and pattern of the social order. All this has meant a weakening of religious authority, a defiance of moral discipline, an equivocal attitude to the rule of law.[13]

On another occasion Brodie explained that his was 'an age which is called upon to meet a crisis involving the possibility of civilisation itself. Ultimately the crisis is moral.'[14] An improvement in morality was required of humanity to try to help it to progress beyond the critical position in which he believed it had become mired.

In 1965, approaching retirement, Brodie himself acknowledged that upon reflecting on the themes of his Chief Rabbinate there were two that had been dominant. We have already noted the influence that the Shoah exerted on his thought. The second theme that pervaded his theological utterances was the significance of the State of Israel, officially created in the same year that he assumed the office of Chief Rabbi. Brodie focused on the hope that he believed had been offered by the creation of a Jewish State. In many of his sermons and addresses he expressed his dream that the State of Israel could develop into a paradigm of the ideal moral state. The clearest expression of these hopes is to be found in a radio broadcast he made during a visit to Australia in 1952. On that occasion he proclaimed:

> I believe the State of Israel has come into being for high purposes – to demonstrate the possibility of a modern state with all its complexities – economic, social and cultural – pervaded by religious faith and founded on absolute social justice – a state that has succeeded in adjusting the inherent rights and freedoms of the individual, and the rightful claims and powers and authority of the group of which the individual is a member.[15]

The relationship between the two themes in Brodie's thought was encapsulated in a Passover address in which he expressed his hope that the suffering of the Shoah could in some way be resolved through the State of Israel:

> All the prayers and soul-searchings and sufferings and martyrdoms for the sake of Heaven and for the survival of Israel's faith

are justified, if the renewal of the national life is guided and stimulated by the fundamental spiritual and moral teachings derived from the Law and the Prophets.[16]

Brodie's expectations for the State rested on lofty religious ideals. Whether he truly believed that Israel could live up to his dreams remains unclear. Whether it was possible for any country to fulfil such expectations must be doubtful. It represented, seemingly without reference to an achievable reality, every ideal and solution to the world crises that dominated Brodie's thoughts. His own need for a source of optimism and inspiration, the needs of Anglo-Jewry, and also of human civilization, he hoped could all be answered by the creation of a paradigmatic Jewish homeland.

Hertz's theological system, in contrast to the various ideas to be identified in Brodie's thought, focused on a long-term goal: preparing Anglo-Jewish youth for their encounter with the modern world. His promotion of a progressive conservative theology provided the basis for a system of education and a methodology for interaction with the modern world that was intended to sustain a Jewish youth that could synthesize the teachings of Judaism with the ideas of modernity. No such clearly thought-out system is identifiable in the work of Israel Brodie. Rather, it is simply the pervading fear and bewilderment of the 1950s and 1960s that dominated his thought. One goal that Brodie sought to promote through his Chief Rabbinate was the achievement of what he termed the 'integrated personality'. Prima facie, this term may conjure up visions of the ideal progressive conservative Jew, a Jew who effects an appropriate Hertzian synthesis. However, as Brodie was to interpret the term it meant something rather different:

> Abraham was conspicuous through the fact that in all that he did he followed the will of the Almighty … He was an integrated personality in all his acts and in all his thoughts. He was always aware of the Almighty.[17]

The knowledge and awareness of God, and the fear that Brodie hoped this would inculcate, represented this Chief Rabbi's central theological message. He was desperate for humanity 'to re-learn the elements of moral hygiene, the fundamentals of social ethics'.[18] In his Installation sermon he had declared: 'We of this generation have the opportunity of giving a convincing and memorable response … despite these puzzling, momentous times'.[19] The new Chief Rabbi would fail to provide the lead in guiding Anglo-Jewry to such a response. He offered the community a reactive theology that was unable to look beyond the crises created by the Shoah. It lacked systematic thought and focused instead on the need to improve morality as the only means of saving the world. Perhaps it is inappropriate to expect anything more from Brodie in the period in which he served. Ministering to a community that has been characterized as unthinking, perhaps his focus on the need to improve personal morality was sufficient. It would, however, appear instructive to consider how both his predecessor and, as we shall see, his successor as Chief Rabbi, placed Jewish education at the heart of their theologies.

The absence of a comprehensive theological system denied Brodie access to the tools through which he might have been able to assert the authority of his office, however diminished that authority might have become. A comprehensive theological system could have provided him with a specific and principled position that he could have defended against the influences and advances of others. No matter how amenable his personality and notwithstanding his eagerness to avoid conflict, if Brodie had entered his Chief Rabbinate with a well thought out theology he would have been able to secure a sound base from which to assert his opinions. Lacking this, the Anglo-Jewish Orthodoxy that he was supposed to lead became susceptible to the influence of other leaders in the community.

11

Right-Wing Orthodoxy

As we have already seen, Hertz had recognized that the viability of a representative leadership figure rested on his capacity to represent a majority of the community. Representation of only a minority of Anglo-Jewry would make a mockery out of his office's right to the title of Chief Rabbi. Those influenced by his decisions would be too few in number and too many other members of the community could claim that his opinions were too unrepresentative to be valid as the 'official' opinion of Anglo-Jewry. Despite the pre-Second World War immigration which strengthened the outer poles of Anglo-Jewry, the right-wing Orthodox and the Progressives, in terms of pure numbers it was the centrist position, which Hertz had defended throughout his Chief Rabbinate, that maintained its dominance in the community. Therefore, it was their position that the new Chief Rabbi had to represent if he was to adopt a viable leadership position.

Nonetheless, the strengthening in numbers and the presence of strong leadership figures, particularly in the person of Solomon Schonfeld, ensured that right-wing Orthodox Judaism was in a position to exert considerable influence on the Anglo-Jewish community and most especially on the Chief Rabbi. A key factor in the right wing's success at exerting this influence lay in its outspoken assertions of its importance as the only group upholding a true form of Orthodox Judaism. Their claim was that

> only with us and through us can genuine Jewish life be kept alive in the country. And let us never forget that the true classic Judaism which we keep alive is not only worthwhile, but that it is the civilisation which is the goal and haven of mankind.[1]

It has already been noted that the impact of the Shoah can be discerned in the theology of Israel Brodie; it eroded the new Chief Rabbi's capacity for optimism. It also affected the London Bet Din, who came to view their activities with greater gravity in the aftermath of the Shoah. The dayanim's newly important role within a European Judaism that had lost its greatest centres of religious authority led to a fresh zeal in their halakhic decision-making. This introduced a strictness and rigidity to their interpretation of the teachings of Judaism that had not been noticeable under Hertz's mediatory leadership. In addition, the Shoah exerted an influence over the theological development of the right wing in Anglo-Jewish Orthodoxy. It heightened the perception that a greater responsibility now fell upon members of their own group to preserve a faithful remnant of Orthodox Judaism. They were highly conscious of the fact that the Shoah had destroyed eastern Europe's centres of learning and piety. Their assessment was that the burden to sustain Orthodox Judaism fell upon the European Jewish community that had escaped unharmed. However, the concern amongst the right wing of Anglo-Jewish Orthodoxy was that the majority of the community, those contained under the umbrella represented by the centrist position that Hertz had sought to defend, were insufficiently strict in their observance of Orthodox Judaism. They perceived that the burden of sustaining a remnant was therefore restricted solely to their own members and those within the ultra-Orthodox camp.

The method right-wing Orthodoxy adopted to achieve this goal was religious separatism. By reducing contact with those who were either less Orthodox or non-Orthodox, they believed that they were more likely to succeed in preserving their own Judaism intact. In particular, they secured the provision of a separate and stricter control over *kashrut*, they focused on providing suitable Jewish education for the youth of their communities, and they encouraged the construction of *mikvaot* in order to improve observance of the laws of family purity.[2]

Of course religious separatism was a phenomenon in Anglo-Jewry that predated the Shoah. The perception that the mainstream of Anglo-Jewish Orthodoxy was insufficiently Orthodox had been clear when the Machzike Hadath had been established in 1891. The formation of the Machzike Hadath had been designed to separate those Jews who were more exacting in their practice of Judaism. It provided them with an appropriately strict *shechitah*, and enabled its members to disassociate from mainstream Orthodoxy, which was viewed as complicit in allowing Jewish practices that simply were not deemed to be sufficiently Orthodox. The name chosen by these earlier seceders in Anglo-Jewish Orthodoxy to designate their group demonstrated the perception they entertained regarding the nature of their role. The epithet *Machzike Hadath*, aside from connections to its Galician forbears, identified its members as part of the Assembly of those who Strengthen Judaism. When Bernard Homa came to write the history of this group, the title that he chose for his book further captured the attitude of its adherents. Published in 1953, it pointed to current sentiment in perceiving adherents of separatist Orthodoxy as *A Fortress in Anglo-Jewry*. Both are names that capture the mentality of members of separatist Orthodox communities. They point to a self-perception of their group as a pious minority fighting a lonely struggle on behalf of righteousness. This was the mentality that developed as a by-product of religious separatism. It was also evident amongst members of the Adath Yisroel and then the UOHC who championed a number of the causes that had previously been fought for by the Machzike Hadath.

The UOHC would come to represent two types of Orthodox communities in Britain. Those of mostly Germanic origin dominated the UOHC. In addition, Jews with eastern or central European origins developed devout enclaves in Gateshead and Manchester, and certain London suburbs, notably Stamford Hill. As has been noted, the groundwork for religious separatism in the UOHC is to be identified in the theology of Samson Raphael Hirsch. In 1864 Hirsch espoused the principle of the *Austrittsgemeinde*. This was an approach to the concept of the Jewish community that was antithetical to the attitude that had dominated in Anglo-Jewry, where the Chief Rabbi was a symbol of the community's unity. *Austritt* was the notion that sectarianism, separation from the main Jewish community, was necessary in order to preserve the Orthodox integrity of one's own community intact. It was feared that sustained unity with those whose opinions and practices differed from those of Orthodoxy might subvert the strictly observant. The principle of self-preservation, the concern to avoid the erosion of one's own Judaism, legitimized the creation of division in a community. As Solomon Schonfeld explicitly acknowledged, the value of leading others to righteousness becomes secondary if one's own religiosity could be threatened.

> Our minority is often challenged to infiltrate into and to infuse the general community. The chance of spreading some good far and wide is to be eagerly grasped. But if it may cost only some of one's own intensity, then Orthodoxy says no. The price is too heavy.[3]

Within the context of Anglo-Jewish Orthodoxy, the principle of *Austritt* could not be applied in the same manner as it had in communities such as Frankfurt, Vienna and Berlin. This had been recognized by Victor Schonfeld, who only sought to exercise separatism in England where it was feasible. On one occasion he had explained his refusal of a wedding invitation by asserting that, 'I do not want to make a rule of attending functions in the United Synagogue because I do not regard it as a strictly Orthodox institution'.[4] However, he also recognized that 'our Synagogue was never established as an *Austrittsgemeinde* in the continental sense. Legal, social and religious conditions are quite different here.' He argued that we differ from many an Austrittsgemeinde who, as a rule do not care a jot as to what happens on the other side of the fence … I said in … a sermon that we must have our windows open to communicate with Jewry outside.[5]

The evolution of Hirsch's principle of *Austritt* was influenced by the political and legal nature of Jewish communities in Germany. The Jewish *Gemeinde* was a forced rather than voluntary organisation that levied a tax on all its members and thereby provided for the community's religious, social, educational and welfare needs. German law, the *Gemeindezwang*, dictated that Jews either had to be members of the local Jewish community or they had to renounce their Jewish identity altogether and convert to become members of a Christian Church. Hirsch's objection to this scenario arose when the *Gemeinde* came under the control of Reformers. Once the Reformers gained a majority in a community, they were able to impose religious reforms in the communal institutions. The Orthodox members of the *Gemeinde* were forced to continue to contribute to the upkeep of these bodies through the communal taxes and if they wished to set up alternative Orthodox institutions they were forced to provide for these themselves.[6]

In 1844, when Leopold Stein (1810–82) was appointed Chief Rabbi of the Frankfurt Jewish community, liturgical reform came to be introduced. Initially this included the introduction of a choir, German prayers for the government and community, and the abolition of the sale of Torah honours. By the end of his first year, more prayers were translated into German, whilst some prayers were simply removed from the liturgy. By late 1846 a triennial cycle of Torah reading was adopted and the *Haftarah* (additional reading from Prophets) and its blessings also came to be recited in German. The silent recital of the *Musaf* (additional) prayer and the prayer calling for the restoration of sacrifices were eliminated.[7] For the Orthodox members of the community to provide Orthodox religious facilities for themselves, they effectively had to subject themselves to a double taxation: forced to continue paying the communal tax but also having to bear the cost for Orthodox provisions from their own resources. The Reform majority in the Frankfurt community ensured that a proposal in 1851 that the *Gemeinde* should provide at least limited facilities for the Orthodox was rejected by 302 votes to 126.

The impetus for Hirsch's crusade over the right to secession came in October 1864 when the emancipation of Frankfurt Jewry was completed. Hirsch argued that emancipation enabled all citizens to be recognized as equals; the significance of religious denomination had been removed by law. The state was therefore practising inequality by continuing to interfere in the religious beliefs of Jews. He asserted that forced membership of the Jewish community interfered in a Jewish citizen's right to freedom of religious conscience. He came to view membership of a Reform-dominated *Gemeinde* as an unacceptable endorsement of the Reform community and its activities. In 1873 the Prussian Parliament's passage of the May Laws enabled Catholics to leave a Church if they disagreed with its doctrines, without having to reject Christianity. This was the precedent upon which Hirsch focused. On 18 July 1876 the *Austrittsgesetz*, the Law of Secession, was passed enabling Jews to secede from the Jewish community. Hirsch rejected all the compromises and concessions which the *Gemeinde* offered to introduce in an attempt to avoid schism, and in September of 1876 he made use of his right to secede from the Frankfurt Jewish community. In November, he published *Der Austritt aus der Gemeinde*, in which he asserted that the passage of the Law of Secession transformed membership of the community into a voluntary act, as the Jewish community had been transformed into a voluntary association.[8] He argued that all communities must be either religious or political. Since emancipation had brought an end to any political standing of the Jewish community, he insisted that it was not possible to separate the religious issues and thus enable Orthodox Jews to remain within its confines. Even if the community offered concessions ensuring that Orthodox services would be provided for those who wished to make use of them, Hirsch argued that association with Reform was forbidden. The obligation on Orthodox Jews to secede from a Reform-dominated *Gemeinde* was therefore established in his mind. In reply to the suggestion that large-scale secession would result in the collapse of the community, Hirsch insisted that this simply proved that Orthodox affiliation to an essentially Reform community was only helping to sustain an institution to which the Orthodox were opposed. It lent a legitimacy to the Reformers that Hirsch was unwilling to tolerate.

Hirsch's battle to secure the right to secede from the *Gemeinde* and establish a separatist Orthodox community was based on rather different precedents to those which existed in Anglo-Jewry. The legal constitution of the community differed drastically and the perceived threat posed by the non-Orthodox was of an altogether different nature. The halakhic argument on which Hirsch based his principle of *Austritt* was that the Reform movement from which the Orthodox were cutting off their associations represented 'wilful heretics'. According to Jewish law, association with this category of heretics was entirely forbidden. Hirsch argued that they were beyond salvation, which was why there was no benefit to be gained from remaining in contact with them; there was only the potential for Orthodox Judaism to be harmed.[9] On this point the situation was very different in Anglo-Jewry. Orthodoxy, rather than Reform, remained the dominant religious belief of the community. This was a fact that Solomon Schonfeld had himself acknowledged.

> [T]he vast majority of Jews in Britain and the British Dominions subscribe to Traditional Judaism, if only with lukewarm interest. They pay allegiance to one central Chief Rabbinate and to the general principles of Orthodox Judaism. There is thus a more or less uniform official Faith in British Jewry.[10]

Separation was effected by the right wing because the Judaism of the mainstream in Anglo-Jewry was deemed to be too lenient in its practice of Orthodoxy, not because it was Reform. It was not viewed as a viable means of sustaining a faithful remnant of Orthodox Judaism intact. It did pose a threat to what the right wing viewed as an authentic Orthodox Judaism. Nonetheless, Anglo-Jewish Orthodoxy was not deemed to have pushed itself beyond the boundaries of the Jewish people. It was not engaged in wilful heresy. As Victor Schonfeld had suggested, it was possible to allow the windows of their shuls to remain open to them. A method for welcoming those who recognized the righteousness of the right wing should be maintained. However, it should be made clear that the possibility for change or compromise was only in one direction, it was too dangerous actually to allow the doors of their synagogues to be left open in welcome. Separatism was an important principle in the attempt to maintain a remnant.

The separatism advocated by Hirsch related specifically to internal Jewish relations. It was distinct from the other major pillar of his theology: the concept of *Torah im derekh eretz* – the synthesis of Torah living with the modern world. Hirsch's reputation as one of the founders of the phenomenon of 'Modern Orthodox' Judaism had developed following the 1836 publication, initially under a pseudonym, of his seminal *Neunzehn Briefe über Judenthum, von Ben Uziel*. In this work he sought to present a model of a modern Orthodox Judaism that had no need to be fearful of interaction with the surrounding non-Jewish society. Indeed, in Hirsch's thought, Jews potentially had much to gain from secular studies provided that an appropriate knowledge of Judaism, out of its own sources, was attained first. When this was combined with an awareness that synthesis was not to be effected thoughtlessly, external engagement could enrich Judaism. Whilst Hirsch advocated separatism in contacts between Orthodox Jews and Reformers, he advocated engagement with the world outside the Jewish community. He saw in this method a means of undermining the Reformers' argument that presented Orthodoxy as a relic that could not function in the modern world. In his *Nineteen Letters* he laid out the Jewish education that provided the foundation for his theology. This educational programme was designed to ensure that interaction with non-Jewish sources of wisdom could only enhance rather than weaken Judaism.

Between the publication of his *Nineteen Letters* and his battle for Jews' right to secede from a Reform-dominated Jewish community, Hirsch developed a growing belligerence. In his study of the place of Hirsch in the development of a modern Orthodox response to emancipation, it was the contention of Robert Liberles that:

> When Hirsch came to Frankfurt in 1851, he was known as the most progressive leader of German Orthodoxy, but he gradually emerged as its most uncompromising and militant defender.[11]

As Hirsch's focus narrowed so did that of his followers. The principle of internal separatism came to influence interpretations of the *Torah im derekh eretz* element of his theology.

This tendency was perpetuated following his death, when he was succeeded by his son-in-law, Solomon Breuer, a disciple of Abraham Sofer, son of Moses Sofer, in 1888.[12] In the build-up to the Shoah and certainly in its aftermath, additional influences were brought to bear to further undermine the role of *Torah im derekh eretz* in Hirschian theology. The appeal of the modern world was diminished. In considering the role of German Jews in Anglo-Jewry, Julius Carlebach noted how 'the experience of German Jewry did much to dissipate the seductive influence of Englishness'.[13] The Shoah had clearly demonstrated modern civilization's capacity for evil. This helped shift the focus of Hirschian adherents away from the relevance of the theological principle of *Torah im Derekh Eretz* towards a greater emphasis on the axiom of *Austritt*, now extended to all spheres outside one's own *Adath*. Hirsch's notion that there were things to be learnt from non-Jewish cultures was subverted. Rather than examining what could be gained from a careful synthesis of certain ideals from non-Jewish sources of thought, the imperative fell simply on preserving Orthodox Judaism intact. The Shoah helped inculcate the sense that there were in fact no positive ideals to be identified in the realms that existed beyond the fixed confines of right-wing Orthodox Judaism. This point was explicitly stated by Leo Jung, in an editorial comment on an essay treating Hirsch in his *Jewish Leaders*. He suggested that although the interpretation of Hirsch's principle of *Torah im derekh eretz* had originally been intended to designate '"[t]he combination of Judaism and Modern (Western) Culture". The fall of Western culture provoked a revolt against the combination.'[14]

As will become clearer in subsequent chapters, the concept of 'compartmentalisation' developed whereby engagement in the surrounding world for the sake of one's livelihood was to be per-mitted, but the ideas encountered in this world were to be segregated from the dominant Jewish aspect of one's mind. This inclination to reinterpret Hirsch is striking in a new translation and commentary of his *Nineteen Letters*. In this work it is asserted that Hirsch's 'writings make it clear that … he never thought of synthesis'.[15] The concern to present Hirsch as an opponent of synthesis, and thereby attempt to undermine its practice within Orthodoxy, results from a fundamental failure to grasp the meaning and implications of the exercise of synthesis. I have suggested that in the theology of Joseph Herman Hertz the term synthesis is to be understood as a rigorous attempt to fuse two separate elements into one complex, yet viable, whole. All attempts to effect any such synthesis are to begin with the revealed word of God, as understood within traditional Jewish thought. Synthesis with non-Jewish ideas that contradict teachings of Judaism is rejected. However in a post-Shoah world that is deemed to have lost the capacity to impart wisdom, the scope for synthesis is removed to the point where it can be reinterpreted as having never been present.

Hirsch's presentation of the concept of *Austritt* had been directed solely at the Reformers within a Jewish community, yet the principle came to be extended and more harshly defined. His own community in Frankfurt had not been strict in its demands of those who affiliated to Orthodoxy without fulfilling all its requirements.[16] Moreover, Hirsch had not applied the notion of *Austritt* to the non-Jewish world. Yet secession came to be interpreted and applied in a more rigorous fashion on both planes. It led to the separation of the right-wing Orthodox from all other Jews who failed to maintain their exacting standards of Jewish practice *and* from all sources of wisdom and truth that originated outside Judaism.

Although the principle of religious separatism existed in Anglo-Jewish Orthodoxy before the Shoah, the experience of that *Tremendum* nonetheless contributed significantly to the attitude of the right-wing Orthodox. We have already noted how Hitler's rise to power increased the number of Jews in England who had been adherents of the *Austrittsgemeinde* in Continental Europe. This strengthened the practice of religious separatism in England, although the nature of the Anglo-Jewish community prevented a complete implementation of the principle of *Austritt*. After the Shoah, justification for separation, not only from the mainstream of Anglo-Jewish Orthodoxy, but also from modern English society, became easier and more tenable.

In the 1950s an additional impetus towards separatism was provided by the arrival of Jewish refugees from Communist Europe, particularly Hungary. Besides increasing the Hasidic presence in

Anglo-Jewry, the influence of Hungarian Jews was of considerable importance in strengthening eastern and central European sectors of Orthodoxy that practised a non-Hirschian form of Orthodox Judaism inspired by the teachings of Moses Sofer, known as the Hatam Sofer. This would further build up Orthodox communities, such as those in Manchester, Gateshead and Stamford Hill in London, whilst also pushing the UOHC itself further to the right.

A symptom of right-wing Orthodoxy's policy of religious separatism was religious triumphalism. We have seen that there was a perception amongst separatist communities that they were engaged in a lonely struggle for righteousness. This sentiment inculcated feelings of self-righteousness. The notion that right-wing Orthodoxy provided a 'fortress' for Anglo-Jewry, that its adherents fought to defend a small corner of spiritual territory for Judaism, to maintain a faithful remnant to which others were incapable of contributing, sets up the scenario of a battle between the right-wing Orthodox and those who were either non-Orthodox or insufficiently strict in their Orthodoxy. Religious separatism was practised as a result of the conviction that one's own group was fighting for the survival of Orthodox Judaism. Religious triumphalism was nurtured by the belief that one's own methods for defending Orthodox Judaism represented the only suitable and viable formula for sustaining a faithful remnant. In an article seeking to explain the *Role of the Orthodox Union*, Solomon Schonfeld acknowledged this perception that they were engaged in a battle. On the one hand Schonfeld stated that

> the importance and rights of the Union are not to be measured by statistics. But even statistically, if 3,000 Union members attend 700 services per annum each and 280,000 Jews [the number of Jews estimated to reside in Greater London] on an average attend three, four of five services per year – who wins?[17]

A scale of religious values was being calculated here, a scale that established a hierarchical structure that could only help advance an attitude of self-righteousness.

Religious triumphalism fostered the conception that the right wing (alongside the ultra-Orthodox) offered the only correct method of practising Orthodox Judaism and therefore the only sustainable form of the religion. Consequently, they believed that they were integral to the survival of Orthodoxy in Anglo-Jewry. Bernard Homa's study of the Machzike Hadath and the growth of right-wing Orthodox Judaism demonstrates the manner in which this perception was entertained by the separatist communities of Anglo-Jewry. Discussing the activities of the UOHC he asserted:

The leaders of the Union ... pursued their lone and uphill course, encountering many difficulties, but without deviating from their uncompromising attitude to traditional Judaism ... This has all been to the good, for it has brought about a general raising of religious standards.[18]

Celebrating the twenty-fifth anniversary of the UOHC, Schonfeld wrote in the *Jewish Chronicle* outlining his understanding of the development of the institution and the role that it had performed. He suggested that:

The Union knows its role to be that of a Right-wing minority in opposition to Jewish religious indifference and ignorance, an advance guard of Jewish religious learning and observance.[19]

He argued that despite its size, thanks largely to its strong leadership, it had 'weighted the communal scales towards the right'. By leaving their windows open, even if the doors were firmly locked and bolted, a route for religious elevation of the mainstream of Anglo-Jewish Orthodoxy had been maintained. Moreover, Schonfeld asserted that the mainstream had conceded the value of this role that right-wing Orthodoxy performed in the community: 'The Adath had, by dint of sustained effort in constructive spheres of Torah life, attained wide-spread recognition as the guardian of Orthodoxy in Anglo-Jewry.'[20]

In an article published later in 1951 in *The Jewish Post*, the news-paper of the Agudat Yisrael in England, Schonfeld expressed his contention that right-wing Orthodoxy acted not merely as guardians of Jewish life, practice, and belief. He declared that

the minority of Orthodox devotees: the sabbath observers and *koshere Yidden* and those among them who militate against the flouting or neglect of *mitzvos* [*mitzvot* – commandments]. They represent the conscience of the nation.[21]

By maintaining such a conscience, pointing to what they characterized as genuine Orthodox Judaism, and through their perception that this was a vital activity of the separatist communities, Schonfeld suggested that they fulfilled the task not merely of sustaining a faithful remnant but also of encouraging others to understand the importance of their role. In an article explaining the role of the UOHC, Schonfeld suggested that 'through the existence and activity of its separatist groups the larger mass of Jewry is reminded of the higher religious standards at which all should aim'.[22] He further explained that

One can disobey or ignore conscience, but only the depraved
taunt and flout it; all healthy persons do at least respect it. And
this is the first step in healthy Jewish communal life – respect for
the right-wing, the 'fanatics' for Torah.

It was precisely the respect that the right-wing Orthodox community
was able to command from Israel Brodie that enabled them to gain
the foothold that would allow them truly to exert an influence over
the mainstream of Anglo-Jewish Orthodoxy. Lacking his own comprehensive theological system and conscious of the self-righteousness,
assertiveness and assurance with which right-wing Orthodoxy
followed its course, Brodie was susceptible to their influence.

An admiration for the activities of right-wing Orthodoxy, the conception that they provided an exemplar for mainstream Orthodoxy,
and an interest in following their lead to advance their ideals, may be
seen to creep into Brodie's comments. He came to acclaim the religious
activities of Orthodox groups who existed outside the mainstream of
Anglo-Jewish Orthodoxy. These were groups who would seek to shift
the centrist theology of the community rightwards, away from the
beliefs and practices of the majority of the community, uninterested in
the Orthodox umbrella that the Anglo-Jewish leadership had sought
to create to preserve unity and harmony in the community. These were
therefore groups that were liable to foster religious polarization and
undermine the capacity for the Chief Rabbinate to be representative as
the central leadership figure of Anglo-Jewry.

Three key influences located outside the mainstream were acknowledged and commended by Brodie for their help in the gradual
rejuvenation of Anglo-Jewish Orthodoxy towards the theology and
practices of right-wing Orthodoxy. The first was the Jewish Day
School Movement, whose importance in influencing both children and
parents in the community to improve their observance of Orthodox
Judaism was significant. Addressing the 1953 Conference of Anglo-
Jewish Preachers, following a pastoral visit to Melbourne, Australia
the previous year, Brodie contrasted the Orthodoxy which he had
encountered in the city when he had served there as its Minister to that
to be found on his return in 1952. He argued that:

The measure of the changes which have taken place in the intervening years is provided by the general attitude to the Jewish
Day School Movement which has achieved striking success.[23]

The effect that these schools could have on Anglo-Jewish families was
commented upon by Chaim Bermant in his *Troubled Eden: An Anatomy
of British Jewry*. He noted how: 'In an earlier age many housewives had

to keep a Kosher home for the sake of an aged parent; some now have to do so for the sake of a demanding child.'[24] Jewish schools, by educating children in a strict Orthodoxy, could succeed in spreading this Orthodoxy into the homes of its students. Solomon Schonfeld was well aware of this effect. In his report to the Council of the UOHC in 1958 he noted:

> alongside of our strengthening of internal *Yiddishkeit* in its various forms, we were able to continue our efforts for the improvement of religious standards in Anglo-Jewry at large. We were able to develop the Jewish Secondary Schools Movement and to bring some thousands of children from the general community under the orthodox teachings and influences of our schools.[25]

At the opening of a Lubavitch Centre in London in 1961, Brodie acknowledged the value of a second influence that had begun to affect Anglo-Jewish Orthodoxy. He stated that:

> During the short period since the Lubavitch Foundation was established in our metropolis, it has shown that it has a most important contribution to make to the re-invigoration and strengthening of the religious life of Anglo-Jewry.[26]

The Lubavitch are part of the Hasidic movement in Judaism, yet although they are a Hasidic sect, they are an anomaly in Orthodox Judaism. Their attitude of separatism from non-Jewish sources of wisdom is maintained alongside an active outreach programme in which they vigorously mix with less Orthodox or non-Orthodox Jews in order to encourage them to practise Orthodox Judaism. The Orthodoxy that they promote is *haredi*, rejecting the modern world as a potential reservoir of truth. As such, it represented a theological position that had little affinity with the attitude of the majority of Anglo-Jewry. Thus the Chief Rabbi was here praising a religious group whose Orthodoxy was far removed from mainstream Anglo-Jewish Orthodoxy.

In a special supplement to the *Jewish Chronicle* in January 1964 on 'Jewry in the North-East', Brodie contributed an article in which a third key influence can be identified in the right-wing transformation of Anglo-Jewish Orthodoxy. In a considerable shift from the position expressed by Hertz, Brodie suggested that the Jewish learning institutions of Gateshead and Sunderland were of significant benefit to the wider Jewish community. He noted how they provided a number of highly qualified Jewish teachers for the Jewish Day School

Movement and other educational establishments in Anglo-Jewry. In addition, he suggested that they were succeeding in creating 'the nucleus of a learned laity'.[27] His own attraction to the theological position of right-wing Orthodox Judaism, to its assuredness that it provided the only method for sustaining Orthodox Judaism, led Brodie to advocate a religious rejuvenation for Anglo-Jewish Orthodoxy that followed its guidelines and practices. A religious rejuvenation that was facilitated by the input of right-wing and ultra-Orthodox teachers, rabbis and laity. That the Orthodoxy of the *Yeshivot, Kollelim* (advanced Talmudic institutions) and Women's Seminary of Gateshead and Sunderland might have been able to exert these influences on Anglo-Jewry, and have such influences appreciated by the Chief Rabbi, suggests that the theology of the community's religious leader had shifted considerably further to the right than had been possible during the tenure of his predecessor. Hertz had opposed their theology as a system of thought that was inappropriate for Anglo-Jewish Orthodoxy. He opposed their extremist position on the right wing of Orthodoxy and the internal and external separatism that they championed. However, under Brodie the influence of the right wing was being allowed to exert itself on mainstream Anglo-Jewish Orthodoxy in a manner that had never previously been possible.

Brodie came to lend his support to a religious rejuvenation that moved in a completely antithetical direction to the theological position advocated by Hertz. He came to promote the value of a theology that practised separatism or compartmentalization rather than a theology of synthesis. This separatism isolated its adherents from those Jews who failed to adhere strictly to its own practices; as such the promotion of religious polarization lay at its heart. Moreover, in a contemporary society, it promoted detachment from the modern world which, certainly post-Shoah, was deemed to have lost its potential (if any such potential had previously existed) to offer ideals or interesting values which it might have been appropriate to attempt to synthesize with Judaism. This shifted Brodie's theology away from a centrist position and undermined his role as Chief Rabbi. The importance which Brodie placed on the need for a rejuvenation in Orthodoxy, an emphasis that was informed both by the pervading fear which dictated the path of his theology, and by the influence which the right wing were able to exert upon him, had led this Chief Rabbi to enable a considerable shift in religious orientation to occur in the leadership of Anglo-Jewish Orthodoxy.

12

The Jacobs Affair

The last five years of Brodie's Chief Rabbinate were to be the most significant. The theological developments to which Anglo-Jewish Orthodoxy had been subject in the preceding years came to be encapsulated in this period in an episode that was to become known as the Jacobs Affair.

Rabbi Dr Louis Jacobs was a promising and prominent member of the Anglo-Jewish ministry. He had entered the rabbinate of the United Synagogue in 1954 when he assumed the pulpit of the New West End synagogue, one of the most prestigious pulpits in London. At that time, as Jacobs himself recalls with irony, Norman Cohen had written an article on the increasing trend for Anglo-Jewish Orthodoxy to veer towards its religious right wing. In this article, Cohen had presented the appointment of Jacobs as rabbi of the New West End Synagogue as a clear example of this religious shift. He believed that although Jacobs had accepted a position in the United Synagogue, theologically he was affiliated to rabbis on the right wing of Judaism who were exerting an increasing influence on the Chief Rabbi and, through him, on Anglo-Jewry.[1]

Jacobs did represent the new forces that were growing in authority in the institutions of the Anglo-Jewish community. Although born in England and the son of British-born working-class parents, he was a product of the eastern European immigration of the 1880s and not a member of the native Anglo-Jewish community. Jacobs' grandparents were Lithuanian immigrants who had arrived in England with the general influx at the end of the nineteenth century. Born in July 1920 in Manchester, he had been brought up in a home which he characterized as traditional in its observance of Jewish laws but not strict. However, following his Bar Mitzvah, his father had been persuaded to allow him to attend classes at the Manchester Yeshiva and there he encountered a rigid Orthodoxy. The prevailing sentiment in the yeshiva was that the attainment of a secular education was a distraction, a waste of time that detracted from the task of Torah study. As Jacobs recalls, on the occasion of his rabbinical ordination the Rosh Yeshiva of Manchester, Rabbi Moshe Yitzhak Segal, had expressed his hope that his rabbinical students would pursue the traditional Rabbinic role and spend all [their] free time studying the Torah, not wasting time on studies no doubt suitable for those training to be English ministers but not for those who had graduated from a traditional Yeshiva like that of Manchester.[2]

At the age of 15 Jacobs had enrolled as a full-time student in the yeshiva. The undercurrent to the thoughts of the Rosh Yeshiva served to dissuade students from aspiring to attain a university education. Instead, Jacobs was to pursue his studies at the yeshiva for a total of seven years before deciding, at the age of 20, to further his Talmudic studies in Gateshead, where a new Kollel was being opened. He returned to Manchester Yeshiva in 1941 to obtain his *semikhah*.

Regardless of any laxity in the Orthodoxy that he experienced in his home life, by completing his religious education in Manchester Yeshiva and Gateshead Kollel Jacobs had come to be explicitly located on the right wing of Anglo-Jewish Orthodoxy. Each of these provincial centres of Talmudic learning were bastions of right-wing Orthodoxy and Jacobs immersed himself into the so-called ultra-Orthodox cultures which both offered. His identification with the ultra-Orthodox model was further confirmed when he chose to continue devoting his time to learning following his marriage.[3] The importance attributed to Torah study in the ultra-Orthodox world breeds a culture in which Talmudical students are willing to accept financial support from others to facilitate their learning, rather than give up time which could be devoted to study in order to provide for themselves. Instead of undertaking a career in the rabbinate, or any alternative profession, for the first year of his marriage Jacobs accepted the financial support provided by his father-in-law and spent his time engaged in the study of Torah. In the light of this educational background, Cohen's perception of Jacobs as a member of the right wing appeared to be utterly valid.

Jacobs did come to decide that it was inappropriate to rely on his father-in-law for the maintenance of his own family. His decision to accept a rabbinical position nonetheless continued to demonstrate his alignment with the right wing of Orthodoxy, since his first appointment was as assistant rabbi to Eliyahu Munk at the Golders Green Beth Hamedrash. As we have already seen, the Golders Green Beth Hamedrash was a synagogue founded in 1934 by German refugees who arrived in England from the *Austrittsgemeinde* of cities like Frankfurt, Berlin and Vienna. The congregation was fiercely independent, even refusing to affiliate with the UOHC. It was one of London's centres of separatist Judaism.

The Hirschian background of the Golders Green Beth Hamedrash distinguished it from the theological approach that Jacobs had encountered in Manchester and Gateshead. Most notably, reflecting the Hirschian principle of *Torah im derekh eretz*, the absolute antipathy towards university education was absent in the new environment in which he found himself. Both members and rabbis of the community were at liberty to pursue a university education. Consequently, it was whilst Jacobs was in London, working at the Golders Green Beth Hamedrash, that he decided to disregard his Rosh Yeshiva's exhortation and enter University College London to study for a BA in Semitics, after which he proceeded to commence work on a doctorate.

Notwithstanding its acknowledgement that a university education was of value, the outlook propounded in the Golders Green Beth Hamedrash was in line with the transformation in emphasis that has already been noted in the practise of late nineteenth- and twentieth-century Hirschian Judaism. It was not expected that the principles acquired in a university education would actually be meaningfully integrated and synthesized into one's understanding and practice of Judaism. The term 'compartmentalization' captures the theological and practical methodology of such a community, explaining the processes which enabled compatibility to be perceived between the attainment of a university education and a right-wing approach to Orthodox Judaism. The two spheres of knowledge were partitioned off from one another, each contained in their own realm. The principle of synthesis had been removed from their thoughts. The notion that ideas learnt from a non-Jewish source could be fused together with one's Jewish knowledge, to create a complex yet viable whole that could truly contribute to one's understanding of Judaism, had been undermined. It was acknowledged that university education imparted cultural knowledge to its students and provided access to the professions and the opportunity to earn a livelihood. The value in the attainment of these goals was recognized. Nonetheless, heightened fears about the importance of fighting to preserve a remnant of Orthodox Judaism intact had served to downgrade the value perceived in the benefits of a university education. The ideas learned in that environment were subsequently prevented from being allowed to exert any real influence over the beliefs or practices of Judaism.

Despite the influences to which he was subject in his synagogue community, Jacobs' encounter with the academic world caused a transformation in his theological outlook. He failed to effect the process of compartmentalization that was appropriate for the religious environment in which he was located. Rather, his insight into academia's approach to religious issues, particularly pertaining to the origins of the Jewish Bible, led him to question the tenets of Orthodoxy

that he had imbibed in the yeshiva world and which he was expected
to extol in the Golders Green Beth Hamedrash.

In his autobiography, *Helping With Enquiries,* Jacobs recalls that at
this time he made the decision to remain in the rabbinate and seek to
resolve the inner turmoil which he was experiencing from within a
synagogue pulpit rather than in the academic world. He was therefore
glad to be presented with the opportunity to return to Manchester in
1948 and assume the post of rabbi in the city's Central Synagogue.

Manchester's Central Synagogue had grown out of the Chevra
Walkawishk, one of a number of *chevrot* established in Manchester by
eastern European immigrants. The Chevra Walkawishk had been
founded in 1871 by Jews from the Walkawishk neighbourhood of
Lithuania. In his history of Manchester Jewry, Bill Williams characterized the Orthodoxy of the Manchester *chevrot* thus:

> dedicated as a whole to the strictest religious standards of the
> Eastern European ghetto ... the *chevroth* were sustained by a flow
> of immigration which kept up until the First World War and by a
> line of the most uncompromising Polish rabbis, of whom the
> prototype was Susman Cohen of the Chevra Walkawishk.[4]

The Central was therefore an Orthodox synagogue, which perceived
in Jacobs a rabbi who could maintain this tradition, equipped with
considerable Jewish learning, but also able to preach in either Yiddish,
or English, as new situations sometimes dictated. In Jacobs' attempts
to accurately capture the nature of the community he noted that
'[t]hese people were the salt of the earth: pious, hard-working, respect-
ful of Jewish learning, regular in their synagogue attendance'.[5]

Despite his intention to use his time in this synagogue as an opportunity to confront the questions raised by his university education, the
doubt he was experiencing remained intact. Jacobs began to realize
that it was inappropriate for him to remain at the Central Synagogue.
Indeed he began to feel that it was improper for him to be a rabbi in
any community that was 'at least nominally Orthodox ... subscribing
evidently to a fundamentalist approach that I could not share'.[6]
Against this background he decided to return to London and assume
the pulpit of the New West End Synagogue. He made two assumptions. The first was that his religious position would be perfectly
acceptable to the members of the New West End Synagogue. He
viewed the Orthodoxy of this community as far less steadfast than that
with which he had previously been associated. His second assumption
was that this congregation would provide him with a more amenable
environment in which to work out the religious difficulties from which
he was suffering.

Jacobs' characterization of his new community was as follows:

> The New West End Synagogue in St Petersburgh Place, Kensing-
> ton, was the Anglicised synagogue *par excellence* ... The result was
> typical Anglo-Jewish compromise. While men and women were
> seated separately (the latter in the special ladies' gallery) there
> was a mixed choir, situated in the choir-loft built over the Ark.
> The part of the Musaf prayer calling for the restoration of the
> sacrificial system was not recited aloud by the Cantor, but silently
> by those who wished to recite it.[7]

By 1954, when he assumed the pulpit of this synagogue, Jacobs had
completed a process that was to align him far closer to the more
established native community of Anglo-Jewish Orthodoxy than the
new breed with which he had previously been identified. Moreover,
his appointment as rabbi of this prominent congregation, who were
unaware of the motivations that had led him to accept the position,
established his reputation and heightened perceptions about his
future role in the community. It set him on a path to become the Rabbi
expected to take over the Principalship of Jews' College and then move
into the Chief Rabbinate, an office that was to be vacated by Brodie in
1965 when he reached the newly instituted retirement age of 70. Not
only did Jacobs' Orthodoxy remain unquestioned, as was attested to
by Norman Cohen's comments at the time of his appointment, it
appeared that he was being groomed for the position of Chief Rabbi.

As Jacobs himself recalls, it was during this period that Chief Rabbi
Brodie invited him to deliver the sermon at a service of dedication
for London teachers at the Central Synagogue, on 8 May 1955. On
7 September 1955, when Brodie was recovering from an illness, it
was Jacobs who was asked to deputise for the Chief Rabbi and install
the new minister at the consecration of the Slough and Windsor
Synagogue. Earlier, in March 1955, Brodie attended, as guest of
honour, a dinner celebrating the first anniversary of the study group
instituted by Jacobs at the New West End. At the end of 1959 Jacobs
resigned from the pulpit of the New West End to take up a position as
Lecturer and Moral Tutor in Jews' College, a move that prompted the
United Synagogue President, Ewen Montagu, to declare:

> From the point of view of the community as a whole there has
> been no better news for a long time than that of the appointment
> of Rabbi Dr Louis Jacobs as a teacher at Jews' College.[8]

The hopes and expectations that were invested in Louis Jacobs were
becoming more apparent. There was an awareness that, following the

introduction of a retirement age for chief rabbis, it was important to identify a suitable candidate who could be prepared to take over the role. In addition to this, leading figures amongst the laity of Anglo-Jewry, such as Ewen Montagu, concerned by the religious polarization that was occurring in the community, had come to view Jacobs as the rabbi most likely to strengthen the centrist position in Anglo-Jewish Orthodoxy. At face value he was well equipped to perform this role. He represented an unusual blending of the old and new in Anglo-Jewry. A rabbi trained in the strictly Orthodox worlds of Manchester and Gateshead who was capable of ministering to the highly Anglicized members of the New West End Synagogue.

Jacobs insists that his decision to accept a position at Jews' College, and resign from his prestigious ministry at the New West End Synagogue, was based on the understanding that he would assume the Principalship of the College upon the retirement of the incumbent Isidore Epstein. This position was later confirmed by Felix Levy and Lawrence Jacobs, who had been Joint Treasurers on the Executive Council of Jews' College at the time of the appointment. Approached by the *Jewish Chronicle* for clarification of exactly what Jacobs had been told when he accepted a position at the College they stated that:

> The Honorary Officers (other than the Chief Rabbi) indicated to Dr Jacobs at the time of his appointment as Tutor and Lecturer that, subject to the Chief Rabbi's approval of his candidature, they intended to recommend to the Council his appointment as Principal when the post became vacant.[9]

Epstein, who had been on the faculty of Jews' College since 1928 and Principal since 1948, was due to retire in September 1961 upon reaching the age of 65.[10] In July 1959 the College formally ratified this position. Recording the announcement of Epstein's scheduled retirement, a *Jewish Chronicle* editorial took the opportunity to note that 'Jews' College must now consider the kind of personality whom it would wish to succeed to the principalship'.[11] With this acknowledged need to find a successor it was no coincidence that Jacobs' appointment was made within just a few months of the announcement. It was quite obvious that Jacobs' appointment to the faculty was a means of lining him up for the post. Since Brodie had fulfilled a similar role in the College before his appointment to the Chief Rabbinate, Jacobs' position in Jews' College was viewed as an appropriate penultimate step to the assumption of the office of Chief Rabbi, for which many people were coming to see him as suitable, when Brodie's turn came to retire.

It was an open secret that Epstein had no desire to leave Jews'

College upon reaching 65. Raymond Apple, a former student of his, asserted that 'he bitterly resented his forced retirement'.[12] Conscious that Jacobs was being manoeuvred into a position to assume his role following his retirement, Epstein also felt resentment towards Jacobs. Consequently, Jacobs received no support from Epstein when attempts were made to ratify the verbal agreement concerning his appointment to the Principalship. However, since a number of members of the Executive Council of Jews' College had been party to this agreement, they rallied to his cause.

The final ratification for the appointment lay in the hands of the Chief Rabbi, who was president of the College. Although the Council viewed the appointment as a foregone conclusion, Brodie repeatedly failed to give his authorization. Moreover, there was no sign that his approval would be forthcoming. Jacobs' frustration with his predicament grew. His supporters on the College Council also became exasperated at Brodie's procrastination. The situation finally erupted at a Jews' College Council meeting in December 1961. Alan Mocatta, Chairman of the College, tabled a resolution at this meeting formally seeking the Chief Rabbi's approval of Jacobs' appointment. He stated

> Here we have an outstandingly successful minister, a man who appeals to young people, a man who himself leads a pious life, and whose object is to teach others to do so, a man born and bred in this country. He would be admirable in the post of Principal.[13]

Brodie refused to respond, insisting that discussion of the entire issue should be postponed until a later date. The only explanation he offered for his refusal was a concern to avoid creating 'divisiveness' amongst the College Council. Mocatta noted that Jacobs had already tendered his resignation, subject to being persuaded that he should remain at the College, and that it was therefore imperative that they dealt with the issue immediately. However, it became clear that Brodie would neither agree to discussion of the appointment nor give his approval to Jacobs being promoted. Mocatta, along with the Joint Treasurers of the Council, Felix Levy and Lawrence Jacobs, Frederic M. Landau, and Isaac Levy, Honorary Secretary and lecturer at the College, subsequently tendered their resignations in protest.

These events made the front page of the *Jewish Chronicle* and remained a constant feature in subsequent months. The background to this drawn out dispute over Louis Jacobs' suitability for the principalship of Jews' College lay in his publication of a book entitled *We Have Reason to Believe*, in 1957. This book outlined Jacobs' response to the ideas he had encountered in the university world. It represented his attempt to reconcile academic conceptions about the genesis of the

Bible with the traditional Jewish understanding of the origins of the
Torah in which he had been brought up to believe. In the light of
modern critical theories on the evolution of the Hebrew Scriptures,
Jacobs came to question the traditional Jewish doctrine of *Torah min
hashamayim*, which, in his view, taught that 'the Torah simply dropped
down from heaven ready-made'.[14] He questioned the veracity of the
dogma that the Torah was literally dictated by God to Moses at Mount
Sinai. In *We Have Reason to Believe* he sought to construct a synthesis
between the ideas of these two worlds that would prevent him from
engaging in intellectual dishonesty but would nonetheless be compatible with Orthodox Judaism. He believed that this solution was
provided by the recognition that the Jewish People's history of interaction with God provided them with the tools by which to reach the
Divine. He explained that performance of the *mitzvot* served to create
a ladder connecting Jews with Heaven, securing a Jewish understanding of the Divine Will. The teachings of the Torah provided testi-
mony to this. He argued that the practices that it prescribed therefore
retained their validity regardless of their precise origins.

When Jacobs had chosen to record in his autobiography the fact that
he had made a conscious decision to remain in the rabbinate following
his experience of a religious crisis, he was acknowledging that this
could have been viewed as a strange choice. In the light of his doubts,
it might have been viewed as more appropriate to leave the Orthodox
rabbinate and continue his study of Judaism in an academic rather
than religious environment. His decision to remain in the rabbinate
and seek to resolve his religious crisis within a communal setting was
motivated by the apprehension that he was not alone in encountering
such theological difficulties. His impetus in writing *We Have Reason to
Believe* stemmed from a desire to attempt to construct a work that
could, in some ways, act as a Maimonidean *Guide to the Perplexed* for
Jews of his own era. He hoped that it could provide a method for
modern Orthodox Jews to perpetuate their interaction in the non-
Jewish world without the experience of intellectual dishonesty. In a
new Preface to the fourth edition of *We Have Reason to Believe*,
composed in February 1995, Jacobs clearly expounded his goals.

> The task of the Jewish theologian is not to try to defend the
> medieval picture of how Judaism came about. Such a picture has
> gone, never to return. The modern Jewish theologian, true to the
> tradition, has to try to understand how, now that Judaism is seen
> to have had a history (which means that there is a human element
> in revelation), the traditional views of Torah Min Ha-Shamayim
> can be reinterpreted while still retaining its ancient vigour and
> power.[15]

In his resignation letter to Jews' College, dated 14 November 1961, Jacobs asserted:

> I remain firmly convinced that the approach to traditional Judaism I have sketched in these books is one that must commend itself to all who are aware of modern thought and scholarship. I have tried to show that intense loyalty to Jewish tradition and observance need not be synonymous with reaction and fundamentalism.[16]

Although four years had been allowed to elapse between the publication of this book and the Chief Rabbi's questioning of Jacobs' Orthodoxy, it was the ideas presented in *We Have Reason to Believe* which lay behind Brodie's refusal to confirm Jacobs as a suitable principal of Jews' College. Brodie impugned Jacobs' scholarly credentials, as well as his Orthodoxy, when he finally made public his veto over the appointment at the Annual meeting of Jews' College Governors and Subscribers in May 1962. He suggested that, in addition to 'his published views', he had been encouraged to reject Jacobs 'having regard to the standards of outstanding scholarship and other qualifications required of a candidate for the office of Principal'.[17] However this was a smokescreen designed to try and shift attention away from the controversy surrounding Jacobs' theological opinions. Thanks to the coverage given to the Affair by the *Jewish Chronicle*, these events received a prominence that was unwanted by the Chief Rabbi's office. The story had even been covered in the national press.[18] This explains the unwarranted attempt to malign Jacobs' scholarship in order to divert attention away from the theological issues. Nonetheless, at least one version of the true motivations for the rejection of Jacobs had already been publicized in February 1962, three months before the Chief Rabbi himself publicly disclosed his refusal to accept Jacobs as Principal. At that time the Bet Din had issued a statement to the *Jewish Chronicle* making it clear that, in essence, the problem was one of Orthodoxy. Their assertion was as follows:

> The Chief Rabbi found himself unable to agree to the appointment of Dr L. Jacobs as Principal of Jews' College, an institution for the training of Orthodox rabbis, ministers, readers, and teachers. The particular reason for his inability to agree, which Dr Brodie stressed again and again to the Dayanim and others, was his deep concern for the views expressed by the candidate in his writings and addresses, which the Chief Rabbi considered to be in conflict with the fundamental beliefs of traditional Judaism.[19]

Jacobs was left without a job. He had resigned from the pulpit of the New West End in order to take the position at Jews' College; now he had felt compelled to resign from that institution. This provided the impetus for the creation of a Society for the Study of Jewish Theology, of which he was appointed Director. Established by a number of his supporters, the Society was founded in order to ensure that he remained in England and to create a role for him in the Anglo-Jewish community. These supporters did not want him to give up the fight and leave for America, where he had received an invitation to join the faculty of the JTS.[20] The inaugural meeting of this group was held on 26 September 1962 and, thanks to the public furore surrounding Jacobs, attracted an unexpectedly large attendance of 700 people.

Jacobs' continued presence in England allowed the issues underlying the Affair to fester. Primarily, it appeared to be principles of theology that lay at the heart of the dispute. His supporters and opponents were fighting over the definition of what was and was not Orthodox. However issues of authority were also caught up in the Affair. Questions about the function of the office of Chief Rabbi were raised. There was a renewed interest in examining exactly how far the power of the Chief Rabbi's office extended.

The authority of the Chief Rabbinate came to be fully examined in the second stage of the Jacobs Affair. As we have already seen, there were two clearly established spheres of power in which the Chief Rabbi was able to hold sway over religious matters. The first of these was in the Board of Deputies where, particularly in the case of certification of orthodox synagogues for marriage secretaries, the Board acknowledges the religious authority of the Sephardi Haham and the Chief Rabbi. The United Synagogue represented the second setting in which the Chief Rabbi was truly able to govern. Power struggles had occurred regarding the precise extent of the office's religious authority over this institution, but the principle had always been clear and it would be firmly asserted in Stage II of the Affair.

When Jacobs had moved to Jews' College, Chaim Pearl was appointed to his post at the New West End Synagogue. At the end of 1963 Pearl indicated his intention to resign in order to take up a position in America.[21] The Board of Management of the New West End viewed this as an ideal opportunity to reinstate Jacobs and try to bring an end to the whole Affair. As Chaim Bermant has suggested: 'There is nothing like exclusion to make a man radical, and nothing like office to tame him.'[22] In January 1964 they therefore offered him the opportunity to return to the ministry of his former synagogue. However, Brodie once again chose to intervene, exerting his religious authority over a constituent member of the United Synagogue. The constitution, character and organization of the United Synagogue have already been examined. The nature of the institution meant that rabbis of individual communities were able to oversee the day-to-day requirements of synagogue members but always had to refer weightier matters to the centralized leadership of the United Synagogue. In an interview with Raymond Apple, who entered the United Synagogue ministry in 1960 when he assumed the pulpit of the Bayswater Synagogue, he recalled his shock and frustration upon realizing that authorization from 'Head Office' was required in all decision-making. 'I had to seek permission before pinning a sign up on the shul notice-board.' Jacobs himself noted how the Chief Rabbi acted as religious leader over all the synagogues under his authority in the United Synagogue.

> Ministers were not, in fact, employed by their own synagogue at all but by the United Synagogue … The advantage of the system for ministers was that it made them independent, in a sense, of the members of their own congregation, who were not their employers and to whom they were not beholden. Provided a man did his job properly, no matter how much he quarrelled with his congregation and how unsatisfactory his sermonising, nothing could be done to get rid of him. Carrying out the duties laid down in his contract with the United Synagogue was all that was required of him and he had tenure for life … however … according to the Constitution of the United Synagogue, the Chief Rabbi's word was law. It was the Chief Rabbi, the rabbi of the organisation as a whole, who was, in fact, the rabbi of the local congregation as well. No innovations in the service, for example, were tolerated, even if desired by the local minister and his congregation, unless sanctioned by the Chief Rabbi.[23]

As was noted earlier, it is a requirement that all prospective ministers of United Synagogue pulpits receive the approval of the Chief Rabbi before a rabbinic appointment can be made. Brodie made use of this power to intervene in the decision-making of the members of the New West End and prevent them from re-appointing Jacobs to the pulpit of their synagogue. Although Jacobs had received certification before he had first assumed the pulpit of the New West End, Brodie insisted that any attempt to reinstate him would also be subject to the approval of the Chief Rabbi's office. He refused to provide such certification unless Jacobs was willing to renounce the theological opinions that had provided the impetus to the whole Affair.

Jacobs had explicitly stated that in the light of his academic studies he had become unable to uphold a belief in the traditional understanding of the doctrine of *Torah min hashamayim* without engaging in intellectual dishonesty. Having made his position on this matter so clear, he could never truly have been expected to rescind his views, to

give way to Brodie's demands and endorse something he had charac-
terised as 'intellectually schizophrenic'. The Chief Rabbi similarly
refused to compromise his position. The stalemate that ensued could
not be resolved.

The Honorary Officers of the New West End composed a letter
to the newly elected President of the United Synagogue, Sir Isaac
Wolfson, explaining their position. They stated that

> while anxious to maintain the Chief Rabbi's authority and the
> integrity of the United Synagogue, the Board of Management of
> the New West End was making known to the United Synagogue
> its intention to take all necessary steps to obtain the minister of
> the congregation's choice.[24]

On 1 March 1964 an Extraordinary General Meeting of members of
the New West End was convened. According to the *Jewish Chronicle*,
an 'overwhelming mandate' was given at this meeting to both the
Honorary Officers and Board of Management of the synagogue to
contest the Chief Rabbi's objection to the appointment of Jacobs as its
rabbi.[25] Since the synagogue received no further word from the Chief
Rabbi, either to retract or reinforce his opposition to Jacobs, following
the celebration of the Passover Festival the Honorary Officers invited
Jacobs to put on his canonicals and return to the minister's seat and
pulpit. On 18 April he was asked to address the congregation from the
pulpit. Responding to these actions the United Synagogue Council
called a Special Meeting the following week, at which Wolfson gave
his support to the position adopted by the Chief Rabbi and put
forward a resolution that the Honorary Officers of the New West End
be discharged from their positions. The very next day, 24 April 1964,
the Secretary of the newly installed Honorary Officers sent a letter
to Jacobs informing him that he was longer permitted to attend the
synagogue in his canonicals. He was only to be welcomed as a
member and worshipper. At a meeting on 3 May, 300 members of
the New West End Synagogue assembled to agree to form a new
congregation. The New London Synagogue was established as an
independent, yet Orthodox synagogue whose theology Jacobs
explained as follows:

> If by Orthodoxy you mean an attitude of mind which shows no
> hospitality to modern scholarship and modern thought and the
> inquiring mind, then I would say that we shall certainly not be
> Orthodox and we shall be proud not to be Orthodox ... However,
> if by Orthodoxy you mean – and the words are not ours ...
> 'Progressive Conservative', then we are as Orthodox as the next
> man.[26]

The emergence of an independent synagogue on the religious left wing of the United Synagogue was the end product of Brodie's decision to assert the powers of his office, first over Jews' College and then over a constituent member of the United Synagogue. This laid the groundwork for the creation of what would eventually become an entirely new synagogal organization in Anglo-Jewry, the Masorti Movement, which in time came to identify itself with the Jewish Conservative Movement of America. Through the events of the 'Jacobs Affair' the theological position espoused by Jacobs and those members of the New West End Synagogue who followed him to the New London had come to be officially marginalized. It was classified as outside the religious spectrum embraced under the umbrella of the United Synagogue, an institution that was supposed to represent the centrist religious position of Anglo-Jewry, encompassing the greatest possible proportion of the Anglo-Jewish community who wished to affiliate to Orthodox Judaism. As a recently retired leading member of the Anglo-Jewish ministry acknowledged:

> The Jacobs Affair changed all of us in a way. We have now said that he isn't Orthodox. Now we have got to be Orthodox. The woolly things to which we turned a blind eye now had to be changed.[27]

The events of the Jacobs Affair helped to effect a change in the theological position of Anglo-Jewish Orthodoxy. Its experience of polarization was sharply intensified as the centre of Anglo-Jewish Orthodoxy was subsequently forced to shift rightwards; and attempts to sustain the United Synagogue as a viable umbrella body were critically undermined.

13

Interpretations of the Jacobs Affair

Jacobs himself has asserted, and this is a commonly held view, that Brodie's actions in the first stage of the Affair were heavily influenced by the opinions of the Bet Din regarding Jacobs' potential suitability for a leading role in Anglo-Jewish Orthodoxy. In Jacobs' autobiography he expressly attributes blame for the first stage of the Affair to the office of the Bet Din. He has argued that it was not until this body had raised its concerns with Brodie, asking questions about his Orthodoxy, that the Chief Rabbi considered questioning his promotion at Jews' College.

Jacobs' reading of events gains considerable support from the fact that Brodie failed to intervene when Jacobs was first appointed to a position in Jews' College. His appointment as lecturer and tutor had been made two years after the publication of his *We Have Reason To Believe*, implying either that Brodie had failed to read the book or that having read it he was unconcerned by its contents. We have already suggested that, as the Bet Din feared, Jacobs' appointment had been made in order to position him for promotion to the principalship of Jews' College and ultimately appointment as Chief Rabbi, following Brodie's retirement. Brodie's failure to act at the time of Jacobs' initial appointment at Jews' College was interpreted by Jacobs' supporters as the Chief Rabbi's signal of his acquiescence in this planned course of events. He appeared to have no quarrel with Jacobs' theology.

Having made his own investigations into the background to the Affair, Jacobs has stated that Isidor Grunfeld was the specific member of the Bet Din who had directed Brodie's attention to the theological problems to be identified in *We Have Reason To Believe*.[1] He had expressed the Bet Din's concern with Jacobs and sought to impress upon Brodie the unsuitability of Jacobs for promotion. The manner in which the Bet Din had usurped much of the religious authority that had previously been exercised by the Chief Rabbi has already been demonstrated. Moreover, Brodie's eagerness to avoid confrontation with both the Bet Din and the lay leadership of the United Synagogue has been noted. The potential for the Bet Din to exert an influence over Brodie and encourage him to refuse to give his rubber stamp to the promotion of Jacobs, a promotion that he was never expected to question, therefore emerges as a real possibility.

The Bet Din's decision to issue a statement expressing their dis-approval of the theology espoused by Jacobs, and their assertion that their opinion matched that of the Chief Rabbi had already exhibited the dayanim's willingness to become involved in this matter, months before Brodie had publicly made a decision on Jacobs' appointment.[2] Even before that statement was issued, in the first week after the resignations at Jews' College, following the front page headlines in the *Jewish Chronicle* questioning the rejection of Jacobs as a suitable Principal of the College, the Bet Din had immediately expressed their thoughts on this issue:

> [I]n response to many inquiries received at the Beth Din, the Dayanim feel it necessary to state; considerations of special scholarship and other qualifications apart, some of the views expressed in recent years in publications and articles by the proposed candidate are in conflict with authentic Jewish belief and render him unacceptable.[3]

Ewen Montagu, in his role as president of the United Synagogue, condemned the dayanim of the Bet Din for interfering in this matter. He was keen to note that: 'The Chief Rabbi alone has a veto on the appointment of the Principal of Jews' College.' Moreover, he was eager to remind the Bet Din that, officially at least, it was the Chief Rabbi who remained in control of religious matters in the community.

> The Chief Rabbi is the religious authority of the Orthodox com-munity. In that enormous responsibility he has the benefit of being able to ask for, and to consider, the advice of his Beth Din before *he* makes *his* decision.
> The slightest degree of loyalty to their Chief Rabbi – even the slightest decent feeling – would have told the Dayanim, his advisers, that they of all people could not possibly publish their views on the point ... 'Pressure!' It will need all the courage of a great man for the Chief Rabbi now to give *his* decision if, on reflection, it conflicts with that of the Dayanim.[4]

Montagu was here pointing to a traditional English understanding of the dayanim's role as 'Ecclesiastical Assessor to the Chief Rabbi', signalling the dayan's function as an adviser and aide to the Chief Rabbi rather than an independent religious functionary. However, with a chief rabbinate that had already been weakened by the trans-ferral of much of its powers, and with an incumbent who lacked the strength of personality to assert the power he retained, the Bet Din had attained an influence in religious decision-making which it had never previously enjoyed or may have expected to exercise. Perceptions about the role of the Bet Din had consequently altered. This was perhaps best exemplified by comments made by the dayanim and the Chief Rabbi in an interview with the *Jewish Chronicle* on the occasion of the Bet Din's relocation to Woburn House in July 1959. In an article discussing the activities of the Bet Din, the dayanim and Chief Rabbi had been asked for information on the structure of the office. They asserted that, far from being assistants to the Chief Rabbi, 'the Beth Din is completely independent'. Furthermore, whilst acknowledging that the official English title of the office of dayan may have been 'Ecclesiastical Assessor to the Chief Rabbi', they explicitly dispelled this notion of the dayan's role. They argued that this title should be considered 'an obsolete term dating back to the time when the Chief Rabbi decided virtually every case'.[5] Both the Chief Rabbi and the Bet Din were willing to confirm that there had been a considerable overhaul in the powers of the Bet Din and the nature of its relationship with the Chief Rabbinate. In these changed circumstances the connotations of the dayan's official English title had become inappropriate and confusing and the interviewees were eager to invest the office with greater prestige.

Notwithstanding the Bet Din's role in inciting the Jacobs Affair, according to members of the United Synagogue rabbinate who were serving at the time, the real impetus to the Affair is to be identified in a review of Jacobs' work written by John Rayner, a Liberal rabbi.[6] Rayner had stated in his article that the views expressed by Jacobs were 'almost completely non-controversial from a Liberal Jewish point of view'.[7] He had also suggested that: 'Naturally one cannot help wondering how a scholar of such a liberal mind can continue to identify himself with the Orthodox "establishment".' It was this suggestion that encouraged both the Bet Din and Brodie to act against Jacobs. Isaac Levy recalled speaking to Brodie after these comments by Rayner were used to influence the Chief Rabbi; he approached him with incredulity to ask 'if the devil quoted Scripture would you reject it?' In Levy's interpretation of the Jacobs Affair the underlying problem was not only Brodie's weak personality and the Bet Din's willingness to exert pressure on him, rather he lamented that: 'The tragedy was that Brodie was influenced by whoever spoke to him last.' This was a judgement of the situation that would appear to gain credence from a statement Ewen Montagu issued at a United Synagogue council meeting in January 1962. In that statement he insisted that the Chief Rabbi had assured him that he was not vetoing Jacobs' promotion because he was impugning his Orthodoxy.

> From very early on in this problem the Chief Rabbi made it clear that this was not a question of Orthodoxy. On more than one occasion he stated quite categorically, to me and to others, that he

had no complaint as to the Orthodoxy of Rabbi Dr Jacobs and that he regarded Rabbi Jacobs as a completely Orthodox man or he would not have approved of his appointment to the most important office of Tutor.[8]

The February statement issued by the Bet Din, referred to in the last chapter, was in clear contradiction to Montagu's comments. Indeed, the dayanim of the Bet Din explicitly stated:

> The sentiments in this matter attributed to the Chief Rabbi by Mr Montagu are in striking contrast with the distress and expressed opinion of the Chief Rabbi on the attitude of Dr Jacobs to Jewish fundamentals and the religious concepts of traditional Judaism as propounded by the leading Jewish authorities.[9]

On the assumption that neither side in this argument was being untruthful, the contrasting understandings of Brodie's attitude to Jacobs, exhibited by Montagu and the Bet Din, can only be understood by reference to Levy's suggestion that the Chief Rabbi was influenced by whoever spoke to him last. Brodie was inconclusive on this matter and susceptible to influence.

In Jacobs' account of Stage II of the Affair he has argued that:

> The Chief Rabbi was in the position of a leader accused of weakness and who therefore felt obliged to demonstrate his strength and courage even when wisdom dictated a more conciliatory attitude.[10]

Brodie was fully conscious of how his role in the first stage of the Affair had been portrayed. He realized that he had widely been perceived as weak and subject to the influence of the Bet Din. This provided him with the impetus to firmly uphold his decisions in the second stage of the Affair and refuse to be influenced or back down on this occasion; although most who advised him viewed Jacobs' reappointment to the pulpit of the New West End as the ideal resolution of the Affair. Jacobs has asserted that he was informed 'on good authority' that the Bet Din had been amongst those who advised the Chief Rabbi to give up his interference in the appointment since in their opinion

> whatever my views, they would be capable of doing no harm in a pulpit long recognised as being somewhat outside the normal United Synagogue patterns in its 'reformist' tendencies.[11]

Jacobs was also told that Wolfson acted on his behalf, seeking to influence Brodie to relent. Ultimately, however, the requirement that United Synagogue ministers gain certification from the Chief Rabbi, attesting to their religious and moral suitability, was unquestionably an area over which the Chief Rabbi alone retained responsibility. Although the United Synagogue President and Bet Din had usurped a considerable portion of the influence and authority exercised by the office of Chief Rabbi, on this matter they were powerless to intervene and force Brodie to change his mind. Moreover, despite Brodie's eagerness to avoid dispute and his willingness to be moulded by the opinions of others, his overriding concern at this juncture was to try to avoid the appearance of weakness and assert the limited religious authority that was at his disposal. The tragedy on this occasion was that his decision to ignore the advice of others paved the way for the creation of a new independent synagogal movement in Anglo-Jewish Orthodoxy that effected the religious polarization of the community. The absence of a comprehensive theological system of his own ensured that Brodie lacked any of the ammunition that had empowered Hertz in his Chief Rabbinate. Brodie had none of the tools that might have strengthened him during the events of the Jacobs Affair. These might have enabled him to follow his own theological path, defending a strong and confident centrist position for Anglo-Jewish Orthodoxy that could preserve the United Synagogue as an umbrella organization, capable of withstanding the influences either of spiritists or those on its right and left wings.

The Editorial of the *Jewish Chronicle* in the week after the Jacobs Affair first erupted had asserted:

> The smouldering dispute which has finally flared into the open at Jews' College is not simply a conflict of personalities but the symptom of a fundamental cleavage in Anglo-Jewish religious attitudes: its outcome is likely to be decisive in shaping the community's future. The issue at stake is not merely who shall be the next Principal of Jews' College. It is whether the Orthodox Establishment in this country will successfully negotiate the transition to twentieth century Western life while maintaining Judaism's spiritual vigour, relevance and communal unity. The alternative is to lapse into narrow, dogmatic rigidity which must inevitably bring about disunity and decline.[12]

Whilst this description of events might be said to contain an element of hyperbole, the importance of the 'Jacobs Affair' in any study of the Anglo-Jewish community in the twentieth century cannot be questioned. Subsequently a number of opinions have already been published which attempt to explain the causes and the significance of the actions which made up this Affair.

The relevance of a weakened Chief Rabbinate and a recently strengthened Bet Din has already been made clear. The development of these two institutions in this direction and the potential problems which this posed have been acknowledged from the outset. The potential for polarization can be said to have been created by the election of Brodie and his installation into an office that had been diminished by the considerable transferral of power to the Bet Din. As we have seen, Louis Jacobs has presented the weakness of the Chief Rabbi and the capacity for influence exerted by the dayanim of the Bet Din as the most important factors in any attempt to explain the events that made up the Jacobs Affair. These factors must not be overlooked, nor should one disregard the relevance of the machinations of the lay and religious leadership of Anglo-Jewry, whose actions had conspired to create this very situation. However, analyses of the 'Jacobs Affair' have led some to suggest that it was a contrived event that was used by any one of three sections of Anglo-Jewry to further their own ends.

The *Jewish Chronicle* is one body that has frequently been accused of having blown the events surrounding the Jacobs Affair out of all proportion in order to further its own aims. The basis for this accusation was the presence of William Frankel as editor of the paper in this period. Frankel had assumed the editorship of the *Jewish Chronicle* in 1958 with the expressed intention of making use of the paper's supposed role as 'The Organ of Anglo-Jewry'.[13] An analysis of the paper during his time in charge and throughout the Jacobs Affair elicits a perception of an editor increasingly concerned with the fate of Anglo-Jewry and the direction in which its Orthodox section was moving. As David Cesarani has noted, in his study *The Jewish Chronicle and Anglo-Jewry, 1841–1991*, Frankel made use of the paper as a forum through which to question something the editor termed 'militant orthodoxy on the offensive'.[14] Frankel himself has recalled that his concerns were really inflamed by a series of articles he commissioned, under the title of 'The Man behind the Pen'.[15] This was a series of interviews with 'a number of young Jews in Britain who, in the 1950s were making names for themselves in the literary world but had little, if any, connection with the Jewish community'.[16] In Frankel's perception, the sentiments elicited in this series highlighted the problems Anglo-Jewry was facing in its attempts to retain the religious allegiance of its youth. He believed that amongst the membership of the United Synagogue Judaism had become moribund; Anglo-Jewish youth was detached from its religious heritage, and the rabbinic leadership was unable to engage its audience:

there was no search for new and contemporarily relevant meaning in Judaism ... But the communal leadership was more concerned with throwing bricks at the red light rather than drawing the warning signal to the attention of rabbis, teachers and parents.[17]

Frankel was amongst those members of Anglo-Jewry's lay leadership who pinned their expectations on Louis Jacobs' perceived ability to help reinvigorate the religious life of the community. He viewed him as a leading light of Anglo-Jewry, a rabbi in whom hopes for an intelligent interpretation of Judaism could be placed. His perception of the need for such leading rabbis in the community was demonstrated in an editorial lamenting the decision of Alexander Altmann to leave England for a university position in America.

Dr Altmann is one of the few rabbis in this country to enjoy a reputation of international dimensions. He has taken the lead in pursuing theological and philosophical studies within a Jewish framework; he has had the courage to approach the relationship of modern literary and historical criticism to Jewish belief; and he has strengthened Orthodox Judaism by showing that neither obscurantism nor violent diatribes against other forms of belief need accompany a whole-hearted commitment to its tenets.[18]

Frankel argued that Anglo-Jewry was in need of rabbis who would honestly seek to explain how and if a synthesis between modernity and Orthodox Judaism was possible. In his description of Altmann's qualities he outlined the attributes he perceived to be essential for the sustenance of Anglo-Jewry. His fear was that the apathetic attitude of Anglo-Jewry's communal leadership not only prevented the community from maintaining the faith of its youth, but also served to deter the rabbis who might have been able to deal with these problems from remaining in the community. Noting the departure of Altmann, Frankel was eager that a similar fate should not also befall Jacobs. However, Frankel's interest in Jacobs extended beyond the personality of the particular individual caught up in the events of the Jacobs Affair. Rather, his focus rested on the theological direction in which he hoped this rabbi might be able to move the community. Frankel had a vested interest in his paper's coverage of the Jacobs Affair, viewing it as an ideal opportunity to promote his own vision for the future direction of the religious life of the community.

Frankel's willingness to manipulate the *Jewish Chronicle*'s coverage of the Jacobs Affair did not pass unnoticed. The Chief Rabbi and Bet Din were prominent critics of the paper, claiming that the Jewish press had played a central role in inflating the issues surrounding Jacobs' appointment to the Principalship of Jews' College and his reinstalment in the pulpit of the New West End. On 5 May 1964 Brodie issued a *Statement to Rabbis and Ministers* in which he publicly levelled this accusation against the *Jewish Chronicle*, condemning it for the manner in which it had manipulated the entire Affair to suit its own ends.

> Whilst we believe in the freedom of the Press, we should not allow this freedom to be abused and even turned into a tyranny as is attempted by the *Jewish Chronicle* which in recent years, no doubt for reasons of its own, has not presented an objective picture of the Anglo-Jewish scene, nor has it reflected the tradition and sentiment of Anglo-Jewry.[19]

Of course the Chief Rabbi and the Bet Din were both bodies who had their own vested interest in seeking to apportion blame for the Jacobs Affair to others. However, these bodies were not alone in sensing that Jacobs was exploited by Frankel and the *Jewish Chronicle* in order to serve the specific aims of the paper's editor. The Jacobs Affair provided an ideal opportunity to undermine the theological position that was gaining dominance in the community under Brodie's Chief Rabbinate and it was an opportunity that Frankel seized. Chimen Abramsky, for example, has commented that, in his opinion, Jacobs' books offered no truly new theological approach to the question of the divine origins of the Torah. The furore surrounding its ideas therefore appears to Abramsky to be out of all proportion to the facts and only occurred as a result of the intervention of certain interested parties.

Besides the accusations levelled against the *Jewish Chronicle*, both the right wing and those who maintained a spiritist approach to Orthodox practice have also stood accused of being exploiters of the Jacobs Affair. On the right wing it has been noted that certain rabbis intervened and sought to exert an influence upon decisions in which they had very little direct interest. The decision to intervene was motivated by the perception of an opportunity to further their own aims. They believed that the Affair might provide the chance to push Anglo-Jewry in an opposite direction to the one that Frankel was promoting through the *Jewish Chronicle*. This point has been argued by Isaac Levy who, in our discussions, recalled the manoeuvrings of rabbis such as A.M. Babad of Sunderland, who sought to influence Brodie by highlighting the supposed heresies of Jacobs during the first stage of the Affair. Levy found this to be an absurd scenario since rabbis such as Babad had no concern whatsoever for Jews' College as an institution. It was a Jewish learning environment at which they sneered, a point which Jacobs himself made when he noted the contents of an addendum to the Ethical Will of Shalom Moskovitz, the Shotzer Rebbe, in which he had stated:

> One of the root causes of the disease from which the Anglo-Jewish community suffers is the existence of Jews' College, where are trained rabbis, reverends, ministers – that is to say, ignoramuses with an acceptance of false beliefs, opposed to the tradition of our holy sages, of blessed memory, by whose mouth we, the people who are old Israel's children, live.[20]

Levy acknowledged that the *Jewish Chronicle* had been influential in 'adding fuel to the fire and embittering Jacobs' opponents'. However, he insisted that:

> The right wing generated their own prominence out of the Jacobs Affair.
> Jacobs didn't set himself up to cast aspersions on Orthodoxy; he was an Orthodox Jew himself.

The exploitation of Jacobs by the spiritist wing became most apparent in the second stage of the Jacobs Affair. The Chief Rabbi's decision to interfere in the appointment of a rabbi at the New West End Synagogue was viewed by certain members of Anglo-Jewry's native community as a further example of how new influences in the United Synagogue were seeking to take over their institution; to challenge the values which its founders had sought to promote and which their descendants wished to perpetuate. They viewed these events as an opportunity to wage a battle in defence of their position, fighting against the changes that they believed were being imposed on the community from outside.

Aubrey Newman, in his study of the history and development of the United Synagogue, has argued that the older generation gave their support to Jacobs precisely because it gave them a chance to pitch themselves against a United Synagogue, which although they had been instrumental in creating, they had ceased to recognize. For the native community the United Synagogue had become an institution that had 'developed in ways they found unpleasant'. The changes in theology and attitude which had occurred led Newman to suggest that, in fact, rather than remaining at the New West End 'it must be admitted that the founding fathers would certainly have felt at home in the synagogue of which Dr Jacobs became the minister'.[21]

In Newman's opinion, the Jacobs Affair elicited the response it received from certain members of the spiritist wing because it related to deep problems in the United Synagogue that had been waiting to be aired for some time. Many of the events of the 'Jacobs Affair' took place in a United Synagogue that for the first time was being led by a president, Isaac Wolfson, who did not come from Anglo-Jewry's Cousinhood and who in fact was of immigrant stock. The transferral of power from members of the native community to descendants of the immigrant community was viewed with suspicion by those who were being displaced. Changes in the lay leadership of the United Synagogue were seen to have exerted a shift in the institution. As Newman noted

> the sort of people who were now available for election as honorary officers were different from their predecessors, and because they were different they had entirely different concepts of the United Synagogue as an institution from those held by their predecessors. These were the years that saw the end of the Grand Dukes in United Synagogue affairs and the attitudes that went with them.[22]

When the Chief Rabbi demonstrated his willingness to be influenced by those who were part of the 'changing balance of forces within the United Synagogue by the new generations and the new families',[23] there were members of the native community who were motivated to attempt to wage one last fight for the integrity of the spiritist values which the United Synagogue had once encompassed. Once this failed a number of them were willing to leave the United Synagogue and become involved in the creation of a new, independent synagogue, because they finally realized that their Orthodoxy was no longer mainstream and acceptable to the new leadership – religious and lay – of the United Synagogue. This position was perhaps best summarized in an article published by *The Times* when the Jacobs Affair had first erupted. Despite Anglo-Jewish concerns to keep communal affairs within the confines of the community, a person *The Times* had described as a 'leading member of the Jewish community in London' had divulged the story to the national press. In his explanation of the beginnings of the Jacobs Affair he had elucidated the situation thus:

> There is no real rift in the Anglo-Jewish community but a number of Jewish scholars who have come to Britain from abroad in recent years now occupy positions of authority. Their outlook is very different from what we regard as the more tolerant Anglo-Jewish outlook and it would seem that the present crisis was brought to a head because of the influence which some of these scholars have been able to bring to bear on the Chief Rabbi.[24]

The theology formulated by Jacobs, the ideas which had supposedly precipitated the Affair, were of little concern to those members of the native community who were on the spiritist wing of Anglo-Jewish Orthodoxy. Their primary concern was with the future of the Judaism with which they identified, and practised in their own particular ways, rather than thought about deeply. As has been noted, the absence of a thinking Jewish laity was a trait that characterized Anglo-Jewish Orthodoxy. This was a point that was acknowledged by Raymond Apple who suggested that, rather than being interested in beliefs about the origins of the Torah, 'the niceties of Anglo-Jewish theology meant that greater concern was directed at what one wore on being called up to the Torah'. Jacobs had provided his supporters at the New West End with an outlet for their battle, just as he had provided the right wing, and the editor of the *Jewish Chronicle* with an opportunity to promote their missions.[25] In each case, Jacobs' actual theology played a rather minor role and his personality was little more than symbolic.

14

A Re-interpretation of the Jacobs Affair

It should be evident that there are certain parallels to be drawn between the theologies of Jacobs and Hertz. Both rabbis had been seeking to create and defend a method for interaction in the modern world with its alternative sources of wisdom and truth. Both sought to create syntheses to effect some kind of compatibility between the two realms. They had both been attempting to prepare Anglo-Jewish youth for their encounter with the non-Jewish world and had been aware, or in the case of Jacobs had become aware, of the difficulties that this world could pose for Orthodox Judaism. Conscious that this encounter was an inevitable feature of existence for a minority religious community located in the midst of a host society with which it was able to freely interact, they both exhibited a concern to impart a confidence in Jewish youth that would enable them to approach the task of synthesis with an absence of fear, confident in the vitality of their Judaism.

In his autobiography, Jacobs explained how he had retained the conviction that he could assume the principalship of Jews' College with the views he had evolved. Furthermore he explained how he believed that it would have been useful for him to assume this post. He asserted that:

> My intended policy, if I did become Principal, was not to promote 'heresy' in an institution strongly committed to fundamentalism – Jews' College was never that – but to try to make more explicit that which had long been implicit in all that was taught there: that modern scholarship has shown the developing nature of Jewish thought and practice. Moreover, right-wing Orthodoxy had always considered the College to be a non-Orthodox institution, so that whatever the official theological position of the College, its very existence would be taboo to the right wing. *I believed that the College could only hope to enjoy success if it firmly nailed its colours to the mast. For the College to be constantly looking over its right shoulder could only result in dislocation of the neck and the head resting on it.*[1] [my emphasis]

In July 1959 a *Jewish Chronicle* editorial had similarly noted that, 'the college needs to be strengthened in self-confidence'.[2] Since Jews' College was an institution in which students for the rabbinate were also required to study for a university degree, interaction with the non-Jewish world and its ideas was an inescapable reality. It was not a yeshiva in the traditional sense; it was a centre of training for rabbis who would serve a laity that interacted in the non-Jewish world. Any attempt to make the college appear a yeshiva-like institution in the perception of rabbinical leaders on the right wing of Anglo-Jewish Orthodoxy was destined to failure. As long as its training was devoted to the creation of Anglo-Jewish 'ministers', rather than rabbis, it would be looked down upon by the rabbis of the yeshiva world. If, however, Jews' College ceased to produce such ministers and sought to train yeshiva-educated *rabbonim* it would fail in its duty to provide the Anglo-Jewish laity with the rabbinical leaders required by the United Synagogue membership. Recognizing the role that the College was required to perform, Jacobs hoped to lead it in this mission with confidence about the validity of this role. Moreover, he was eager to prevent the college's performance of its function from resulting in its students experiencing what he had termed 'religious schizophrenia'.

He had evolved a personal confidence in the synthesis he had come to create to enable his Orthodox Jewish beliefs to remain compatible with his interaction in the modern world, with its conceptions about the evolution of religion and its alternative sources of wisdom and truth. This was a confidence that he wished to impart to those who might have required it if they were to interact with modernity whilst seeking to remain true to their religious heritage. He was conscious that he was not alone in experiencing theological difficulties as a result of his encounter with the ideas of the university world. His impetus in writing *We Have Reason to Believe* stemmed from a desire to attempt to construct some type of *Guide to the Perplexed* for Jews of his own era, although he never expressed it in these terms. In Jews' College he hoped to further this programme, acknowledging the perplexities that could arise from interaction and responding to them. He has explicitly stated that he never intended to undermine the faith of those who were comfortable with the dogmatic interpretation of the concept of *Torah min hashamayim*. His goal was to provide one possible resolution to the problems related to a modern Orthodox existence for those who were in need of such a resolution. His aim was to ensure that Jews' College did not experience fear as a result of its advocation of inter-action; and to address the problems that arose out of such interaction by its students.

One of Jacobs' greatest concerns was the manner in which the College appeared to ignore the fact that its students might experience theological difficulties as a result of their university studies. In our discussions with him he recalled the stories he had heard regarding Adolf Buechler's attendance at meetings of the Society for the Study of Religion. Although in that context the Jews' College Principal would refer to 'the Maccabean Psalms', back at the College these texts were portrayed as the work of King David. Jacobs also noted how, as an Examiner for Jews' College, Epstein had set a question concerning the historicity of the patriarchal figures of the Pentateuch. Jacobs argues that it was absurd to set such a question, having provided the students with the tools by which to answer it, and then expect that the answers provided would simply be ignored when the attention of the student was turned to Judaism as understood within Orthodox parameters. To Jacobs' mind 'It was schizophrenic!' Nonetheless, he has noted that this approach characterizes Anglo-Jewry in general. It reflects the community's basic lack of interest in directing too much thought to their Judaism. As we have already seen Raymond Apple acknowledge, in Anglo-Jewish life little attention was directed to considerations of theology. The focus rests upon the performance of practices fulfilled out of respect for tradition rather than theological thought. As Jacobs explained: 'The *din* [Jewish law] was the Jewish way and you did that ... It was more a kind of, I would see it as a British muddling through, pragmatism.'

It was the transmitted traditions that the Anglo-Jewish community had received from previous generations that were of importance. The ideas behind these practices, or their consequences, simply were not fully considered. This was not the priority, which was precisely why a student could be expected to consider the historicity of a biblical character like Abraham without then allowing these ideas to influence his actions. Jacobs has pointed to Ewen Montagu's insistence that his tailor always ensure that his suits were sent away to be tested for *shaatnetz* as another example of this Anglo-Jewish mentality of performing practices that, when contemplated rationally, might well have been questioned. The laws of *shaatnetz* offer a particularly good model of a Jewish law that would appear obscurantist if subjected to rational questioning. Ensuring that no garments of a Jew's clothing contain a mixture of wool and linen would appear to serve very little practical or spiritual religious purpose. Nonetheless, Ewen Montagu continued to perform this ritual, as Jacobs explained, because it was a tradition handed down to him by his father and his grandfather before that. Montagu's rationalism led him to choose to be cremated on his death, contrary to the Jewish law that requires that Jews be buried; but during his life he performed the Jewish law of *shaatnetz*. The particular problem for Jacobs was that this same attitude prevailed at Jews' College.

> Jews' College; they also muddle through. You see, take the
> question of Biblical Criticism ... they taught the whole of the
> critical position and yet they were taught *Dinim*. I'm not saying
> that the two were incompatible, but there was no attempt made
> to make them compatible. Whereas the interesting thing is ... in
> the Jewish Theological Seminary they studied Criticism with
> regard to Psalms and Ecclesiastes and so on, but they didn't touch
> the Pentateuch. But here it was worse because they did touch the
> Pentateuch and the boys were given the impression that it was all
> right for the *goyim* [non-Jews], or to get a good degree ... They
> were not told how it could be reconciled.

It was his intention to bring an end to the common practice of
expecting students to 'muddle through' the crises they experienced by
acknowledging that religious turmoil could result from the encounter
with modernity but arguing that it need not truly threaten Orthodox
Judaism.[3]

The question of whether his proposed methods for resolving these
issues were correct, or offered anything new, is largely immaterial to
an understanding of the motives behind Jacobs' actions. The halakhic
propriety of his opinions became largely extraneous as the disparate
forces at work in the Jacobs Affair sought to make use of events for
their own purposes. The laity, of course, also expressed little interest in
the intricacies of the theology, preferring to focus on the commotion
created around the Jacobs Affair. Consequently, an examination of the
actual resolutions Jacobs composed to the theological difficulties
raised by the principle of *Torah min hashamayim* is less important than
the responses his ideas elicited. Nonetheless, it must be acknowledged
that Hertz would not have agreed with the attempted synthesis
created by Jacobs on this issue. Hertz opposed the theories of Higher
Criticism that had led Jacobs to question the origins of the Torah.
Following Solomon Schechter's position, he condemned Higher
Criticism as 'Higher Antisemitism', seeing it as a method for undermining Judaism and the confidence Jews may have in their faith. It
was his contention that the Bible critics were seeking to diminish
Judaism's claim to be a source of morality through their attempts to
demonstrate that the teachings of the Torah, rather than being the
word of God, teaching new moral principles, reflected the sentiments
of men writing in a later age expressing the practices of the time.[4] Such
questioning of Judaism's contribution to other societies contrasted
with Hertz's interpretation of the religion's passage through history
and impinged on his argument that a Jew's religious heritage should
provide a source of pride. Although Hertz and Jacobs may have
shared common goals, the theories which moved Jacobs to create a

synthesis were based on ideas which the Chief Rabbi had suspected would impair rather than enhance the all-important experience of confidence in Judaism. However, notwithstanding these differences, Hertz might still have been expected to sympathize with the predicament in which Jacobs had found himself following his encounter with the ideas of the university world. It had been precisely the religious crisis that Jacobs faced which Hertz had sought to prepare Anglo-Jewish youth to avoid. It is also worth considering how the situation might have differed if the Jacobs Affair had occurred during Hertz's Chief Rabbinate rather than that of his successor. Hertz's refusal to countenance the opinions of those on both the spiritist and right wings of Anglo-Jewish Orthodoxy might have enabled him to treat the events of the Jacobs Affair free from the undue influence of characters whose only real interest in the proceedings was to manipulate events in their preferred direction.

A crucial difference to note between the approaches of Hertz and Jacobs to the task of synthesis is the fact that the Jewish education which Jacobs had received before entering university had in no way provided him with the tools which Hertz had considered essential for young Jews entering the modern world. He had not gained a training in the educational programme of positive historical Judaism advocated by Hertz. Jacobs had been faced with stark contradictions between his yeshiva training and the ideas he was being taught at university; and he had obtained no advance preparation for this experience through a knowledge of Jewish responses to such situations in the history of earlier encounters with non-Jewish sources of wisdom and truth. Of course Jacobs' Jewish educators in the yeshiva world had not wished him to engage in the ideas of the modern world, as was clearly evidenced by the comments of the Manchester Rosh Yeshiva when Jacobs received his *semikhah*. Having chosen to ignore Segal's exhortation to concentrate solely on traditional Torah study, Jacobs came to be faced with a stark dilemma. He could practice a theology of compartmentalization, separating the ideas he had learnt at university from his faith and practice of Judaism, preventing the former from meaningfully influencing the latter. The practice of compartmentalization was the response he viewed as intellectually dishonest. This was the theological position that characterized the educational programme that Jacobs had discovered at Jews' College (and at the Golders Green Beth Hamedrash). He had already rejected it when he wrote his *We Have Reason to Believe*, and he recognized the difficulties it created when he encountered it at Jews' College. Having been taught the critical theories on the origins of the Pentateuch and the evolution of the Jewish religion he felt unable to dismiss these ideas simply because they contradicted the beliefs he had been taught at yeshiva; and he was unwilling to relegate them to a locked compartment of his mind. The alternative was to accept the validity of critical theory and, in an attempt to uphold his Orthodox Judaism, seek to reconcile the opposing ideas he had learnt in university and yeshiva. His task was to construct a theology of synthesis without a prior knowledge, which Hertz's educational programme would have provided, of how such syntheses had been effected in earlier stages of Jewish history.

Significantly, in our discussions with Jacobs, he recognized the importance of Hertz's educational programme suggesting that Anglo-Jewry's failure to sustain a Hertzian progressive conservatism resulted from an abandonment of the principles which defined Hertz's approach to education. Jacobs was keen to note that perceptions about the nature of Jewish education for Anglo-Jewry have shifted. When asked to explain the theological development of Anglo-Jewry towards its right wing, he asserted: 'If I were to put it in one sentence it would be that the whole historical approach to Judaism has been abandoned.' Without the apprehension of Judaism as a positive historical pheno-menon the potential for misunderstanding the history of the religion is increased. Alongside this, the capacity for Jews to experience self-contempt grows. Each of these experiences inculcates feelings of fear, rather than confidence, concerning the religion's ability to engage in spheres of thought whose sources of wisdom and truth differ to those of Judaism. The rejection of Hertz's educational policies therefore exacerbates the difficulties that emerge out of the attempt to maintain Orthodox Jewish practice and beliefs intact in a Jewish community that exists as a minority group within a non-Jewish host society. Engagement with the host society is an inescapable component of the Anglo-Jewish reality. The importance of creating a number of different levels of confidence for Jews in this encounter was recognized by Hertz. However, this process is impaired by the failure to provide Jewish youth with the appropriate religious education.

In attempts to fully understand the Jacobs Affair, the true signi-ficance of Jacobs' educational background extends beyond the fact that he had not received the training advocated by Hertz. His religious upbringing in institutions that represented bastions of ultra and right-wing Orthodoxy was a key factor in the furore that surrounded his supposed heresies. In May 1964 when Brodie delivered a *Statement to Rabbis and Ministers*, seeking to present his version of events in the Jacobs Affair, the relevance of Jacobs' background in the yeshiva world was acknowledged. Brodie recalled the comments he had made to the *Southern African Jewish Times* in July 1962 when he sought to explain how Jacobs might have been led to believe that he would assume the Principalship of Jews' College. In the interview Brodie suggested

I consented to his appointment as Tutor, though I knew that some of his views were not completely acceptable, but *bearing in mind his background and early training, I felt that an act of faith on my part would be justified,* and that with the passage of time, and with further study of Jewish sources and continuing research, he would modify his views.[5] [my emphasis]

Brodie's subsequent requirement that Jacobs agree to publicly rescind his views in order to be allowed to return to the pulpit of the New West End evidently pointed to the Chief Rabbi's belief that a man of Jacobs' educational background would, ultimately, be persuaded to uphold the traditional interpretation of the concept of *Torah min hashamayim*. The fact that a person with his background could question the traditional interpretation of *Torah min hashamayim* following his interaction with the university world, and refuse to compartmentalize or reject the new ideas he learned, was what was so truly shocking and significant in the Jacobs Affair.

Jacobs has suggested in our discussions that he was a 'symptom' of his age, that the treatment he received during the Jacobs Affair was simply characteristic of the religious direction in which Anglo-Jewry was heading at the time. This perception reflects the point of view of two of those groups who exploited the Jacobs Affair for their own purposes. For William Frankel at the *Jewish Chronicle* and certain members of the native community of Anglo-Jewry, Jacobs' treatment was a symptom of the transformation that was occurring in Anglo-Jewish Orthodoxy. This interpretation views the rightward swing in the ideological position of the community as inevitable; a result of the influence exerted on the religious institutions of the community by the arrival of such large numbers of immigrants from the 1880s onwards. This is an oversimplified interpretation of Anglo-Jewry's development. If any immigration was significant in the rightward shift it was the arrival of Nazi refugees in the 1930s, rather than the immigration of the 1880s. However that too did not set Anglo-Jewry on an irreversible path towards religious change. The pivotal factors were Hertz's waning health and subsequent death at such a crucial juncture in the community's history, the appointment of Brodie to a Chief Rabbinate whose power had been weakened, the presence of dayanim who usurped much of the religious authority in the community for the Bet Din, and the implications that were drawn from the religious background of Louis Jacobs. His acknowledgement that he had experienced a theological crisis following his encounter with the ideas of the university world was critical.

Ostensibly, it was the Shoah that had acted as an influential factor in the practice of separatism and the fear of interaction that was inculcated amongst the right wing of Anglo-Jewish Orthodoxy. The importance of preserving intact a remnant of Orthodox Judaism had become more urgent; and the onus was seen to fall more heavily on right-wing and ultra-Orthodoxy in England since the traditional centres of Jewish life and learning of Continental Europe had been destroyed by the Shoah. The perception that Orthodox Judaism could be undermined by interaction, both internally with those deemed to be insufficiently strict in their Orthodoxy and externally with the non-Jewish world, fostered an atmosphere of fear towards this endeavour. Alongside the practice of separatism a theology of compartmentalization was also advocated. This was designed to ensure that if interaction did occur the ideas encountered in non-Jewish sources of wisdom could be prevented from exerting an influence over Orthodox Judaism.

Quite aside from the heightened concern to preserve a remnant in its aftermath, the atrocities of the Shoah also weakened the allure of interaction. The Shoah appeared to demonstrate that modernity was bereft of any redeeming values that could be of interest to Jews. The moral depravity illustrated by the Shoah pointed to the possibility that there was actually nothing to be gained from interaction in modernity and provided further justification for the practice of separatism. The Shoah had seemingly revealed the true colours of modernity, confirming the legitimacy of its rejection by right-wing Orthodoxy.

In truth, the rejection of modernity had preceded the Shoah. Fear of the effects of engagement with modernity had featured in right-wing circles of Continental European Jewry since the offer of emancipation had first been presented to Jews. The Shoah substantiated fears that had already been prevalent. The potential offered by emancipation had been apprehended with fear by rabbinical leaders from the outset. They recognized that it would relax the ties that held the community together, weakening the hold of traditional religious authority. The increased potential for interaction would increase the likelihood of assimilation.

Although Hirsch had argued in defence of the potential value of a careful synthesis of the two realms, we have already seen how the focus of his theology was shifted by his successors. When Hirsch had defended synthesis he had recognized, as did Hertz the following century in Anglo-Jewry, that members of a Jewish community who were located in the midst of a non-Jewish host society that was willing to admit Jews into its environment were likely to practice interaction. Both Hirsch and Hertz promoted theological systems whose focus rested on preparing these Jews for such interaction. Yet their models for interaction and synthesis were ignored by right-wing rabbinical leaders who preferred to advocate separatism, focusing on the potential for harm rather than the benefit that could accrue from interaction. At its heart, the right-wing position rested on an absence of confidence in the ability of Jews to interact in non-Jewish spheres without undermining their Orthodoxy.[6]

Jacobs has argued that in the hands of those he has termed fundamentalists the doctrine of *Torah Min hashamayim* has had to evolve in utterly static terms. 'Everything is the word of God. Rebbe Moshe Feinstein becomes the word of God.' Instead of *Torah min hashamayim* 'it is "Orthodoxy *min hashamayim*".'[7] Jacobs insists that he can maintain a traditional life of Jewish observance with his dynamic interpretation of the doctrine of *Torah min hashamayim*. He believes he has achieved an acceptable synthesis between certain ideas of rational modern thought that he was unable to reject and his Orthodox Judaism. He argues that it is not necessary to make a clear choice between traditional Jewish belief and an existence in the modern world. Yet he notes that those he terms fundamentalists, on the right wing of Orthodox Judaism, have presented the doctrine of verbal inspiration as an either/or. That is, if it is rejected all of faith is undermined. Jacobs exclaims that:

> It is this either/or that those of us who are not fundamentalists find intolerable. We refuse to accept that the only choice before us is the stark one of either rejecting all modern knowledge and scholarship or rejecting belief. We believe that we can have both. *It is because we have faith in Judaism that we have confidence in its power to survive without an artificial buttressing of untenable theories.*[8] [my emphasis]

Once again, the importance of confidence is raised as a pivotal factor in the ability to maintain a modern, Orthodox, progressive conservative Judaism. Confidence is a facilitator of interaction and a foundation stone for theologies of synthesis. It is the contention of this study that with fear acting as the underlying motivator in the activities of the right wing, an interaction with modernity that allows for the possibility of synthesis has to be precluded.

Louis Jacobs had substantiated these fears of the right wing. Rather than being a symptom of the inevitable transformation of Anglo-Jewish Orthodoxy, he acted as a catalyst for the changes that were to occur. Here was a young Anglo-Jew brought up in the new strongholds of a more stringent Anglo-Jewish Orthodoxy – Manchester Yeshiva, Gateshead Kollel, the Golders Green Beth HaMedrash – yet even his Jewish faith had been unable to withstand the influences of the non-Jewish world. The university world, in particular, had demonstrated its power to corrupt. Jacobs provided the right wing with the paradigm through which their fears could be justified; and their rejection of a Hirschian or Hertzian model of synthesis legitimized. Even with his knowledge of Orthodox Judaism Jacobs had been persuaded to question a central tenet of Orthodoxy. His background therefore enabled the right wing to demonstrate to Jews outside their community that interaction and synthesis were rightly to be feared. Jacobs provided them with a model of interaction that they could hold up to justify, defend and promote their practice of separatism. He served as the catalyst for the right wing's promotion of a theology of compartmentalization that helped them to effect the theological transformation of a broader spectrum of the community.

Jacobs was unable to succeed in his attempt at empowering Jewish youth to interact meaningfully with modernity. The Jacobs Affair which surrounded his theology only succeeded in empowering the right wing to demonstrate that synthesis simply was not possible; that the modern world and the values it offered were things to be feared. In the aftermath of the Shoah, the urgent need to sustain a remnant of truly Orthodox Judaism had been established. Through the events of the Jacobs Affair the right wing appeared to have conclusively proven that confidence in the possibility for interaction was misplaced; that the attitudes of separatism and compartmentalization, attitudes which had been gaining dominance in Anglo-Jewish Orthodoxy since the late 1930s, were the only viable methods for ensuring the survival of the remnant.

In Brodie's *Statement* he noted some of the different influences that were brought to bear upon him and to which he claimed he was impervious. It seems interesting to note one of his comments:

> I was also urged to think of the verdict of the future historian of Anglo-Jewry who would describe me as the Chief Rabbi who split the community from top to bottom. To forestall such a verdict, I should change my decision. I do not presume to dictate to any contemporary or later historian. I hope, however, he [sic] will give thought to the fact that the Chief Rabbi, after much prayer and deliberation decided in accordance with his principles, and that spiritual leaders and many laymen in this country and overseas sustained his stand.[9]

Brodie's reference here to the fact that he had received support for his position from various people in England and abroad acknowledges, even in this attempt to defend his position, the fact that he was far from impervious to the opinions of others. For this reason, if for no other, the blame for the Jacobs Affair and the divisions that it created in Anglo-Jewish Orthodoxy cannot be directed solely at the Chief

Rabbi. Brodie need not have feared that this particular study of the Jacobs Affair would identify him as the direct cause of the theological transformation that subsequently occurred in Anglo-Jewish Orthodoxy. The Chief Rabbinate that Brodie had inherited on assuming the position in 1948 had been weakened before he even entered the office. The groundwork for religious polarization had already been put into place by the time he was elected. Actions by representatives of both the spiritist and right wings of Anglo-Jewish Orthodoxy had ensured that the new Chief Rabbi's hold on authority had been weakened to prevent him exercising the power that Hertz had previously wielded. The absence of a comprehensive theological system further diminished Brodie's ability to defend the authority of his office and promote a mediatory position for the religious institutions of Anglo-Jewry. Aside from considerations about the positive image that Brodie offered the community, he had specifically been chosen as Chief Rabbi because of his weaknesses and his willingness to defer the authority of his office to others. With Brodie as the incumbent at the time of the Jacobs Affair, the Chief Rabbinate could not reasonably have been expected to provide a source of strength, defending Anglo-Jewish Orthodoxy against a rightwards shift in its theological position. Once Jacobs had provided those on the right wing of Anglo-Jewish Orthodoxy with a method for confirming and promoting their fear of interaction and synthesis, the transformation of the theology advocated within the religious institutions of the community became an inevitability. The propriety of the right wing's attitude of fear became established. The principle of separatism and the construction of theologies of compartmentalization could now more easily be instituted as the best method for maintaining Jewish identity in a religious minority group that was located in the midst of a host society that espoused the values of an alternative religious system.

Conclusion

The Jacobs Affair altered the theological makeup of Anglo-Jewish Orthodoxy. It helped to foster the belief that synthesis was to be feared, that interaction was dangerous, and that the practice of compartmentalization provided a safer method for engaging in the non-Jewish world. With Brodie in place as Chief Rabbi, the community lacked the religious leadership figure who could have opposed the promotion of a theology of compartmentalization.

Brodie had easily been persuaded that fear was the appropriate response to the age. He lacked the confidence to assert the powers of his office. He had no particular theological system to promote boldly and he exhibited no trust in modernity's potential to contribute useful values. On the right wing, the Shoah undoubtedly heightened the concern to attempt to maintain a faithful remnant of Orthodox Judaism through the practice of separatism. However, their stance toward the modern world had already been influenced by the fear with which traditionalist rabbis on the Continent had initially responded to the offer of emancipation. Fear, of the freedom emancipation provided for Jews to interact, ultimately defined much of the right-wing response to modernity. This fear led to the advocation of compartmentalization that was seen to represent a far safer method of responding to the modern world's offer of tolerance. Overriding any interest in the potential benefits that the non-Jewish world might offer was fear of the potential consequences of interaction with its ideas. As we have seen, in Anglo-Jewry Jacobs was used to justify the expedience of these practices.

The right wing in Anglo-Jewry had succeeded in establishing themselves as the 'conscience of the nation' through whose activities 'the larger mass of Jewry is reminded of the higher religious standards at which all should aim'.[1] This created a tendency in the mainstream of Anglo-Jewish Orthodoxy to look over its right shoulder to seek the approval of the right wing. Jacobs had identified this disposition in Jews' College. Brodie demonstrated it through the manner in which he became impressed and influenced by their practices and outlook. By gaining, through the Jacobs Affair, a method for promoting their fear, the right wing were provided with the means of exerting their influence across a broader spectrum.

Purely in terms of numbers, their impact on the community at this stage was small. The growing acceptance of the principle that the right wing's fears were correct and that compartmentalization was justified did not cause large numbers of British Jews to change their practices. Nor did it result in a rash of disaffiliation from the United Synagogue in protest at the theological position it had adopted. Yet this was merely symptomatic of the general theological malaise of Anglo-Jewry. Compartmentalization rests on the principle that the Anglo-Jewish ideology of meaningful interaction has to be forsaken. Yet interaction characterizes Anglo-Jewry, since that is the nature of a community located in the midst of a host society with which it may freely engage. The Chief Rabbi's ability to act as a representative body was therefore impaired by its incumbent's willingness to accept the validity of compartmentalization. The United Synagogue's capacity truly to act as an umbrella organization, fostering harmony and unity across a broad spectrum of the community, was similarly diminished. By defining the theology of Jacobs as outside the confines of the Orthodoxy advocated within the mainstream institutions of the community, the theological position of the Chief Rabbinate and United Synagogue became more rigid, representative of a far smaller section of the religious spectrum in Anglo-Jewry.

Hertz had provided a model for synthesis and interaction. His theology delineated his method for securing Jewish identity in a community that, by its very nature, would engage in interaction. Jacobs was seen to have provided an alternative paradigm that undermined Hertz's model by demonstrating that his theological position was not a sufficiently reliable method for maintaining Orthodox Judaism intact, even though Jacobs lacked the theological training advocated by Hertz. The replacement of Hertz's theology of synthesis with a theology of compartmentalization was presented as the only assured means of defending the Jewish identity of a minority community. It is predicated on the requirement that members of a modern religious community separate themselves from their host society, compartmentalizing the ideas with which they come into contact. However, this ignores the realities of the Anglo-Jewish community.

Right-wing Orthodoxy has developed a triumphalist confidence in the legitimacy of its approach to the life of a religious community in an alien host society, viewing it as the only certain method of maintaining Orthodox Judaism intact. Nonetheless, its confidence is based on fear. The story of Anglo-Jewish Orthodoxy's theological development is a tale of two theologies; the shift from a theology of synthesis to a theology of compartmentalization. At its heart, the theological position of the community is predicated on the presence of confidence or fear.

Todd Endelman, in his examination of the phenomenon of radical assimilation in modern Anglo-Jewry, argued that an inherent feature of the English culture that provided a host society to the Jews was the perception that its own values represented the only truly valid ideal, regardless of how tolerant it was of other approaches to life. Endelman contends that English culture was inhospitable to all forms of diversity. 'It was ruthlessly genteel, monolithic, and exclusive and did not include alternative modes of being authentically English.'[2] As a consequence, it offered Jews a toleration that he characterized as 'subtly qualified'. By suggesting that this was perfectly adequate for those Jews whose 'sense of self-worth was not linked exclusively to their reception in gentile circles',[3] Endelman has inadvertently pointed to the relevance of Hertz's programme for Anglo-Jewry. Precisely what Hertz had recognized was that Anglo-Jewish youth needed confidence in its religious heritage. This was the prerequisite of interaction, since it ensured that Jews could judge their religion against their own standards rather than against the standards set for them by others: either English culture, or right-wing Orthodoxy. The programme for religious education that Hertz defended throughout his Chief Rabbinate was designed to impart this confidence. This was his method for maintaining Jewish identity intact. Jacobs was seen to have undermined the viability of Hertz's model, demonstrating that Hertz's confidence had been misplaced. Of course Jacobs had not approached the non-Jewish world with a background in the religious education that Hertz had advocated. Nonetheless, the fact that the Jacobs Affair occurred during the Chief Rabbinate of Brodie ensured that there was no confident religious leader in place to defend a centrist theology. This enabled the alternative, triumphalist confidence exhibited by the right wing to emerge as a religious standard to which Jews should aspire. This in turn facilitated the theological shift from synthesis to compartmentalization as Anglo-Jewish Orthodoxy was taught that it should forsake its ideology of meaningful interaction if its religious identity was to remain intact.

Epilogue

As Anglo-Jewish Orthodoxy entered the twenty-first century it had altered radically from the community Hertz had been appointed to serve in 1913. The spectre of a divided community has become very real. The ability of the Chief Rabbi to represent this community and provide it with religious leadership appears to have been diminished, to the point where its viability has to be questioned. The Jacobs Affair and Brodie's retirement from the Chief Rabbinate in 1965 brought to a close a pivotal era in the theological development of Anglo-Jewish Orthodoxy. It signalled a change in the religious leadership of the community that altered the nature of the theology espoused for Anglo-Jewry. Since 1965 two subsequent Chief Rabbis have entered the post. Each has asserted their intention to seek to re-establish the authority and confidence of their office; to provide genuine leadership to the community; and to attempt to restore a sense of unity. Although the Chief Rabbinate of the present incumbent, Jonathan H. Sacks, has been marked by infamous failures and has enjoyed limited successes, it is inappropriate to judge his tenure whilst he still seeks to exert an impact on the theology of the community. However, the influence of Brodie's immediate successor, Chief Rabbi Immanuel Jakobovits, later Lord Jakobovits, may provide a means of examining some of the effects of the community's shift in theology.

In 1991, as Jakobovits' Chief Rabbinate came to an end and the incumbency of Sacks began, a review of the United Synagogue was initiated by the organization's honorary officers. The report that was produced the following year exposed a crisis in this central institution of Anglo-Jewry. Membership of the United Synagogue was in decline, which had precipitated a financial crisis. This fall in members was harming the institution's ability to raise funds, which in turn was impairing its historical role as the major provider of religious functions for the community. Still more worrying was the review's analysis of the demographic make-up of the membership that had retained its affiliation to the various congregations of the institution; this identified an ageing community that was liable to exacerbate the decline in the coming years. Entitled *A Time for Change*, the report concluded that the crisis in the United Synagogue had one root cause: 'a drift away from the fundamental goals or "mission" of the organisation'.[1] If the United Synagogue wished to try to arrest its decline the report stated that it needed to reclaim its Mission, which was clearly outlined in the following terms:

> The historic responsibility of the United Synagogue is to provide for the broad majority of Anglo Jews, offering a place for every Jew who wants to identify with the community within a traditional framework. The United Synagogue should pursue this fundamental goal by adopting, as its mission, the need to expand its membership under the banner 'including Jews within tradition'. This should be the basis of future policy development and strategic planning.[2]

The findings of the United Synagogue Review appeared to suggest that the theological shift amongst the religious leadership that had occurred in the aftermath of the Jacobs Affair had seemingly been perpetuated during Jakobovits' Chief Rabbinate. This shift had alienated many Jews who formed the natural constituency of the United Synagogue and Chief Rabbinate.

The research carried out in preparation for this report, including surveys, consultations with broad cross-sections of the community, and focus groups, identified an abiding attachment to the values represented by the United Synagogue.

> On the one hand we encountered a deep sense of frustration and disillusionment with the United Synagogue. On the other hand, market research revealed an equally deep and pervasive loyalty to the moderate, contemporary Orthodoxy with which the organisation was identified.[3]

The survey of United Synagogue members found that '[t]he key issue was seen as reversing the trend to the right and preventing the marginalisation of the non-Orthodox'.[4]

Although the report claimed that it had not refrained from considering the possibility that the United Synagogue had lost its relevance and had ceased to serve a useful purpose, its conclusions favoured the maintenance of this Anglo-Jewish institution. It lauded the functions traditionally provided by it and expressed a hope that these former glories could be restored. Yet it argued that to achieve this goal certain changes would have to be introduced.

> The United Synagogue was once a great institution. It shaped the religious character of Anglo-Jewry. It provided a spiritual home

for the vast majority of London's Jews. It fostered the growth of new congregations. It supported the institutions – most obviously, the Chief Rabbinate – which guided the development of provincial and Commonwealth Jewry as well. *It represented a Jewish ethos that combined loyalty of halakhah with tolerance, inclusivism and an openness to the challenges of the modern world.*[5] [my emphasis]

Reinforcing the sentiments of the United Synagogue's *Deed of Foundation and Trust*, which laid down no test of individual observance as a condition of membership, the report called on the United Synagogue to reassert its strengths.

The traditional strength of the United Synagogue lies in its 'inclusivist' approach. This needs to be refocused to meet contemporary circumstances and to help retain and increase membership … All facets of the organisation must be responsive to the basic purpose of the United Synagogue, namely, to include as many Jews as possible under the umbrella of traditional Judaism.[6]

This recommendation to reclaim the model of the 'umbrella' starkly contrasted with the views propounded by Immanuel Jakobovits, who had served the community as Chief Rabbi between 1967 and 1991. From the time of his Installation address Jakobovits disavowed the usefulness of umbrella models.

I will do my best to serve and unite all sections of the community, but I am not prepared to replace the Torah by an umbrella, either open or closed, as the symbol of my office. In any event, I anticipate fair weather rather than rain or hail, and we should not require any umbrellas.[7]

The potential for disunity, communal fragmentation and religious polarization had re-emerged towards the end of Hertz's Chief Rabbinate. The effect this had on the community was identified in the United Synagogue Review. As previously, the challenge for the community's religious leadership was to sustain Anglo-Jewish Orthodoxy by promoting a form of Jewish identity and practice that could be perpetuated amongst a minority group that was located in the midst of a host society that espoused an alternative value system.

Prior to the appointment of Hertz's successor, the manoeuvrings of certain lay and religious leaders had already diminished the authority of the Chief Rabbinate. The incumbent's ability to provide genuine leadership to the community was thereby impaired. Brodie's election and tenure as Chief Rabbi, culminating in the Jacobs Affair, had enabled right-wing Orthodox influences to shift the community's religious leadership away from its natural constituency. Internally, this led to a move away from the umbrella model for Anglo-Jewry, as the principle of 'strength in numbers' increasingly ceased to be viewed as a prudent means for securing the survival of Jewish group identity. Externally, the one assured method for maintaining Jewish identity intact was perceived to be a Judaism that feared its encounter with the ideas of the surrounding society. The retirement of Brodie and the appointment of a new chief rabbi could have provided an opportunity to redress these theological shifts. In light of the findings of the United Synagogue Review, the subsequent election of Jakobovits to a Chief Rabbinate that had already lost so much of its capacity to exert control, may be construed as having done little to arrest the trends that led to a strengthening of right-wing theological dominance, the growth of religious polarization, and increasing rates of disaffiliation.

IMMANUEL JAKOBOVITS

Jakobovits was the eldest child in a family of four sons and three daughters. Born in 1921, in Koenigsberg, where his father, Julius, served as rabbi of the Orthodox congregation, he and his family moved to Berlin in 1928, when his father took up a new appointment as a Dayan to the mainstream community in the city, rather than the separatist Adath. Notwithstanding his father's affiliation with the main community, his children were educated at the school of the Adath and were thereby raised in the world of *Torah im derekh eretz*. Fearing the rise of Nazism in Germany, Jakobovits' family sent him to England in 1936 to complete his schooling and to study for rabbinical ordination in London. He was later joined by the rest of his family after the events of *Kristallnacht* persuaded his father that it was no longer safe to remain in Germany.[8]

In England, Jakobovits decided to enrol at both Jews' College and Etz Chaim Yeshiva to pursue his rabbinical studies.[9] Each institution represented a different type of Orthodoxy and both differed from the world in which he had been raised. He would later comment on the absence of a unifying ideology at Jews' College, contrasting it unfavourably with the Hildesheimer Rabbinical Seminary in Berlin, and noting how this prevented graduates of the College from being taught a specific theology.[10] In deciding where to obtain his *semikhah*, Jakobovits chose the more Orthodox framework of Etz Chaim. However, although he was deeply influenced by Rabbis Elia Lopian and Nachman Greenspan, his teachers at Etz Chaim, from whom, with the addition of Rabbi Loeb Gurewicz, he received his *semikhah* in 1947, Jakobovits always cited his father as the greatest influence on his theology.

He secured his first rabbinical appointment whilst still a student, entering the United Synagogue as temporary minister of the Brondesbury congregation in 1941. He later served at the South-East London and the Great synagogues before accepting an appointment as Chief Rabbi of the Jewish community in Ireland, in 1948. It was during this ministry that he married Amélie Munk, the daughter of a rabbinical family from Paris, who would remain at his side and become a significant personality in her own right. He served there for ten years until assuming the ministry of a newly established Orthodox community in Manhattan's Fifth Avenue.[11]

Jakobovits characterized the circle of friends with whom he mixed whilst in Berlin as, 'followers of the "Torah *im derekh eretz*" school … They possessed wider horizons and sought values also in the general culture and its literature, and, of course, in the world of science.' More generally, he acknowledged how in his upbringing, '[a]t any rate, I was raised from an early age in an atmosphere that the world around was not to be ignored, but was to be related to, albeit critically, and at times with reservations'.[12] The principles of *Torah im derekh eretz* provided the basis for the theological system that Jakobovits would champion throughout his life. In his sermons and writings Jakobovits clearly promoted the value of Jewish interaction in the surrounding world. Certainly he expressed reservations about the study of Judaism in the university, feeling that this inevitably undermined the religion.[13] However, following the example of his father, who studied for a doctorate at the University of Berlin, and acknowledging his own university studies, undertaken at University College London, where he completed a doctorate on Jewish medical ethics,[14] Jakobovits supported Jewish engagement in the ideas of the secular world.

Appearing to uphold a theology that could be suitable for Anglo-Jewry, he lamented the manner in which sections of Orthodoxy segregated themselves from the world. However, notwithstanding this critique, he expressed understanding of how and why this situation had emerged. Explaining the waning appeal of synthesis, Jakobovits pointed to the effects of the Shoah on Orthodox thinking and psychology.

> Germany's betrayal of civilisation, culminating in the Holocaust, produced a terrible disillusionment with all Western culture and science. Our generation can no longer accept the inevitability of civilisation's progress and of man's enlightenment, as assumed by Hirsch.[15]

Moreover, in addition to the Shoah undermining belief in the potential value of secular society, he noted the 'widespread disillusionment with the sham values of our contemporary society and civilisation', which drove Jews to prefer 'the security of spiritual insulation to the risks inherent in exploring unknown paths or venturing into alien territory'.[16]

Although noting that this was a dominant feature of right-wing Orthodoxy, in truth, it is possible to discern in Jakobovits' thought a sense that the nature of interaction had, in fact, changed across a broader spectrum of Orthodoxy. Jakobovits frequently evinced the belief that his contemporary society had become morally vacuous, driven by materialism and a focus on individual rights rather than duties.[17] Under these circumstances, the practice of interaction came to be reinterpreted. Whilst it remained a laudable principle in theory, in practice Jakobovits viewed interaction with the surrounding society as a means for Judaism to impart morality to that society. He had essentially lost the sense, if he had ever genuinely imbibed it, that Judaism could gain from the encounter.

An examination of Jakobovits' thought demonstrates how, despite his avowed acceptance of the principle of *Torah im derekh eretz*, he was unable to restore the community's ideology of interaction. In fact, the views he expressed highlight the manner in which the Hirschian principle of *Torah im derekh eretz* has come to be subverted in its modern guise amongst contemporary adherents of this theology. As has been noted above, a subtle shifting of emphases occurred in interpretations of Hirsch's teachings.[18] As there was a diminution of the belief that non-Jewish sources of wisdom and truth had the capacity to impart teachings of value to Judaism, the interpretation of *Torah im derekh eretz*, the promotion of interaction in the surrounding society, shifted. As we have seen, many supposed followers of the Hirschian school simply diverted their focus onto Hirsch's secessionist principles. Amongst those who remained willing to acknowledge that *Torah im derekh eretz* was a central teaching of Hirsch's thought, interaction came to be reduced to what can be viewed as a mission theory. This viewpoint suggested that *Torah* provided a means of influencing the *derekh eretz* but precluded this process from also functioning in the opposite direction.

The importance of the Jewish mission to the nations of the world, to impart the teachings of monotheism, was always an important feature of Hirsch's theology. In his *Nineteen Letters*, the principle of the Jews' mission provided a framework around which Hirsch sought to present an understanding of Judaism that would retain an appeal to Jewish youth and thereby discourage them from embracing Reform, or rejecting Judaism in its entirety. His argument revolved around the idea that, although all of humanity had been put on earth to help recognize God and shape the world according to the divine will, the Jews had been set apart as a chosen people in order to provide an example of how this goal was to be achieved. Their role was to serve as a light unto the nations to enable all humanity to fulfil its task. This reading of Judaism provided one basis for Hirsch's educational programme. He argued that Jews needed to acquire a full understanding of their Judaism in order to cherish it for themselves and enlighten others through the example provided by appropriate performance of its teachings. However, Hirsch's educational programme also involved engagement in the ideas of the surrounding cultural, social and intellectual milieus. As he explained in his commentary on Genesis 3:24, the ideas of the surrounding society, the *derekh eretz*, provide an alternative means of accessing Truth; the Torah is needed to complete this understanding but to discard the *derekh eretz* is to limit one's knowledge of truth. So long as a suitable Jewish education is put in place, knowledge of the *derekh eretz* can serve as a means of expanding one's general understanding of Judaism as well as truth.[19] Nonetheless, as subsequent followers concentrated on the moral vacuity of the secular world and its potential to undermine Judaism, the mission aspect of Hirsch's notion of *Torah im derekh eretz* came to be emphasized at the expense of the idea that Judaism could gain from the encounter. Hence Joseph Elias, in his commentary on Hirsch's *Nineteen Letters*, insists that the principle of *Torah im derekh eretz* is to be understood only in terms of how Torah can influence the world with which it interacts, not vice versa: '*Derech Eretz* represents the setting in which, and upon which, Torah is to operate.'[20]

In an insightful study on Hirsch and the contemporary influence of his teachings, Jakobovits identified some of the shifts that have occurred in understandings of Hirschian theology. A loss of belief in the worth of the surrounding society has been combined with a new focus for Jewish life provided by the creation of the state of Israel: 'The emphasis today is on self-preservation and on the reclamation of Jews. All our energies are fully engaged in the mission to the Jews, not to mankind.'[21] When Jakobovits emphasized the importance of the broader Jewish mission to the wider world, he therefore felt comfortable presenting himself as an advocate of the *Torah im derekh eretz* school. He noted that Hirsch 'sees the ultimate Jewish national purpose in the mission to the nations'.[22] He did not recognize the restrictions that have been imposed on understandings of *Torah im derekh eretz* as fear of the surrounding society has been allowed to exert a stranglehold over Judaism. To focus on this mission role, in an understanding of *Torah im derekh eretz*, requires a clear shift in emphasis. The sense in which interaction and the scope for synthesis represent two-way processes, characterized by Hertz as 'cross-fertiliza-tion', appears to have been removed.

Whilst Brodie's Chief Rabbinate had similarly identified a wide-spread moral decline in society at large, Jakobovits' interest in the Jewish mission led him to actively address the issue and seek to exert an influence, rather than merely apprehend contemporary morality with fear. Somewhat in the model of Hertz, Jakobovits was happy to promote his views to any audience willing to listen. These views famously appealed to Margaret Thatcher, so that, as Bermant notes, 'the Chief Rabbi came to be regarded as chaplain to the [Tory] party and father confessor to the Prime Minister'.[23] His opinions on gender, sexuality and AIDS were highly conservative, but it was his views on the role of the individual in society which appeared to confirm his affinity to the Tory Party, although he always denied that he identified with any single political party. In 1985 Jakobovits composed a response to the *Faith in the City* review of inner city decline carried out under the auspices of the Archbishop of Canterbury. In his *From Doom to Hope: A Jewish View on 'Faith in the City', the Report of the Archbishop of Canterbury's Commission on Urban Priority Areas*, Jakobovits appeared almost to regurgitate Tory party policy in the guise of Jewish teaching, as he promoted the value of self-help and refused to apportion the blame for urban ghettos on government policy.

When Jakobovits was later elevated to a peerage in the 1988 New Year's Honours list, there were some who suggested that the views he had expressed in his *From Doom to Hope*, and his general affinity to the Tory Party, had been highly influential. Regardless of the veracity of this viewpoint, it is clear that in a period when Anglican Church leaders were often accused, particularly by Tory MPs, of moral ambivalence, Jakobovits had secured an important place for himself in British society as a religious spokesman who could be relied upon to provide forthright opinions.[24] As the first chief rabbi to be honoured in this way, Jakobovits was seen to provide reflected glory for the Anglo-Jewish community as a whole, even amongst those who disagreed with his views. The public image of the chief rabbinate thus remained a significant feature of the office.

In addition to influencing his activities in the wider British society, Jakobovits' focus on Judaism's divine mission in the world would deeply influence his Zionist ideology. He followed the pattern, already demonstrated by Brodie, of calling for the Jewish state to function as a light unto the nations. As Jakobovits acknowledged in his study of Hirsch, this Zionist belief conflicted with Hirschian thought, which clearly adopted early nineteenth-century patriotic values. Rather than segregating themselves in an independent Jewish state, Hirsch directed Jews to serve as an example by acting as good citizens in the countries they inhabited.[25]

In examining Jakobovits' Zionism it is possible to identify the influence of German Orthodox thought. He expressed clear concern at Jewish nationalism and its messianic undertones. He explained that he had not been willing to adopt the religious Zionist formula of praying for Israel as 'the first flowering of the redemption'; and he warned that 'I see secularism, and possibly even idolatry, in the worship of the Land'.[26]

Nonetheless, on the basis of his mission theory for Judaism, Jakobovits proceeded to explain '[o]n the other hand, as I noted, I accept the potential – if not actual – religious significance of the State of Israel'.[27] Throughout his life, Jakobovits expressed a strong and committed attachment to Zionism, attested to in his only auto-biographical work, which charted the role of Zionism in his activities and thinking, entitled *'If Only My People ...' Zionism in my Life*.

His sense of the importance of Israel's mission fostered what could be viewed as the greatest controversies of his Chief Rabbinate. At various junctures, he flew in the face of widespread, largely unquestion-ing, worldwide Jewish support for Israel by forcefully voicing his disagreement with the State's policies on the Palestinian issue, and criticizing the involvement of religious authorities in the political processes of the country. He lamented the moral weakening of Israeli society that was being caused by a variety of State policies. He decried the Orthodox support for many of these strategies. His comments focused on security issues and peace talks, Jewish education in Israel, and the general role of Judaism and its teachings in the life of the State.

> I spelt out the fallacy of secular Zionism in fostering the illusion that Jewish Statehood would solve the Jewish problem and eliminate anti-Semitism; I expressed the realization that Israel had neither a claim nor the ability to prevail if it surrendered its unique spiritual purpose; I stressed the need to separate religion from politics if Judaism and the Jewish State were to be united; I underlined the challenge to religious leaders to promote our people's regeneration, to interpret current events in the light of Jewish teachings, and to be ready to make territorial concessions if true peace could thereby be secured; and I stated the need to fight for Jewish survival by resisting the evil of ignorance and assimilation with the same grim determination as the attacks of Israel's enemies in battle.[28]

With regard to political matters in Israel, it was Jakobovits' contention that '"Zion will be redeemed through justice" even more than through the might of armies and the location of borders'.[29] In religious matters, he opposed the manner in which Orthodox political parties failed in their duty to impart moral teachings by focusing their attention on the passage of government legislation that often amounted to religious coercion. It was not that Jakobovits favoured the separation of powers between religion and state, rather he was concerned by the adverse consequences of a haphazard mixing of religion and politics. He observed how the decisions and actions of Orthodox representatives had enabled the secular left in Israel to adopt the moral high ground:

> it is mainly the religious element which supports and keeps in power a government which has set Israel and the Jewish people on the present course, leaving it to the secularists to articulate the Jewish conscience and salvage the Jewish honour. What a perverse reversal of our roles![30]

The criticism that Jakobovits was willing to direct at Orthodox authorities for their policies on Israel also extended to a more general critique. As we have seen regarding external relations, he argued against complete disengagement from the surrounding non-Jewish society, even though the nature of the engagement he would advocate was greatly limited. Internally, he also expressed grave concerns. These were directed at the growing stringency of Orthodox halakhic interpretation – 'an unconscionable drive towards conformity' –[31] and the burgeoning role of the *roshei yeshivot* – yeshiva heads – as chief arbiters in halakhic decision-making.

> Now we find a growing call for uniformity and a tendency to write off as dissenters or heretics those who do not toe the line drawn by their critics. In the past, every duly qualified rabbi was master in his own house, and his rulings for those under his jurisdiction were unquestioned and unchallengeable. Today, a communal rabbi, however Orthodox, is often subjected to intoler-able pressures, or indeed to the denial of his rabbinic competence, if he refuses to conform with the dictates and anathemas of those who regard themselves, and are upheld by their followers, as the sole custodians of Jewish religious authority.[32]

He noted that the dominance of *roshei yeshivot* removed the halakhic decision-making process from the domain of the community, in which communal rabbis could address the practical concerns of congregants, to an isolated ivory tower which divorced halakhah from reality.[33]

An additional consequence of growing internal Orthodox intran-sigence, which Jakobovits critiqued, was the loss of concern over the fate of the broader Jewish population, outside the Orthodox enclave. Influenced by his father, Jakobovits rejected the secessionist model for Jewish communities. As has already been noted, his father had taken a post in the mainstream community in Berlin. In his previous position, in Koenigsberg, he had eventually persuaded the *austrittsgemeinde* that he served to re-join the main community. Jakobovits' own previous experiences, as Chief Rabbi in Ireland, and to a lesser extent as a rabbi in New York, had also discouraged him from adopting a separatist stance. He likened the separatism of the right-wing Orthodox to the biblical model of Cain, concerned only for themselves at the expense of their brethren, and he lamented this stance.[34] He recalled how during his ministry in New York, he had been willing to accept invitations to lecture in Conservative and Reform communities

> but on condition that I would not speak within their synagogues ... I always said that the Torah was not given only to Orthodox Jews, and I am obligated to teach those who do not accept upon themselves the yoke of the commandments.[35]

However, a further examination of Jakobovits' thought on this issue of internal relations between Jews will, once again, highlight certain complexities that are to be discerned in his theology. In his attitude to external relations, between Judaism and the surrounding world, we have seen that whilst Jakobovits was willing to champion this cause in principle, in practice its scope was greatly reduced. Similarly, although he explicitly advocated engagement with all Jews and rejected the practice of separatism, his attitude could be likened to Victor Schonfeld's recommendation, noted earlier, that the windows of Adath synagogues in Britain be left open, even as the doors remained firmly barred shut.[36] Engagement with a broad spectrum of Jews was intended by Jakobovits to provide a means of influencing and educating the non-Orthodox and the less Orthodox. However, the process could only function in one direction, with no scope for any compromises. Bermant felt compelled to conclude his assessment of Jakobovits' unifying skills in the community by noting that:

> His failures as a bridge-builder, in the last resort, arise not so much from his abhorrence of progressive doctrines as his conviction that the Orthodox have everything to teach and nothing to learn.[37]

Jakobovits' apparent inclusiveness was designed to encourage all Jews to adopt the Judaism that he believed was best equipped to survive in the modern world. As will become clear following further analysis of his thought, notwithstanding the criticisms he was willing to direct at it, the model of right-wing Orthodoxy represented his paradigm.

Nevertheless, from the outset of his Chief Rabbinate, in his Installation address, driven to reject separatism by the sense that many Jews
simply lacked a sufficient understanding of Judaism, he expressed a
concern that Anglo-Jewry was failing itself by providing its community with no more than a child-like understanding of Judaism: 'if
Jewish education ends, instead of starts in earnest, at Bar Mitzvah age,
is it any wonder that the products are juvenile Jews, quite incompetent
to assert their faith in an adult world'.[38] By improving the Jewish
education of Anglo-Jewry he hoped to enhance the understanding of
the religion in a way that would, in turn, enable people to construct a
Jewish identity that could withstand existence in British society.

Within the confines of the United Synagogue, as noted above,
Jakobovits rejected the usefulness of the 'umbrella' model. He had no
desire to perpetuate a situation in which a significant proportion of the
United Synagogue membership was Orthodox in name only. He
wanted to ensure that its members were educated adequately to be
able to advocate a Judaism that was strong enough to be perpetuated
through the generations. He asserted that, '[n]ext to Israel, Jewish
education must become our principal concern and top priority in
communal budgeting'.[39]

By 1971, Jakobovits had succeeded in establishing the Jewish
Educational Development Trust, a fund that would centralize the
supervision of improved Jewish educational provision in the community. In an editorial in the *Jewish Chronicle*, following the launch of
this initiative, it was noted that the Chief Rabbi's accompanying statement of purpose, entitled *Let My People Know*, contained the shocking
statement that, 'no attempt is made here to evaluate the contents of the
Jewish education'. The editorial asked

> But is this not the fundamental question to be answered before
> any plans can be envisaged? ... It would be instructive to know
> what the Chief Rabbi thinks Jewish children should be taught to
> equip them for living as Jews in Britain on the threshold of the
> twenty-first century.[40]

We here identify one of the obvious differences between the Chief
Rabbinates of Hertz and Jakobovits. As we have seen, both men were
authoritative, often courageous leaders who championed the causes
in which they believed. Both placed Jewish education at the heart of
their theologies; both believed that it underpinned the future survival
of the Jewish people. However, Hertz clearly and intricately laid
out his educational programme, whereas Jakobovits was content to
open the schools without specifying the content and indeed, like
Brodie, was happy to promote the types of Orthodox educational

programmes developed in the yeshivot, kollelim and women's seminaries of London, Manchester and Gateshead.[41] The model Jakobovits put in place for the maintenance of Jewish identity in British society, influenced by right-wing Orthodox models that feared the effects of the surrounding world, effectively rejected the traditional ideology of interaction that had existed as an abiding feature of the community.

Between 1967 and 1982 Jewish day school attendance amongst affiliated Jews in Britain rose from 25.2 per cent to 46.9 per cent. Jakobovits was thus able to enjoy far more success than Hertz in creating places at Jewish schools. His efforts were recognized when the benefactors of a new Jewish secondary school decided to name Immanuel College in his honour in 1990. However, during this period, notwithstanding educational improvements, overall rates of synagogue membership in London shrank from 60,066 in 1970, to 50,305 in 1990. If we examine the breakdown of synagogue membership according to religious affiliation in this period, the diminution of the centre and the increasing polarization of the community is clearly demonstrated. In proportional terms membership of right-wing Orthodox synagogues in Greater London more than doubled, increasing from 2.6 per cent in 1970, to 5.3 per cent in 1983. By 1990 it had risen further, to 8.8 per cent. Over this same period, the proportion of households affiliated to Central Orthodox synagogues shrank from 72.3 per cent in 1970, to 66 per cent in 1983, and 58.2 per cent in 1990. The proportion of Reform synagogue membership grew from 11.9 per cent in 1970, to 18 per cent in 1990, and the Liberal movement accounted for 8.7 per cent of those affiliated in 1970, and 11.3 per cent in 1990.[42]

Hertz had argued that the maintenance of Jewish identity in a minority community was predicated on the provision of an appropriate Jewish education. Only in this way could Jewish identity be underpinned with a genuine knowledge and understanding of the religion that could enable interaction without a subsequent waning in practice. The United Synagogue Review of 1992 highlighted the general numerical decline of Anglo-Jewry and a particular crisis in the community's central synagogal institution. It noted a significant shift away from the traditional Anglo-Jewish model of mainstream Orthodox dominance, as the centre lost out to the poles. Although educational provision was improved during Jakobovits' Chief Rabbinate, the findings suggested that where improved religious education was exerting an influence, the subsequent increase in observance appeared to encourage a move away from the United Synagogue to right-wing Orthodoxy. However, in some ways, as we shall see, this polarization can be viewed as an intentional by-product of Jakobovits' Chief Rabbinate.

ELECTION OF A CHIEF RABBI

As was noted previously, some have suggested that a principal reason for the Jacobs Affair was the perception that Louis Jacobs' appointment as head of Jews' College would provide a natural stepping-stone to his candidacy for the post of chief rabbi. The furore erupted as the opposing parties sought to either support or undermine this potential candidacy. The introduction of a retirement age into Brodie's contract had clearly identified the timing of a new appointment, encouraging various interested parties to promote their preferred candidate. With Jacobs shunted out of contention, a search for new candidates was required. Those on the right wing of the community suggested that Brodie's tenure as Chief Rabbi should be extended to symbolize the community's support for the views he had defended during the Jacobs Affair. Of course, this section of the community continued to function outside the jurisdiction of the Chief Rabbi, which somewhat diminished the strength of their argument. The United Synagogue honorary officers insisted on implementing the retirement clause in Brodie's contract and deliberations for the selection of a new Chief Rabbi got underway in 1964, preparing for Brodie's retirement the following year.

A shift in the make-up of the lay leadership of the United Synagogue, from members of the Cousinhood to children of the immigrant community, had begun to exert an influence on the decisions and directions taken by this institution. Nonetheless, when it came to the appointment of a new Chief Rabbi, Sir Isaac Wolfson keenly adopted the established United Synagogue model and as President assumed the role of kingmaker. Bermant records how Wolfson would refer to the United Synagogue as the Great Universal Synagogue, indicating the manner in which he extended his autocratic leadership style from his business to his communal work.[43] He exerted almost total control over the deliberation process in the search for a new chief rabbi so that, as Newman has noted, 'the statement was often heard at the time of the election that Sir Isaac had promised "to find a Chief Rabbi"'. As Newman further explained

> he [Wolfson] tried very hard to ensure that public debate be kept to an absolute minimum, and that there should be no vote as between various candidates. Only in this way could the prestige of the Chief Rabbinate be kept at its highest.[44]

The first Chief Rabbinate Conference had been assembled in July 1964 with the sole task of appointing a Selection Committee. By the time the second conference was convened, in March 1965, in the continued absence of even a long list of official candidates, one of the delegates was reported to have warned that, 'the sacred task of selecting a Chief Rabbi must not be left to one man'.[45] However the precedent had already been set; Wolfson pursued a solo campaign to identify a suitable candidate who could be presented for approval to the Conference by May 1965, to coincide with Brodie's retirement. It subsequently transpired that the delay had been caused by Wolfson's efforts to persuade an unexpected rabbi to enter the fray. Dr Jacob Herzog, son of Isaac Herzog, former Chief Rabbi of Ireland, and Israel, was being cajoled by his mother and the United Synagogue President to accept the appointment of Chief Rabbi in Britain. This, despite never having served as a rabbi, having chosen to pursue a career in Israeli diplomacy following his ordination.

In May 1965 the Selection Committee of the Chief Rabbinate Conference had compiled a list of eleven names; not one of the rabbis on this list was then based in England. The selection was subsequently whittled down to a shortlist of three candidates: Louis Rabinowitz, Immanuel Jakobovits and Jacob Herzog. The candidacy of the British-born, South Africa-based Rabinowitz was compromised by his age: at nearly 60 he fell foul of the conference's recommendation that, ideally, the appointment should be confined to someone no older than around the age of 50. The support he received from the *Jewish Chronicle* may also have diminished his standing since, in the aftermath of the Jacobs Affair, the newspaper was viewed critically by many in authority.[46] Jakobovits, whose qualifications had been, often negatively, debated in the *Jewish Chronicle* throughout much of the election process, had withdrawn from contention the previous month. In a somewhat contradictory letter, he appeared to suggest that he preferred to withdraw his candidacy rather than risk not being selected.[47] Since Herzog had informed Wolfson that he would only accept the post if he was elected unanimously, without recourse to a vote, the committee was eventually persuaded to ratify Wolfson's selection.

However, the optimism generated by this appointment was short-lived. Herzog was forced to withdraw his acceptance of the post of chief rabbi in September 1965, following medical advice. The entire selection process therefore had to be set in motion, once again, at another meeting of the Chief Rabbinate Conference in February 1966. Ultimately, in a re-enactment of the earlier deliberation process, the names of Rabinowitz and Jakobovits came to the fore. At a meeting of the honorary officers of the United Synagogue, prior to the convening of the Selection Committee, in June 1966, it was agreed that Jakobovits was their preferred candidate. At the subsequent Selection Committee meeting, although there was some support for the more religiously liberal Rabinowitz, the dominance of United Synagogue representatives ensured that Jakobovits secured the approval of the committee.

The Chief Rabbinate Conference ratified his appointment in September 1966. Notwithstanding his earlier withdrawal from the contest, and despite it being obvious that he was the second choice candidate, Jakobovits accepted the call to become Chief Rabbi.

In the repercussions of the Jacobs Affair it had seemed that the very viability of the Chief Rabbinate had been called into question. However, the prospect of a new appointment concentrated attention on attempts to restore unity across Anglo-Jewry; optimism was invested in the opportunity for a new appointment to build bridges across the deep chasms that had emerged. Jakobovits assumed the post, conscious that Anglo-Jewry was in need of strong religious leadership. In his Installation sermon he identified the three areas on which his Chief Rabbinate would concentrate. Firstly, he expressed his intention to provide the community with genuine leadership, 'to help in directing the community's internal and external affairs and to suffuse them with religious content'.[48] A second task paralleled the prophetic role, to spread the teachings of Judaism beyond the synagogue, to a broader Jewish community, and to contemporary society. The most important function, which Jakobovits placed at the heart of his Chief Rabbinate, was the improvement of Jewish education

> above all else will be my obligation to promote the study of the Torah.
>
> I want to ensure the inalienable birthright of every Jew to an adequate Jewish education. On this I stake the success of my ministry, for on this will depend Jewish survival.[49]

THE CHIEF RABBINATE OF IMMANUEL JAKOBOVITS

In the early stages of Jakobovits' Chief Rabbinate, conscious of the schisms that had been created, keen to restore the dignity and authority of his office, and intent on mending those bridges that he believed could be fixed, the new Chief Rabbi demonstrated a willingness to meet with non-Orthodox sections of the community, discuss a variety of issues with them, and seek acceptable accommodations. In his Installation address he had pledged that

> it will be my privilege and my duty to do all within my power and authority to close the gaps within our people ... Nevertheless, I recognise dissent as an inescapable fact of Jewish life today. I will seek to befriend those who dissent, and to work with them in Jewish and general causes unaffected by our religious differences.[50]

All sections of the community were represented at his installation ceremony and as soon as he assumed the functions of his office he began to organize meetings with Reform and Liberal leaders, as well as with Louis Jacobs, to try to work out a formula for communal harmony.[51]

The outbreak of war in Israel, just two months after his installation, provided Jakobovits with his first opportunity to provide the community with the leadership he had promised. Support for Israel was an issue that crossed Jewish denominational lines, and at a highly successful gathering of British Jews he called on the entire Anglo-Jewish community 'to mobilise all its resources in defence of Israel'.[52] He also arranged a conference of rabbis and ministers, to which he invited Reform and Liberal 'spiritual leaders', to consider how best to direct the efforts of the community's religious leadership.

In October 1971, Jakobovits demonstrated his willingness to compromise with non-Orthodox sections of the community by recommending that approval be granted to constitutional changes in the Board of Deputies. These would allow consultation with non-Orthodox representatives in religious matters. As the *Jewish Chronicle* explained, the suggested amendment to clause forty-three was intended to create a situation in which, 'for the first time, it also provides that "the board shall consult" the designated religious leaders of the Reform and Liberal sections on all religious matters concerning them'. As the newspaper further noted, these changes had been

> commended to the Orthodox deputies by Chief Rabbi Jakobovits and the Haham 'for the sake of communal unity and in the light of assurances' they had received from the board's President.[53]

Perhaps unsurprisingly, a number of Orthodox deputies at the Board reacted to this recommendation with horror. Unable to gather a majority at the Board to defeat the amendment, yet wishing to protest against the decision, they organized a boycott of the meeting at which the changes would be ratified. Demonstrating a tendency to interfere that had already been apparent during the Jacobs Affair, the Chief Rabbi's Bet Din also voiced their concerns at Jakobovits' decision. Dayan Swift was quoted in the *Jewish Chronicle* suggesting that, '[n]either I nor, I am sure, any other member of the Beth Din would have agreed to the amendment in the form it was put to the board'.[54] Significantly, however, the *Jewish Chronicle* also noted that the rabbinate of the UOHC had been rather more temperate in its support of the Orthodox boycott of the Board. 'It is understood that the rabbinate [of the UOHC] deliberately omitted any public statement of its reasons on halachic grounds to save the Chief Rabbi further embarrassment.'

The relationship between Jakobovits and the UOHC would maintain this type of complicated balance through much of his Chief Rabbinate. Notwithstanding Jakobovits' rejection of separatism and his general willingness to criticize right-wing Orthodoxy, it is clear that he felt most at home in this section of the Jewish world. In Anglo-Jewry, he was viewed, and viewed himself, as a natural member of the UOHC. Discussing his disputes with the Orthodox world, he noted

> Since, however, unlike my predecessors who did not come from the ultra-Orthodox camp, I had grown up among them and had received similar education, they had difficulty in dealing with me. On the personal level I was accepted by them even though I was attacked in their newspapers and charged with too 'liberal' tendencies.[55]

A further demonstration of the true nature of Jakobovits' religious affinities is provided by his six children. As Bermant notes

> they do not belong to synagogues under their father's jurisdiction, but are in no way apologetic for it, as one daughter observed, their father attends the United Synagogue because it is part of his job. If he did not, he would attend the same sort of synagogues as they do. Nor are they apologetic that none of their children attend school under their father's jurisdiction, because they are not the sort of schools which they attended themselves.[56]

Various decisions made by Jakobovits throughout his Chief Rabbinate were met with opprobrium from Orthodox authorities on the right wing. However, compared to the response that other chief rabbis could have expected to elicit for similar actions, the criticisms levelled against Jakobovits were often reasonably muted; although the almost unrelenting Orthodox backlash he experienced against his statements on Israel represent an obvious exception. As Bermant explains, 'Jakobovits enjoys a greater standing among the ultra-Orthodox than any of his predecessors, but so he should, for he has helped to pull the entire community in their direction'.[57]

When Jakobovits assumed the post of Chief Rabbi there was a notable absence of any desire, or perceived need, to prove himself to the right wing. His interest lay in securing his position amongst the centre to whom he was appointed to minister. Nonetheless, the religious triumphalism that had been allowed to burgeon during Brodie's Chief Rabbinate was reaching fruition during Jakobovits' tenure in the post. His own natural identification with right-wing Orthodox beliefs, if not their practice of internal and external separatism, and his sense that it provided the most assured model for Jewish survival, helped exert an additional influence in Anglo-Jewish Orthodoxy's theological shift away from its traditional constituency.

At the centenary celebrations of the United Synagogue Jakobovits commented that

> in this 'either-or' age, compromise and half-commitment are no longer the better part of religious virtue, and one recalls the remark of the sainted *Chafetz Chaim*: in the middle of the road only horses walk.[58]

He commended the growing Orthodoxy of the United Synagogue rabbinate and many of its lay leaders and emphasized the importance of increasing commitment across the community.[59] His support for this trend has been further evidenced, as Bermant notes, by the nature of his appointees to the London Bet Din. Jakobovits was involved in the selection of four dayanim during his Chief Rabbinate, all of whom came from the right wing of Orthodoxy and only one had any background in the United Synagogue.[60]

Jakobovits' relationship with his Bet Din was complex. In a seemingly incidental comment, recorded in Michael Shashar's biography of the Chief Rabbi, Jakobovits noted that when religious questions were directed to him from the Commonwealth communities under his authority, '[b]efore I replied to them, I usually consulted with the members of the Beth Din in London'.[61] The extent to which Jakobovits influenced, or was influenced by, his Bet Din is unclear. Jakobovits frequently noted his belief that it was better for rabbis to exert influence rather than power, since all rabbinical authority had been diminished in the modern world that championed the rights of the individual. The nature of the Chief Rabbinate to which he acceded would often make this a requirement rather than an ideal. Whilst undoubtedly sufficiently courageous to assert his views regardless of widespread support for his opinions, Jakobovits did also demonstrate a willingness to be influenced by others. One example was his sudden unavailability to give the Lily Montagu Memorial Lecture in 1971, despite previously agreeing to take the stage in this Progressive-organized event. However, he appeared comfortable with the nature of his relationship to the Bet Din and he was satisfied with the theological shifts that occurred in the religious leadership of the community.

The United Synagogue Review published in 1992 had uncovered considerable criticism of the London Bet Din. The theology of its dayanim was perceived to be on the right wing of Orthodoxy, too distant from the community for which they provided halakhic rulings. *A Time for Change* recommended that if the United Synagogue were to reclaim its standing in the community, by rejuvenating its traditional mission, it was necessary for all its affiliated institutions, including the Bet Din, to be driven by the same goal.

> If the principle of including Jews within tradition is accepted as the goal of the United Synagogue, it should apply at all levels within the organisation. This means that inclusivist attitudes should have at least a vote, if not a veto, in the development of policy, including religious policy ... There must be a critical relationship between the organization and its mission and the religious leadership. The mission should also influence policy on halakhic matters – within the boundaries of Orthodox halakhic Judaism. It should, for example, be inconceivable for an organisation such as the United Synagogue, dedicated to including Jews, to espouse positions on halakhic matters which are exclusivist, if viable inclusivist halakhic options are available.[62]

During Jakobovits' Chief Rabbinate, before these recommendations were issued, the dayanim of the London Bet Din had again demonstrated their inclination to vocally assert their views when they took the initiative in instigating what came to be characterized as Stage III of the Jacobs Affair. Following Jakobovits accession to the Chief Rabbinate, as part of his attempts to bridge the divides in Anglo-Jewry, he had agreed that the New London Synagogue could be registered by the Board of Deputies as a Jewish place of worship in which marriages could be performed. In September 1983, in what Jacobs characterized as a 'smear campaign', the Bet Din began to suggest that the Jewish status of children produced from marriages performed at the New London might be suspect. In a statement issued to the *Jewish Chronicle*, the Clerk of the Bet Din stated,

> I am instructed to inform the public that marriages performed by Dr Jacobs, even in cases where both parties are eligible for marriage according to Jewish law, have no more halachic validity than marriages contracted in a Register Office in civil law.[63]

Dayan Berger sought to clarify the Bet Din's statement by explaining that the concern had been raised over the validity of the witnesses used at marriages performed under Jacobs' auspices. When pressed by the *Jewish Chronicle* to explain the matter further, Berger would only state that the need for a religious divorce from New London marriages would be dealt with on a case-by-case basis. However he acknowledged that, '[i]n cases where the parties were eligible to marry in

Jewish law, an invalid ceremony itself does not affect the status of the children'. Jacobs insisted that 'no marriages are performed at the New London Synagogue where there is ineligibility'.[64] He asserted that questioning the validity of the witnesses was absurd. He concluded that 'all the talk about the invalidity of our marriages was no more than an attempt to mislead the public'.[65]

Alderman has argued that around this period various attempts were made to reassert the Orthodoxy of the United Synagogue and its affiliated religious institutions.[66] One example was the United Synagogue President's success, in 1984, in implementing a Code of Practice for the Board of Deputies that, effectively, sought to reverse the recognition of non-Orthodox bodies that had been facilitated by the constitutional amendments supported by Jakobovits the previous decade. In light of such activities, the events of the so-called Stage III of the Jacobs Affair could be seen to form part of this general return to a focus on those parts of the community that were perceived to be best-equipped to survive the encounter with British society.

SURVIVAL OF THE FITTEST?

In a study entitled 'The Evolution of the British Rabbinate Since 1845 – Its Past Impact and Future Challenges', Jakobovits praised the right-ward shifts that could be discerned in the community. In comments reminiscent of Solomon Schonfeld's calculations of the differing 'value' of observant and non-observant Jews, whilst lamenting the numerical decline of Anglo-Jewry, Jakobovits asserted that the increased commitment of certain sections of the community served to counterbalance the growing levels of disaffiliation elsewhere.[67] Concentrating on the principle of eschewing the umbrella in favour of securing the survival of a committed remnant, Jakobovits appeared to accept the drift away of United Synagogue members. This could be viewed as a necessary by-product of his attempts to nurture a form of Jewish identity for the community that could be perpetuated amongst a minority group.

> [T]he gains and losses caused by these New Right tendencies seem fairly evenly balanced, at least for the moment; the high calibre minority reclaimed to intensive Jewish living and learning being weighed against the indifferent majority weakening or severing their bonds with the religious community.

Although he was conscious that the increased commitment to Orthodoxy involved only a minority of the community, Jakobovits explained that the minority is bound to prevail ... The others, whatever their present numerical superiority, will stand aside disinterested or opt out altogether from the organised religious community in their inevitable movement towards self-liquidation. Thus will Jewish life ultimately be regenerated.[68]

Nearing the end of his Chief Rabbinate, in correspondence with Rabbi Irving Greenberg, President and founder of CLAL, an inclusive Orthodox institution in America, Jakobovits asserted his belief that 'our [Anglo-Jewish] community should be weaned from its obsession with the unity theme. We should face realities, and not make pretences of common ground where none exists.'[69] This position would appear to conflict with the principle of retaining a single chief rabbi as representative of the entire Anglo-Jewish community. It also fundamentally conflicts with Hertz's understanding of what was required from a chief rabbi if he were to be an effective representative leadership figure.[70]

At a 1977 conference discussing the state of Anglo-Jewry, the continued usefulness of viewing the community as a single, united body was discussed and largely rejected. Sigbert Prais, a consultant in the Board of Deputies' community research unit, stated that:

> My personal impression ... is that it is now more justifiable ... to speak of the polarisation of the community – to speak, if you will, in terms of two nations following very different patterns of lives rather than, as previously, of a single typical way of life for members of the community, with deviations around a norm that were less important than the existence of that central and dominant norm.[71]

He continued by noting how 'we must recognise in retrospect that there has been a movement toward both extremes, and it is the central group that has been unable to retain its adherents'.[72] The findings of the United Synagogue Review of 1992 demonstrated the validity of these perceptions. The survey of United Synagogue members found that only 10 per cent classified themselves as 'strictly Orthodox (Shomrei Shabbat)', whilst 67 per cent identified as 'Traditional (but not strictly Orthodox)'. The data on synagogue attendance found that 29 per cent attended synagogue at least once a week, but 53 per cent attended on 'Yom Kippur only (or a few occasions)'.[73]

A Time for Change called on the United Synagogue and its affiliated institutions – the Chief Rabbinate, the dayanim of the London Bet Din, the congregational rabbinate and Jewish schools – to reclaim their traditional mission in Anglo-Jewry.

> The traditional United Synagogue had a clear message, affectionately summed up in the phrase *minhag Anglia*, a celebration of the twofold blessing of being Jewish and British.[74]

The importance of the principle of interaction in the surrounding society was hereby acknowledged as an abiding feature of the community.

As members of a minority religious group existing in the midst of a tolerant, open society, British Jews were always able to interact with their surrounding social, cultural, political and intellectual milieus. The challenge for this community's religious leadership was how to ensure that the Judaism of their members remained undiminished through this encounter with the host society. During the Chief Rabbinates of Brodie and Jakobovits a fear-induced rightward shift occurred in the theology of Anglo-Jewish Orthodoxy's religious leadership. The value of intellectual engagement was callously undermined; the focus fell instead on its potential to weaken rather than enhance Judaism. Religious boundaries were strengthened in an attempt to protect Orthodoxy from perceived internal and external threats.

The United Synagogue Review discovered that the institution's shift away from its traditional ideology had alienated large sections of its constituency and sent the organization into serious decline. Many members of Anglo-Jewish Orthodoxy remained committed to the ideals of *minhag Anglia*; they wished to celebrate their Englishness as well as their Jewishness and maintain their interaction in the surrounding society. However, those espousing a theology for the community ceased to advocate the principles that would facilitate the maintenance of a religious disposition characterized as *minhag Anglia* – which could also be defined as progressive conservative Judaism. This had led to disaffiliation from the United Synagogue, growing religious polarization, and the end of an era in which a single representative voice was viable for Anglo-Jewish Orthodoxy, let alone Anglo-Jewry as a whole. The United Synagogue Review called on the central institutions of Anglo-Jewish Orthodoxy to address these issues. In a community that had demonstrated an inclination to maintain interaction with the surrounding society, the urgent need, once again, was to find a means of maintaining its Jewish identity intact; to foster what Hertz had described as 'the life consecrated by Jewish religious observance ... in indissoluble union with the best thought and culture of the age, and with utmost loyalty to King and Country'.[75]

Hertz had provided a model for Jewish identity that was predicated on the provision of an educational programme which could ensure that Jews were equipped with a sufficient understanding of their religious heritage, and confidence in its value, to be capable of engaging in the ideas of the host society without fear of any detrimental effects on their Judaism. However, his legacy could be viewed as a failure in two pivotal areas. Not only was he unable to implement the educational programme he championed, he was also frustrated in his wish that the powers of his office be transmitted undiminished to his successor. Consequently, those who inherited his mantle lacked the power of office and the appropriately-developed educational framework to facilitate the promotion of a theology such as progressive conservative Judaism. Significantly, his successors were also influenced by different theological models. These displaced confidence in the value of interaction with fear of its potential ill effects. As we have seen, the Jacobs Affair had been used to substantiate the validity of a theology that sought to sustain Jewish identity by promoting internal and external separatism. Although on some levels Jakobovits argued against this separatism, ultimately he perceived right-wing models for the maintenance of Jewish identity as the best means of securing the survival of the Anglo-Jewish community. If the religious leadership of the community, and the Chief Rabbinate in particular, were to hope to restore their role in Anglo-Jewry, they needed to retrieve a theology that facilitated interaction. Driven by a knowledge of Judaism that inspired confidence, such interaction need not impair Jewish identity, and in fact the Judaism promulgated could even be strong enough to benefit from the encounter.

Notes

PREFACE

1   A. Newman, 'Setting the Scene: Anglo-Jewry in 1870', in S. Levin (ed.), *A Century of Anglo-Jewish Life: Lectures to Commemorate the Centenary of the United Synagogue* (London: United Synagogue, 1971), p.11.
2   Brian Hebblethwaite has suggested that theology, aside from its specific reference to rational thought about God, can include the wider discipline of interest 'with God, man and the universe in their true nature and inter-relation'. B. Hebblethwaite, *The Problems of Theology* (Cambridge: Cambridge University Press, 1980), p.4.
3   See for example A. Eisen, *Rethinking Modern Judaism: Ritual, Commandment, Community* (Chicago: University of Chicago Press, 2000).
4   See for example D. Ruderman, *Jewish Enlightenment in an English Key: Anglo-Jewry's Construction of Modern Jewish Thought* (Princeton, NJ, and Oxford: Princeton University Press, 2000), and his 'Was there a "Haskalah" in England? Reconsidering an old question', in S. Feiner and D. Sorkin (eds), *New Perspectives on the Haskalah* (London: Littman, 2001); T. Endelman, *Radical Assimilation in English Jewish History, 1656–1945* (Bloomington, IN: Indiana University Press, 1990), and 'The Englishness of Jewish Modernity in England', in J. Katz (ed.), *Toward Modernity: The European Jewish Model* (New Jersey: Transaction, 1987).
5   One interviewee has asked to remain anonymous and is therefore referred to throughout as Rabbi A. As a recently retired senior minister in the United Synagogue who entered the rabbinate in 1961 and who has also been a special adviser to the Chief Rabbi's office, he offered a highly informed viewpoint on the make-up of the institutions of London Jewry. The second interviewee was the Rev. Dr Isaac Levy (1923–2005), an ally of Jacobs, who entered the United Synagogue rabbinate in 1936 and was minister of United Synagogue congregations in Hampstead, Hampstead Garden Suburb and Bayswater and was also senior Jewish chaplain in the army. Rabbi Raymond Apple, senior minister of the Great Synagogue in Sydney, Australia since 1972, was able to provide a more detached analysis of Anglo-Jewry. Appointed rabbi of the Bayswater Synagogue in 1960, he remained in the United Synagogue rabbinate until his move to Australia. He was in a position to assess his own experiences in England and the nature of the community with the aid of hindsight, divorced as he is now from personal involvement.

1 INTRODUCTION: ANGLO-JEWISH ORTHODOXY IN 1913

1   It is interesting to note that in the earlier stages of its resettlement in England the Jewish community was involved more in a struggle for naturalization than emancipation, seeking to secure the long-term implementation of the so-called 1753 'Jew Bill' which was repealed by the end of the year. The unofficial nature of the Jews' resettlement in Britain can be seen to have contributed to

the absence of a wide-ranging debate about the Jews' place in society and legislation dealing with them. It may also have reduced the perceived need of Jews in Britain to consider formally the relationship between British and Jewish identity. For a more detailed study of early modern Anglo-Jewry see T.M. Endelman, *Radical Assimilation in English Jewish History, 1656-1945* (Bloomington, IN: Indiana University Press, 1990); and his *The Jews of Georgian England: Tradition and Change in a Liberal Society, 1714-1830* (Ann Arbor, MI: University of Michigan Press, 1999); C. Roth, *History of the Jews of England* (Oxford: Oxford University Press, 1941). See also D. Ruderman, *Jewish Enlightenment in an English Key: Anglo-Jewry's Construction of Modern Jewish Thought* (Princeton and Oxford: Princeton University Press, 2000). For an assessment of the distinctive features of Anglo-Jewry's modern experiences in contrast to other European Jewries see for example T. Endelman, 'The Englishness of Jewish Modernity in England', in J. Katz (ed.), *Toward Modernity: The European Jewish Model* (New Jersey: Transaction, 1987), pp.225–67.

2   For a consideration of how the funds raised by *shechitah* services functioned as an additional, central source of communal income with consequent repercussions for communal unity, see G. Alderman, 'Power, Status and Authority in British Jewry: the Chief Rabbinate and Shechita', in G. Alderman and C. Holmes (eds), *Outsiders and Outcasts: Essays in Honours of William J. Fishman* (London: Duckworth, 1993), pp.12–31.

3   See Cecil Roth, *The Great Synagogue: London 1690–1940* (London: E. Goldston, 1950).

4   For a more detailed description of the formation of this body see Aubrey Newman, *The Board of Deputies of British Jews 1760-1985: A Brief Survey* (London: Vallentine Mitchell, 1987). At the time of George III's accession, the Sephardi community sent a loyal address to the new King which led to a complaint from the Ashkenazi community that they had been excluded. The two communities agreed to send joint representation to the King's mother and agreed to increase cooperation with one another in the future. The Ashkenazim resolved to create their own representative committee which would liase with the committee of the Sephardim. It was this agreement that has been taken to signal the earliest origins of the London Committee of Deputies of British Jews, as it was originally constituted. This body was intended to represent the interests of the whole community on future occasions. Newman has suggested that the formation of this Board, particularly its choice of name, represents another example of Jewish institutions being created to mirror English patterns. He identifies as a model for the Jews the London Board of Dissenting Deputies, established in 1723 by several groups of non-conformist Christian groups to provide them with representation. The Jewish Board only truly gained impetus under the presidency of Moses Montefiore (1838–74), when it flourished into a central institution of the Anglo-Jewish community, representing the Jewish position on various issues and fighting to secure the final elements of emancipation. By 1880 it represented fourteen London congregations and an additional thirteen provincial communities. The Board has nonetheless experienced dissent from various sections of Anglo-Jewry who question its success at being representative of the whole community. Montefiore refused to allow the West London Reform Synagogue to elect deputies after its formation, thereby denying representation to a number of prominent Anglo-Jews. The 1971 decision to allow non-Orthodox bodies to be consulted in religious affairs led to certain Orthodox representatives leaving the Board. It has also always been dominated by

the London community and has therefore been less representative of provincial Jewry. The development of the community has been reflected in the constitutional changes that were forced on the Board, such as accepting the principle that deputies could be elected from non-synagogal institutions such as friendly societies and the B'nai B'rith.

5   For a more detailed description of the emergence of Reform in Anglo-Jewry see A. Kershen and J. Romain, *Tradition and Change: A History of Reform Judaism in Britain 1840–1995* (London: Vallentine Mitchell, 1995). See also D. Marmur (ed.), *Reform Judaism: Essays on Reform Judaism in Britain* (London: RSGB, 1973).

6   Quoted by Kershen and Romain, *Tradition and Change*, p.3. The title of the new synagogue, which pointedly identified its members as *British* Jews, indicated an additional concern to move away from the notion of being Ashkenazi or Sephardi Jews as distinct from British citizens who observed the Jewish faith.

7   The only major religious reform instituted was the abolition of the second day of Festivals.

8   Chief Rabbi Hermann Adler issued a pronouncement declaring the services contrary to Jewish law and preventing any of the congregations of the United Synagogue from providing premises for the JRU. His declaration also persuaded J.F. Stern to end his association with the JRU and A.A. Green resigned from the committee. The West London Synagogue issued a series of conditions that the JRU had to accept before they would allow them to use their premises; these included the requirement to separate the sexes and bring a Torah scroll out of the ark during the service. A full list of the conditions is reproduced in D. Philipson's *The Reform Movement in Judaism* (New York: Ktav, 1967), pp.412f. The JRU chose not to accept the offer.

9   For more detail on the emergence of the JRU and its leading characters see E. Kessler, *An English Jew: The Life and Writings of Claude Montefiore* (London: Vallentine Mitchell, 2002); D. Goldberg and E. Kessler (eds), *Aspects of Liberal Judaism: Essays in Honour of John D. Rayner* (London: Vallentine Mitchell, 2004); E. Umansky, *Lily Montagu and the Advancement of Liberal Judaism: From Vision to Vocation* (New York: E. Mellen Press, 1983). The participants initially included Simeon Singer, A.A. Green and J.F. Stern, ministers of the United Synagogue, and Albert Jessel and Felix Davis, honorary officers of the same synagogal institution whose formation will be discussed below. For a comparative consideration of Progressive Judaism in Britain and its German counterpart, and the influences exerted by the latter on the former, see for example M. Meyer, 'Jewish Religious Reform in Germany and Britain', in M. Brenner *et al.* (eds), *Two Nations: British and German Jews in Comparative Perspective* (London and Tubingen: Mohr Siebeck, 1999), pp.67–83; A. Friedlander, 'The German Influence on Progressive Judaism in Great Britain', in W. Mosse *et al.* (eds), *Second Chance: Two Centuries of German-speaking Jews in the United Kingdom* (Tubingen: Mohr Siebeck, 1991), pp.425–35.

10 V.D. Lipman, *Social History of the Jews in England 1850–1950* (London: Watts and Co., 1954), pp.27ff.

11 Quoted by Endelman, *Radical Assimilation*, p.74.

12 Ibid., p.86. However, it should be noted that British liberal values that facilitated Jewish integration into society did not preclude anti-Semitism, albeit often in somewhat subtle forms. See for example T. Kushner, *We Europeans? Mass-Observation, 'Race' and British Identity in the Twentieth Century* (Aldershot and Burlington, VT: Ashgate, 2004); idem, *The Persistence of Prejudice: Anti-semitism in British Society during the Second World War* (Manchester: Manchester University Press, 1989); D. Cesarani, 'Dual Heritage or Duel of Heritages? Englishness and Jewishness in the Heritage Industry', in Tony Kushner (ed.),

The Jewish Heritage in British History: Englishness and Jewishness (London: Frank Cass, 1992), pp.29–41; C. Holmes, *Anti-Semitism in British Society, 1876–1939* (London: Edward Arnold, 1979); T. Endelman, 'Comparative Perspectives on Modern Antisemitism in the West', in David Berger (ed.), *History and Hate: The Dimensions of anti-Semitism* (Philadelphia: JPS, 1986), pp.95–114.

13 S. Sharot, 'Secularization, Judaism and Anglo-Jewry', in Michael Hill (ed.), *A Sociological Yearbook of Religion in Britain* (London: SCM Press, 1971), pp.130ff.

14 Endelman, *Radical Assimilation*, p.81.

15 Ibid., p.84.

16 For a sociological analysis of the differing attitudes to practice that can be found within Orthodoxy see Samuel Heilman and Steven Cohen, *Cosmopolitans and Parochials: Modern Orthodox Jews in America* (London: University of Chicago Press, 1989). See also Heilman, 'The Many Faces of Orthodoxy', *Modern Judaism*, 2, 1 (1982), pp.23–51, and 'The Many Faces of Orthodoxy, Part II', *Modern Judaism*, 2, 2 (1982), pp.171–98; idem, *Defenders of the Faith: Life Among the Ultra-Orthodox* (New York: Schocken, 1992); S. Heilman and Menachem Friedman, 'Religious Fundamentalism and Religious Jews: The Case of the Haredim', in Martin Marty and Scott Appleby (eds), *Fundamentalism Observed* (Chicago: University of Chicago Press, 1991), pp.197–264.

17 Newman, 'Setting the Scene: Anglo-Jewry in 1870', in S. Levin (ed.), *A Century of Anglo-Jewish Life: 1870-1970* (London: United Synagogue, 1971), p.5. For a detailed analysis of the creation of the United Synagogue, the key figures behind its creation, and some of the developments to which it was subject, see Newman's definitive history *The United Synagogue 1870–1970* (London: Routledge and Kegan Paul, 1976).

18 The formation of the Board of Guardians in 1859 had already centralized responsibility for welfare concerns in the community.

19 Newman notes that Lionel Louis Cohen and Asher Asher were the leading forces behind the creation of the United Synagogue and argues that they had 'very distinct ideas, as early as May 1866, as to the direction in which they wished the discussions to go' (Newman, *United Synagogue*, p.9). Although United Synagogue myth credits Nathan Marcus Adler with providing the impetus towards amalgamation, having raised the idea at a *kiddush* held in his *succah* during the festival of Succot (Tabernacles) in September 1866, Newman asserts that the Chief Rabbi was suggesting something that was already being considered.

20 Newman, 'Setting the Scene', p.1.

21 Quoted by Newman, *United Synagogue*, p.14. The minutes of the United Synagogue from 1870–79, including copies of the act of parliament, *Deed of Foundation and Trust*, and *Final Report of the delegates appointed to take the necessary steps for bringing the scheme for the union of the synagogues into operation*, are held in London Metropolitan Archives (hereafter LMA), Acc.2712/1/1.

22 Clause 5, from the minute book of the United Synagogue 1870–79, LMA, Acc.2712/1/1.

23 Lipman, *A History of the Jews in Britain Since 1858* (Leicester: Leicester University Press, 1990), p.26.

24 See Sharot, 'Secularization, Judaism and Anglo-Jewry', p.130.

25 Geoffrey Alderman, *Modern British Jewry* (Oxford: Oxford University Press, 1992) (hereafter *MBJ*), p.103.

26 The role of the Chief Rabbi as a position akin to an Archbishop, its function in the United Synagogue, and the influence it exerted over the Anglo-Jewish rabbinate as a whole are examined in greater detail in Chapter 3. For a more detailed description of the development of the office of Chief Rabbi see

C. Roth, 'The Chief Rabbinate of England', in his *Essays and Portraits in Anglo-Jewish History* (Philadelphia, PA: Jewish Publication Society of America, 1962); Aubrey Newman 'The Chief Rabbinate and the Provinces, 1840–1914', in J. Sacks (ed.), *Tradition and Transition: Essays Presented to Chief Rabbi Sir Immanuel Jakobovits* (London: Jews' College Publications, 1986); G. Alderman, 'The British Chief Rabbinate: A Most Peculiar Practice', *European Judaism*, 23, 2 (1990), pp.45–58; and his 'Power, Status and Authority in British Jewry: the Chief Rabbinate and Shechita'.

27 The government was keen to avoid establishing structures for ecclesiastical governance of English Jews when it had just disestablished the Church of England in Ireland. Clauses in which reference was made to the religious supervision of the Chief Rabbi, over the institution itself, its synagogues, religious functionaries, preachers, or any other religious duties, were therefore changed. The Deed of Foundation and Trust clearly explained the position in its second clause which stated 'One of the objects of the Institution called the United Synagogue shall be the contributing with other bodies to the maintenance of the Chief Rabbi, and of the Ecclesiastical Board; and the Scheme shall be read and construed as if, in the fifth clause thereof, the words "the maintenance of the Chief Rabbi, and of the Ecclesiastical Board," were substituted for the words "the maintenance of a Chief Rabbi and of other ecclesiastical persons".' In LMA, Acc.2712/1/1.

28 The minutes of a meeting on 14 December 1870 of the delegates who had secured the passage of the Act noted their resolution 'that it is an essential part of the contract between the Constituent Synagogues, that all clauses and parts of clauses which do not receive parliamentary sanction; but which were passed by the Constituent Synagogues, shall form part of the laws of the United Synagogue'. From *The Final Report*, p.11, in LMA, Acc.2712/1/1.

29 Clauses three, seven, and nine, in LMA, Acc.2712/1/1.

30 See Ignaz Maybaum, *The Office of a Chief Rabbi* (London: RSGB, 1964). More generally see Simon Schwartzfuchs, *A Concise History of the Rabbinate* (Oxford: Blackwell, 1993).

31 Roth, 'The Chief Rabbinate of England', p.255.

32 A. Rubens, *Anglo-Jewish Portraits: A Biographical Catalogue of Engraved Anglo-Jewish and Colonial Portraits from the Earliest Times to the Accession of Queen Victoria* (London: Jewish Museum, 1935), No. 48.

33 Roth noted how Hirschell sent one of his *dayanim* (rabbinical judges) to Australia in 1830 to facilitate the issuing of a divorce in the Jewish congregation in Sydney. In 1842 when Abraham Hort emigrated to New Zealand he took an official document from Hirschell authorizing him to establish a Jewish congregation in his new home. In South Africa, no new synagogue was established without a Scroll of the Law from London bearing a license from the Rabbi of the Great Synagogue. However, Roth's account has been subjected to certain historiographical critiques. It does appear to represent a gloss of historical developments, emphasizing a pragmatic, slow process of adaptation to changing circumstances without due acknowledgement of other tensions that were at play. See for example Alderman, 'Power, Status and Authority in British Jewry'.

34 Quoted by Roth, from *Voice of Jacob*, 11 Nov. 1842, in 'The Chief Rabbinate of England', p.259. The *Voice of Jacob* newspaper had been founded in September 1841, preceding by several weeks the introduction of the *Jewish Chronicle*, which was first published on 26 October. After around six months the two journals merged. On the history of the *Jewish Chronicle*, see D. Cesarani, *The Jewish Chronicle and Anglo-Jewry* (Cambridge: Cambridge University Press).

35 The communities that participated are listed in the *Report of the Chief Rabbi's Board*, in LMA, Acc.2712/1/1. Roth identifies only nineteen provincial communities involved in the election. He lists the following (p.258): Birmingham, Brighton, Bristol, Chatham, Cheltenham, Dublin, Edinburgh, Falmouth, Glasgow, Ipswich, Jersey, Liverpool, Manchester, Newcastle, Penzance, Plymouth, Portsmouth, Southampton and Swansea. The list in the Report includes both the old and new congregations of Liverpool, Canterbury and Yarmouth and excludes Ipswich.

36 The *Report of the Chief Rabbi's Board*, 8 May 1871, in LMA, Acc.2712/1/1.

37 He produced an important Jewish work, *Netinah LaGer*, a commentary on *Targum Onkelos*, in 1875.

38 Quoted by Newman, 'The Chief Rabbinate and the Provinces', p.218.

39 Quoted in ibid., p.219 from *Voice of Jacob*, 3 May 1846.

40 *Voice of Jacob*, 7 May 1847.

41 It should be clear that the powers the Chief Rabbi exercised, through his role as a religious authority for the Board of Deputies and the United Synagogue, were not inherent to the office itself, dependent instead on the decision of these institutions to defer to a Chief Rabbi. The impetus that led Anglo-Jewish institutions to centralize authority, as has already been noted, was largely motivated by the interest to create hierarchical structures for the community that provided some sort of mirror to the framework observed in the Anglican Church. Aside from the concern to demonstrate the compatibility between Englishness and Jewish identity that this effort belied, it was symptomatic of a voluntary community; it was also hoped that the structuring of the community in this way would illustrate the religious unanimity of Anglo-Jewry. At times, this interest in presenting an image of unity was not reflective of reality, although this only truly became a problem following the arrival of large numbers of eastern European immigrants. The propriety of this practice has been questioned by commentators of the Anglo-Jewish community, notably Geoffrey Alderman in his paper 'The British Chief Rabbinate: A Most Peculiar Practice'. See also Maybaum, *The Office of a Chief Rabbi*. The existence of the office of Chief Rabbi as a fact of the Anglo-Jewish community is nonetheless taken as given in this work, preventing this question from featuring as an area of examination.

42 C. Bermant, *Troubled Eden: An Anatomy of British Jewry* (London: Vallentine Mitchell, 1969), p.184.

43 Newman, *United Synagogue*, p.49.

44 I. Finestein, 'The Lay Leadership of the United Synagogue Since 1870', in S. Levin (ed.), *A Century of Anglo-Jewish Life 1870–1970* (London: United Synagogue, 1971), p.33.

45 *MBJ*, p.94.

46 See Lipman, 'The Age of Emancipation', in V.D. Lipman (ed.), *Three Centuries of Anglo-Jewish History* (Cambridge: The Jewish Historical Society of England, 1961), p.70.

47 The excuse for these pogroms was the involvement of one Jew amongst the five conspirators in the assassination of the Czar. Lipman has noted that the pogroms were almost entirely confined to southern Russia. 'Immigration to Britain came mainly from Lithuania and White Russia, areas hardly affected except indirectly, by pogroms. But there were underlying economic and demographic factors which contributed to the movement of some 2.75 million Jews from eastern Europe to the West between 1881 and 1914.' Lipman, *A History of the Jews in Britain Since 1858*, p.44. For further consideration of the plight of Russian Jews see John Klier & Shlomo Lambroza, eds., *Pogroms: Anti-*

Jewish Violence in Modern Russian History (Cambridge: Cambridge University Press, 1992).

48 S. J. Prais & M. Schmool, 'Statistics of Jewish Marriages in Great Britain: 1901-1965', *JJS*, Vol.9.2 (Dec. 1967).

49 *MBJ*, p.86.

50 Alderman records some examples of *chevrot* created by immigrants from the same geographic locations such as the Grodno, Kovno, and Warsaw Chevrot. *MBJ*, p.144. There was often also an association with friendly societies and sometimes with Jewish trade unions, see Lipman, *Social History*, pp.119f. In addition, there were *chevrot* whose names reflected the spiritual purposes for which they had been established such as the Chevra Shas or Chevra Tehillim, see Homa, *Orthodoxy in Anglo-Jewry 1840-1940* (London: Jewish Historical Society of England, 1969), p.12.

51 The leaders of the native community in England, alongside their efforts at Anglicizing the immigrants, were also keen to try to reduce the numbers of immigrants arriving in the country. Alderman has recorded their attempts to persuade immigrants arriving in England to continue their journey to America rather than settle in England, even offering financial aid to cover the costs of their onward journey. As an alternative measure they placed advertisements in the Jewish press in Russia and Romania advising potential immigrants against travel to England explaining that they would not receive help from the Anglo-Jewish authorities for the first six months of their stay. They also adopted a policy of repatriation that led to the Board of Guardians repatriating 17,500 cases, which might have represented as many as 50,000 individuals, in the period between 1880 to 1914. See *MBJ*, pp.113ff; and also Lipman, *A History of the Jews in Britain Since 1858*, pp.75f. Of course concern at the impact created by immigrants was not a feature of Anglo-Jewry alone. The desire to acculturate the immigrants once they had settled was quite apparent in other western countries to which the Jews emigrated. Whilst numerous studies have been made of the specific experiences of immigrants in the different countries to which they travelled, an interesting comparison of their differing experiences is provided by Nancy L. Green, 'The Modern Jewish Diaspora: East European Jews in New York, London and Paris', in Todd Endelman, *Comparing Jewish Societies* (Ann Arbor, MI: University of Michigan Press, 1997), pp.113–34.

52 For the immigrant youth these included the Jewish Girls Club (est. 1886), the Jewish Lads Brigade (est. 1895), and the Brady Street Boys Club (est. 1896).

53 Lipman, *Social History*, p.149.

54 For a more detailed account of the establishment of the Federation see G. Alderman, *The Federation of Synagogues 1887–1987* (London: The Federation of Synagogues, 1987); C. Roth, *The Federation of Synagogues 1912–1937: A Record of Twenty Five Years* (London: The Federation of Synagogues, 1937).

55 He was the Liberal MP for Whitechapel between 1885 and 1900 and was elevated to a peerage in 1902, becoming the first Lord Swaythling.

56 Lipman, *A History of the Jews in Britain Since 1858*, p.111.

57 Homa was a grandson of Rabbi Aba Werner, the Rav brought to England to officiate for the Machzike Hadath and lead their battles against Hermann Adler's Chief Rabbinate in the 1890s. The implications of the society's presence in the community are analysed further below, in Chapters 8 and 11.

58 B. Homa, *A Fortress in Anglo-Jewry: The Story of the Machzike Adath* (London: Shapiro, Vallentine, 1953), p.10.

59 Ibid., pp.9ff.

60 Rabbi Aba Werner (1837–1912) born in Tels, Lithuania was appointed rabbi of

Weger at the age of 19 before returning to Tels to become dayan there. He moved to Helsinki in about 1880 to serve as Chief Rabbi of Finland. He was visiting Britain in 1891 to officiate at the wedding of one of his sons in Glasgow when he stopped off in London and was asked by the newly-formed Machzike Hadath to remain in London as their Rabbi, where he stayed until his death. See *MBJ*, p.146.

61 Hermann Adler, 'Installation Sermon', 23 June 1891, in *Anglo-Jewish Memories and Other Sermons* (London: George Routledge and Sons Ltd., 1909), p.81.

62 Ibid., p.92.

63 *MBJ*, p.138. Hermann Adler had been appointed as Delegate Chief Rabbi in 1879 when his father's deteriorating health forced him to transfer some of his duties to his son. Following Nathan Marcus Adler's death in January 1890, Hermann's election as Chief Rabbi in his own right was little more than a formality. See Newman, *United Synagogue*, p.90, for details of the restrictions imposed on Nathan's delegation of his duties.

64 Rabbinical edicts were procured from various leading religious authorities on the Continent to defend the activities of each side. The eventual resolution of the dispute was greatly influenced by a court case in Liverpool, where the local Board of Shechitah were taken to court and forced to pay damages after a similar course of events had occurred. In addition, a negative report by the Admiralty Committee on the practice of *shechitah* persuaded the native community of the importance of presenting a united front on this matter. The financial difficulties experienced by the Machzike Hadath in maintaining a separate *shechitah* also contributed to their willingness to make peace. See Alderman, 'Power, Status and Authority in British Jewry: the Chief Rabbinate and Shechita', for further consideration of the role of *shechitah* in communal disputes and its importance both in financial terms and as a source of authority.

65 See chapter 11.

66 As noted in his Lipman, *Social History*, p.143. See also Lipman, *A History of the Jews in Britain Since 1858*, pp.67ff. More generally see Bernard Gainer, *The Alien Invasion: The origins of the Aliens Act of 1905* (London: Heinemann, 1972).

67 Prais and Schmool, 'Statistics of Jewish Marriages in Great Britain', pp.149–74.

68 Lipman, *Social History*, p.143.

2 JOSEPH H. HERTZ: THE FORMATIVE YEARS

1 In 1961 Rebrin combined with the village of Krasok and the two have jointly become known as Zinplinska Siroka.

2 Esriel Hildesheimer (1820–99) born in Germany, gained a secular education at the universities of Berlin and Halle. He was appointed to the ministry of Eisenstadt in 1851 but left in 1869 for Berlin, where he took up the ministry of the recently established Adass Jisroel synagogue and once again created a yeshivah in which Jewish and secular studies were combined. Hildesheimer's position in Hungary had been made untenable by the principles adopted at the Michalovce Orthodox Convention in 1865. The Orthodox Hungarian rabbinate, ostensibly seeking to restrict reform advances, agreed at this Convention to attempt to prevent any influences of modern culture from penetrating their community. Aesthetic changes, which Hildesheimer had helped introduce, such as the use of the German language in place of Yiddish, were rejected. In addition, the education that could be offered to Jewish students was severely circumscribed, thereby undermining the curriculum that Hildesheimer had

instituted in his Eisenstadt yeshiva. See David Ellenson, *Rabbi Esriel Hildes-heimer and the Creation of Modern Jewish Orthodoxy* (Tuscaloosa: The University of Alabama Press, 1990); Jacob Katz, *A House Divided: Orthodoxy and Schism in Nineteenth-Century Central European Jewry* (New Hampshire: Brandeis Univer-sity Press, 1998).

3   A question mark exists over whether Simon Hertz ever did in fact receive *semikhah*, since two official letters written by Hildesheimer suggest that he is fit for rabbinical ordination but make no mention of him having received it. His tombstone, however, does refer to him as Rabbi.

4   *JC*, 28 March 1913.

5   In discussions with Jeremy Schonfield, grandson of Hertz, he recalled his great aunt, Hertz's sister, informing him that the family had left Rebrin, where they had enjoyed a reasonable lifestyle as plum farmers, because 'more than half the people in the town were antisemitic'.

6   Simon Hertz's interest in Joseph becoming an engineer was discovered by Sefton Temkin from discussions with the Hertz family; see Temkin, 'Ortho-doxy with Moderation: A Sketch of Joseph Herman Hertz', *Judaism*, 24, 3 (Summer 1975), pp.278ff.

7   The Pittsburgh Conference was the stage for the formulation of key principles of Reform Judaism as it had crystallized in the United States. These were released as the 'Pittsburgh Platform'. For a more detailed description of developments in American Jewry at this time and the development of Conser-vative Judaism and the JTS, see Moshe Davis, *The Emergence of Conservative Judaism: The Historical School in 19th Century America* (Philadelphia, PA: The Jewish Publication Society of America, 1963); Sefton Temkin, *Isaac Mayer Wise: Shaping American Judaism* (Oxford: Oxford University Press, The Littman Library, 1992); W.R. Helmreich, *The World of the Yeshiva: An Intimate Portrait of Orthodox Jewry* (New Haven: Free Press, 1986). See also Michael Meyer, *Response to Modernity: A History of the Reform Movement in Judaism* (New York: Oxford University Press, 1988); Marc Lee Raphael, *Judaism in America* (New York: Columbia University Press, 2003); Marshall Sklare, *Conservative Judaism: An American Religious Movement* (New York: Schocken, 1972); Jack Wertheimer (ed.), *Tradition Renewed: A History of the Jewish Theological Seminary* (New York: Jewish Theological Seminary of America, 1997), vol.1.

8   Hertz, 'Sabato Morais: A Pupil's Tribute', in Cyrus Adler (ed.), *The Jewish Theo-logical Seminary of America: Semi-Centennial Volume* (New York: JTS, 1939), p.47. Sabato Morais (1823–97) was born in Italy, and spent five years in England working for the Bevis Marks Spanish and Portuguese Synagogue in London before moving to the Mikveh Israel Congregation in Philadelphia in 1851 to serve as *chazzan*, a position he retained until his death.

9   Alexander Kohut, Aaron Wise, Henry S. Jacobs, Frederick de Sola Mendes, Joseph Blumenthal, Solomon Solis-Cohen and Bernard Drachman are amongst those named as early collaborators in the endeavour to establish the JTS. See Adler (ed.), *The Jewish Theological Seminary of America*.

10   Ibid., pp.6f.

11   Hertz, 'Sabato Morais: A Pupil's Tribute', p.48.

12   Alexander Kohut (1842–94) was born in Hungary and educated at the Breslau Theological Seminary, where he received his *semikhah* in 1867, having received his doctorate from the University of Leipzig in 1864. He arrived in the United States in 1885 after serving several congregations in Hungary and establishing his reputation as a scholar and educator. He immediately became involved in the burgeoning Conservative movement and helped found the JTS, in which he was appointed Professor of Midrash and Talmudic methodology. For a

more detailed analysis of the growth of a Conservative Jewish theology as developed in the Breslau Seminary where Kohut studied, see for example Ismar Schorsch, 'Zacharias Frankel and the European Origins of Conservative Judaism', *Judaism*, 30, 3 (Summer 1981), pp.344ff.

13   Henry Pereira Mendes (1852–1937), born in Birmingham, England was rabbi of the Spanish and Portuguese congregation in Manchester between 1874 and 1877 before leaving for the US, where he was appointed *chazzan* and rabbi of the Shearith Israel, Spanish and Portuguese Congregation in New York. Bernard Drachman (1861–1945) was born in New York. After graduating from Columbia University, he was sent by the Reform Temple Emanu-El to study in Breslau at the Jewish Theological Seminary, during which time he received his doctorate, in 1884, from Heidelberg University. During his time in Germany Drachman's sympathies moved away from Reform towards Orthodox Judaism, and upon his return to New York he ministered at various Orthodox synagogue pulpits. Between 1887 and 1908, he taught several subjects at the JTS as well as serving as Dean. Upon leaving the JTS, he served as president of the Union of Orthodox Jewish Congregations from 1908 to 1920. Joseph Blumenthal (1834–1901) born in Munich, came to the US with his family aged only five. He was a business-man and politician in addition to his involvement in the communal affairs of the American Jewish community. Aside from his activities on behalf of the JTS, he was also president of the Shearith Israel Synagogue at which Mendes served.

14   Davis, *The Emergence of Conservative Judaism*, p.313.

15   Ibid., p.317.

16   They were led by Jacob Schiff and included Leonard Lewisohn, Louis Marshall and Daniel and Simon Guggenheim, all successful men in the US concerned to both reduce the foreignness of the immigrants and also help them.

17   The subject of his thesis was 'The Ethical System of James Martineau'.

18   B.G. Rudolph, *From a Minyan to a Community: A History of the Jews of Syracuse* (Syracuse, NY: Syracuse University Press, 1970), p.83.

19   This is attested to both in Rudolph's *From a Minyan to a Community*, and in Temkin's 'Orthodoxy with Moderation: A Sketch of Joseph Herman Hertz'.

20   Bernard Drachman, *The Unfailing Light: Memoirs of an American Rabbi* (New York: Rabbinical Council of America, 1948), pp.198f. Drachman discusses the problems of mixed seating at some length, since he had also encountered the problem in two of his ministries, which compelled him to resign.

21   When Hertz came to be considered in the elections for the new Chief Rabbi in England, some suspicion was raised over the credentials of his ordination. However, assurances were given of the good standing of his *semikhah*. Furthermore, Temkin, in his 'Orthodoxy with Moderation: A Sketch of Joseph Herman Hertz', discovered that Hertz, in fact, obtained a second *semikhah* in addition to the one he received from the JTS. In a letter to Mr J. Goldreich of Johannesburg dated 31 March 1898, he wrote 'I am a graduate of the Orthodox rabbinical school, the Jewish Theological Seminary of New York. I have furthermore a *Hattaras Horo'h*, or Rabbinical Diploma, from six authorised rabbis.' As the first graduate of the JTS, the form of *semikhah* that would be granted had to be decided upon when Hertz came to be ordained; the *hattarat haroeh* – teaching and making decisions in matters of Jewish law – was not included. Whether it was simply because he wished to obtain the *hattarat haroeh* or because he perceived some use to obtaining a second, more tradi-tionalist *semikhah*, is unclear. Nonetheless he does appear to have obtained this additional *semikhah*. The fact that these rabbis were able to examine and ordain Hertz on the premises of the JTS is also significant. The perceived Orthodoxy of the JTS, at this point in time, is again attested to here.

22   Bernard Drachman, in his autobiography *The Unfailing Light*, recorded that he
       had already encountered these problems ten years earlier. He discovered that
       mixed seating was introduced in synagogues with English-speaking, yet
       Orthodox, rabbis since their communities did not wish to rigidly stick to all
       Jewish religious dictates. They expected some margin for reform.

23   Dora L. Sowden, 'In the Transvaal till 1899', in Gustav Saron and Louis Hotz
       (eds), *The Jews in South Africa: A History* (Cape Town: Oxford University Press,
       1955), p.151.

24   Ibid., pp.151ff.

25   Ibid., p.161. Wasserzug arrived in Johannesburg in 1899 to minister to the
       Johannesburg Hebrew Congregation. In contrast to Sowden's suggestions,
       John I. Simon has argued, in his essay 'Pulpit and Platform: Hertz and
       Landau', in Mendel Kaplan and Marian Robertson (eds), *Founders and Followers:
       Johannesburg Jewry 1887–1915* (Cape Town: Vlaeberg Publishers, 1991), that
       the members of the Johannesburg Hebrew Congregation did not appreciate
       Hertz's attempts to act as a representative for all Johannesburg Jewry. Prima
       facie, Simon's essay may appear to undermine the claim that Hertz's ministry
       in Johannesburg served as useful preparation for his future role as Chief
       Rabbi of the United Hebrew Congregations of the British Empire. Simon not
       only records the Johannesburg Hebrew Congregation's assertion that: 'We
       must take exception to his [Hertz] posing as the representative of the Jews of
       the Transvaal and should he do so we shall be compelled to take such steps as
       we may deem necessary to remove such erroneous impression' (p.185). He
       also notes that following the appointment of Judah Leib Landau to the pulpit
       of that synagogue, in September 1903, 'a bitter mutual antipathy developed
       between these two powerful personalities'. The force of this antipathy was
       such that on hearing of Hertz's appointment to the office of British Chief
       Rabbi, Landau stated 'I wince under the pain, that Jewry should have sunk so
       hopelessly deep as to make such a thing possible'. (Quoted by Simon, from a
       letter to Moses Gaster dated 20 Feb. 1913, p.191.) Nonetheless, Simon notes
       that the two rabbis were able to work together in apparent unity on many
       issues which involved the greater community, such as the Zionist Federation,
       the Board of Deputies, the Chevra Kadisha and the Shechitah Board. He also
       acknowledges that Landau came into conflict with several other rabbis with
       whom he worked, implying that he was not the easiest of men with whom
       to get along. The only cause he could identify for this discord was a spilling
       over of 'inter-congregational rivalry' and it is this factor that may resolve
       the questions which Simon's essay might otherwise appear to have raised.
       The animosities which had existed between the members of the original
       Johannesburg congregation and those who had seceded from it to establish
       a distinct synagogue were perpetuated despite the arrival of new ministers
       for each community. Opposition towards Hertz, from both Landau and his
       community, derived from the former rabbi's position as minister of the
       Witwatersrand Old Hebrew Congregation rather than any obvious flaws in
       his ministry. Indeed the editors of *Founders and Followers* asserted that 'In 1898
       the Witwatersrand Old Hebrew Congregation welcomed one of the most
       outstanding ministers in the history of South African Jewry, the young Rabbi
       Dr J.H. Hertz' (p.29).

26   Hertz, *The Jew as a Patriot: A Plea for the Removal of the Civil Disabilities of the Jews
       in the Transvaal*, rev. 2nd edn. (Johannesburg: M.J. Wood and Co., 1898).

27   The representative role performed by the Zionist Federation and that associa-
       tion's reluctance to relinquish this role is further detailed in Stephen Cohen,
       'The South African Zionist Federation and the South African Jewish Board of

Deputies: Samuel Goldreich and Max Langermann', in Kaplan and Robertson (eds), *Founders and Followers*, pp.197–210.

28   Sowden, 'In the Transvaal till 1899', p.162.

29   Gustav Saron, The Long Road to Unity', in Saron and Hotz (eds), *The Jews in South Africa: A History*, pp.231f.

30   Quoted by Saron, ibid., p.263, without reference.

31   Temkin, 'Orthodoxy with Moderation: A Sketch of Joseph Herman Hertz', has suggested that Hertz began his search for a new appointment following his marriage. He married Rose Freed in 1904. He began to feel that the rugged conditions to be experienced in Johannesburg were inappropriate for his wife and any family they might have.

32   The position went to Joseph Hockman who remained in the post until 1915. John Shaftesley, 'Religious Controversies', in S.S. Levin (ed.), *A Century of Anglo-Jewish Life* (London: United Synagogue, 1973), explains that Hockman resigned before Hertz, then Chief Rabbi, could question the religious position he was propounding in the New West End pulpit.

33   Samson Raphael Hirsch (1808–88) may be viewed as the father of Neo-Orthodoxy. Born in Hamburg, he attended university for a year before being called away in 1830 to serve as *Landesrabbiner* of the Principality of Oldenburg aged just 22. He moved to Emden in 1841 to take up the post of *Landesrabbiner* of East Friesland and then in 1846 accepted an appointment as Chief Rabbi in Moravia and Austrian Silesia. In 1851, he left this rather illustrious position to become rabbi of a newly formed independent congregation in Frankfurt, the *Israelitische Religionsgesellschaft* (IRG) also know as the Adass Jisroel, where he remained until his death. The theology of Hirsch is more fully discussed in Chapter 11.

3   THE ANGLO-JEWISH ESTABLISHMENT AND THE OFFICE OF THE CHIEF RABBINATE

1   As stated in an interview with Hertz in the New York *Jewish Morning Journal* reprinted in the *JC*, 16 Aug. 1912.

2   *JC*, 3 May 1912.

3   C. Roth, *Essays and Portraits in Anglo-Jewish History* (Philadelphia, PA: Jewish Publication Society of America, 1962), p.6.

4   V.D. Lipman, *Social History of the Jews in England 1850–1950* (London: Watts and Co., 1954), p.22, has argued that Hirschell's edict denying the reformers 'communion with us Israelites' was not actually intended as a *cherem*. Regarding the repeal of this edict see A.M. Hyamson, *The Sephardim of England* (London: Methuen & Co., 1951), pp.291ff.

5   Indeed in 1890, preceding the Chief Rabbinate elections following the death of Nathan Marcus Adler, the West London Synagogue was invited to send representation to the Chief Rabbinate Conference which was to appoint Hermann Adler to the office, an invitation which they declined.

6   C. Roth, *History of the Jews of England* (Oxford: Oxford University Press, 1941), p.253.

7   M. Goulston, 'The Status of the Anglo-Jewish Rabbinate, 1840–1914', *JJS*, 10, 1 (June 1968), pp.64f. As Stephen Sharot has further explained in his 'Religious Change in Native Orthodoxy in London, 1870–1914: Rabbinate and Clergy', *JJS*, 15, 2 (Dec. 1973), p.171, 'upper-class acculturated lay leaders mixed socially with Anglicans and they were concerned that Anglo-Jewry should have a religious head who could occupy a position of authority somewhat

parallel to that of the Archbishop of Canterbury in the Anglican Church'.

8   Sharot, 'Religious Change in Native Orthodoxy in London, 1870–1914: The Synagogue Service', *JJS*, 15, 1 (June 1973), p.58. However, it should be noted that a new school of thought has developed in studies of Anglo-Jewish history that suggests that the subtle pressure to conform to established English mores in fact demonstrates a form of antisemitism at the heart of British liberalism. See for example Tony Kushner, *The Holocaust and the Liberal Imagination: A Social and Cultural History* (Oxford: Blackwell, 1994). For more references see above Introduction, n.12.

9   Reported in the *JC*, 1 Dec. 1905. Albert Jessel was a vice-president of the United Synagogue from 1899–1917.

10 *JC*, 22 Nov. 1907. This was a story retold by Sharot, 'Religious Change: Rabbinate and Clergy'.

11 Hermann Gollancz (1852–1930), as well as ministering to the Bayswater Synagogue, taught Hebrew at University College London. He was knighted in 1923.

12 *MBJ*, p.147.

13 N.M. Adler, *Laws and Regulations for all the Synagogues in the British Empire* (London: Office of Chief Rabbi, 1847), p.5.

14 See *JC*, 9 Nov. 1894, and Sharot, 'Religious Change: Rabbinate and Clergy', pp.173f.

15 Aubrey Newman, *United Synagogue 1870–1970* (London: Routledge and Kegan Paul, 1976), p.94, notes that this comment of Hermann Adler was adopted by a United Synagogue sub-committee which had been examining the duties of the Chief Rabbi and the role of the Bet Din in relation to the office of the Chief Rabbinate.

16 C. Bermant, *Troubled Eden: An Anatomy of British Jewry* (London: Vallentine Mitchell, 1969), p.186.

17 Newman, *United Synagogue*, p.47.

18 See below, Chapters 7 and 9.

19 Robert Waley Cohen's business experiences are more fully detailed in a biography by Robert Henriques, *Sir Robert Waley Cohen 1877–1952: A Biography* (London: Secker & Warburg, 1966) (hereafter *RWC*). This edict is quoted by Henriques, p.321.

20 Newman, *United Synagogue*, p.129.

21 *MBJ*, p.120.

22 D. Cesarani, 'The Transformation of Communal Authority in Anglo-Jewry, 1914–40', in David Cesarani (ed.), *The Making of Modern Anglo-Jewry* (Oxford: Basil Blackwell, 1990), pp.115–40. He has suggested that 'in practical terms the agenda of the Zionists in Britain was oriented entirely towards domestic affairs. The ideology of the movement, as in other countries, provided a viable Jewish identity which enabled Jews to remain in the Diaspora and a rhetoric of revolt for middle-class elements denied access to communal power ... Zionism was the vehicle for a middle-class Jewish ethnic identity which first- and second-generation British Jews constructed through ethnic neighbourhoods, community organisation and their immigrant heritage. This process of redefinition was bound to have an impact on communal authority' (p.140).

23 The League consisted of leading lay members of the Anglo-Jewish community; MPs such as Lionel de Rothschild who was president, Louis Montagu the Second Lord Swaythling and Claude Montefiore. See, for example, Stuart A. Cohen, *English Zionists and British Jews: The Communal Politics of Anglo-Jewry, 1895–1920* (Princeton, NJ: Princeton University Press, 1982).

24 *RWC*, p.263. Another example of the native community's concern to preserve

its own image intact, regardless of the effects this might have on the immigrant community, was demonstrated by a number of their activities during the First World War. Their interest in displaying the patriotism of the Anglo-Jewish community interfered with efforts to help immigrants. The Board of Deputies refused to intercede when the government interned Jewish immigrants as enemy aliens in 1915. A far bigger problem emerged with regard to conscription and volunteering for service in the British army. Immigrants who had not been naturalized as British citizens were exempt from conscription and were not keen to volunteer for service. They were reluctant to fight to defend the Russian Czar whose influence many had sought to escape. Herbert Samuel, the Jewish Home Secretary at the time, suggested that Russian immigrants of military age should either volunteer for the British army or return to serve in the Russian army. In July 1917, Britain signed an agreement with Russia to repatriate immigrants who refused to join the British army to enable them to be conscripted into the Russian armed forces. Geoffrey Alderman, in his *MBJ*, p.238, has noted comments made by Samuel in a letter to Lucien Wolf in which he explained the 'disastrous' effect that the immigrants' actions were causing to the reputation of Jews. In its attempts to alter the actions of the immigrant community Alderman notes the decision of the Jewish Soup Kitchen in the East End to decline to serve Russian Jews who had refused to volunteer. The native community's activities during the War led to the creation of a Foreign Jews Protection Committee, which was established outside the control of the lay leaders of Anglo-Jewry. Alderman asserted that 'The emergence of the FJPC amounted to a vote of no confidence in the existing representative institutions' p.241.

4 A CHIEF RABBI FOR 'EAST AND WEST'

1 *JC*, 14 July 1911, and frequently thereafter, throughout the deliberation process leading to the election of the new Chief Rabbi.
2 *JC*, 19 Jan. 1912.
3 These columns were written by Leopold Greenberg, editor and part-owner of the paper. Cesarani details the editorial changes and the identities of various writers who adopted pseudonyms for their columns in his *The Jewish Chronicle and Anglo-Jewry, 1841–1991* (Cambridge: Cambridge University Press, 1994).
4 *JC*, 21 June 1912. Questions were also raised about the methods of searching for this new appointment. Disapproval was voiced at the decision to expect leading rabbis to apply for the post, rather than be sought out and approached by the Selection Committee.
5 Reported in the *JC*, 21 Feb. 1913.
6 The minutes of this meeting are contained in the compilation of data relating to the 1911–13 election process held in LMA, Acc.2712/1/143.
7 *JC*, 12 Jan. 1912.
8 Joseph Abrahams, Samuel Daiches and Hermann Gollancz had each, briefly, thrown their hats into the ring but their candidacies failed to make the shortlist.
9 Hyamson (1863–1949), born in Suwalk, in Lithuania came to England aged just five. He was educated at Jews' College and University College, London and received his ordination in 1882. During the interregnum between the Chief Rabbinates of Hermann Adler and Joseph H. Hertz, Hyamson served as president of the Bet Din, working alongside Asher Feldman, a fellow Dayan, who was acting Chief Rabbi to the community. From 1915 to 1940, having

travelled to New York to take up the ministry at the Orach Chayyim congregation, vacated by Hertz, he held the Chair of Codes of Jewish Law at the Jewish Theological Seminary. Drachman, referred to above in Chapter 2, see n.13, was Rabbi of both the Ohev Zedek community and the Zichron Ephraim congregation at the time of his candidacy for the British Chief Rabbinate and was also president of the Union of Orthodox Jewish Congregations, a post in which he remained until 1920.

10   *JC*, 25 Oct. 1912.
11   As recorded in the *JC*, 7 March 1902.
12   See below, p.47f.
13   *JC*, 21 Feb. 1913, from A.H. Jessel's comments.
14   B. Drachman, *The Unfailing Light* (New York: Rabbinical Council of America, 1948), p.316.
15   From an article by 'Mentor' *In the Communal Armchair*, *JC*, 15 Nov. 1912.
16   As reported in the *JC*, 21 Feb. 1913.
17   Drachman, *Unfailing Light*, pp.316ff. Drachman recalled one particular dinner held in his honour at the home of a United Synagogue minister during his tour of England. Drachman had been led to believe that this minister's observance of *kashrut* was suspect and therefore decided that he could not eat the food he was offered. He identified the offence caused that evening as crucial in the mounting opposition to the perceived stringency of his Orthodoxy. Aside from any such concern about his religiosity, Drachman's candidacy may also have been undermined by Solomon Schechter's deprecatory comments about his scholarship. There was personal acrimony between the former acting president of the JTS and his successor. This ultimately encouraged Drachman to leave the Seminary and it may have impelled Schechter to speak out against Drachman when he became involved in the Chief Rabbinate contest. Harvey Meirovich, in his *A Vindication of Judaism: The Polemics of the Hertz Pentateuch* (New York: Jewish Theological Seminary of America, 1998), has pointed to the influence Schechter's comments may have exerted and reproduced the contents of a letter sent by Schechter to Albert Jessel in which the JTS president stressed his support for Hertz rather than Drachman: 'Hertz is decidedly the greater scholar, even in rabbinics, the greater gentleman, and the great preacher ... The difference between the two candidates is so greatly to the advantage of Dr Hertz as to exclude all comparison ... I know of no greater calamity which could happen to British Jewry than the election of Dr Drachman to the chief rabbinate. Even the extending of an invitation to him is humiliating to English Jewry in the eyes of those who know the man and his position here' p.195, n.74, from JTS Library Archives.
18   *JC*, 3 Jan. 1913.
19   *JC*, 25 Oct. 1912.
20   See editorial of the *JC*, 12 Jan. 1912.
21   Interestingly, this did, at least, ensure that a greater unity was restored between the lay leadership of the Federation and its membership. As reported in the *JC*, on 24 Feb. 1912 a meeting of delegates of the Federation was convened to discuss its representation at the Chief Rabbinate Conference. Concern was expressed at the manner in which the delegates who had been sent to the Conference had been self-appointed, rather than elected by the membership of the Federation. Furthermore, it was noted that no effort had been made to ascertain the opinions of the laity that they represented. The initial decision to secede from the Chief Rabbinate Conference had been made without any consultation with the membership, indeed it was suggested that the majority of Federation members had only learned of what had happened

through the correspondence pages of the *JC*. According to the *JC*'s reporting of the meeting it had been stated that: 'It was absurd to say that the three delegates represented the opinions of the 6,000 and more members of the Federation. It was equally ridiculous and absurd, and, moreover, untruthful to say … that the general body of the Federation endorsed the attitude taken up by the delegates of the Federation.' However, once it was confirmed that the Federation was to be allocated a derisory number of votes, a figure totally out of proportion to the numbers it represented, a June meeting of Federation members agreed that it had been appropriate after all for their institution to withdraw from the election process and they did not feel that they could rejoin the Rabbinate Conference. It was felt that to partake in the elections under the United Synagogue scheme would set an unacceptable precedent concerning the right of the United Synagogue to dominate the entire community as a result of their material wealth.

22 See *JC*, 28 June 1912.
23 *JC*, 3 Jan. 1913. It should be acknowledged that Leopold Greenberg, editor of the *JC* throughout the election campaign, was an ardent Zionist who became involved in the paper when the World Zionist Organisation considered purchasing the *JC* when it came up for sale in 1906. Although the Zionist Organisation did not channel funds into the paper and it remained independent, David Cesarani has stated in his *The Jewish Chronicle* that 'Greenberg certainly did put the *Jewish Chronicle* to the service of Zionism', p.105. Consequently, Greenberg's support of Hertz's candidacy may have been partially influenced by the passionate support that Hertz had already exhibited towards Zionism.
24 *JC*, 17 Jan. 1913.
25 There were a total of 418 votes cast; the twenty-eight which had originally been allocated to the Federation were not re-distributed; of the remaining votes, sixty were abstentions and the other twenty-one were absent from the voting. Votes cast by representatives of synagogues outside the control of the United Synagogue were in favour of Hertz by forty-three votes to twenty-nine.
26 See *JC*, 3, 17 and 31 May 1912.
27 Alfred Lord Milner (1854–1925) had been appointed Governor of the Cape Colony and British High Commissioner in South Africa in 1897. In 1901, he left the Cape to administer over the Transvaal and Orange Free State – the two Boer republics that were annexed by Britain during the Anglo-Boer War. He returned to England in 1905, where he became active in the House of Lords and was appointed to the War Cabinet of David Lloyd George from 1916 to 1921.
28 Quoted by A. Newman in his *Commemoration of the Centenary of the birth of Chief Rabbi Dr. Joseph H. Hertz* (London: United Synagogue, 1972), p.5f.
29 Indeed as Newman recorded, Japhet's diary noted that Rothschild relied upon the recommendations of a Mrs Elsa Cohen for proof of Hertz's Orthodoxy. 'I was nonplussed. Elsa Cohen! our dear sweet little Elsa, without the faintest conception of anything Jewish an expert on the qualifications of an orthodox Rabbi!' Quoted in A. Newman, *The United Synagogue 1870–1970* (London: Routledge and Kegan Paul, 1976), p.101.
30 *JC*, 21 Feb. 1913.

5 THE PROGRESSIVE CONSERVATIVE THEOLOGY OF JOSEPH H. HERTZ

1 J.H. Hertz, 'Opening Address by the Chief Rabbi', *1923 Conference of Anglo-Jewish Preachers* (hereafter *CAJP*) (London: Oxford University Press, 1923), p.19.

2 J.H. Hertz, *The Recall to the Synagogue,* Address by the Chief Rabbi at the United Synagogue Conference, 25 July 1940 (London: Office of the Chief Rabbi, 1940), p.7.
3 J.H. Hertz, *Affirmations of Judaism* (London: Oxford University Press, 1927), pp.150f.
4 Maimonides is now thought to have been born in 1138.
5 J.H. Hertz, 'Opening Address by the Chief Rabbi', *1935 CAJP*, p.13.
6 Ibid., p.10.
7 Ibid., p.11.
8 See J.H. Hertz, 'Bachya and "The Duties of the Heart"', Appendix in *The sixth biennial report of the Jewish Theological Seminary of America* (New York: Press of Philip Cowen, 1898); and his *Bachya: the Jewish Thomas à Kempis, a chapter in the history of Jewish ethics* (New York: Jewish Theological Seminary of America, 1898).
9 J.H. Hertz, *Sermons, Addresses and Studies* (London: Soncino Press, 1938) (hereafter *SAS*), III, p.334.
10 J.H. Hertz, 'The Hallowing of History', in his *The Pentateuch and Haftorahs: Hebrew text, English Translation and Commentary,* 2nd edn (London: Soncino, 1975), p.936.
11 J.H. Hertz, 'The Recall to the Synagogue', *Sermon Preached at the Hampstead Synagogue 17th August, 1940 by the Chief Rabbi* (London: Office of the Chief Rabbi, 1940), p.7.
12 'The Function of Jews' College', in J.H. Hertz, *Early and Late: Addresses, Messages and Papers* (Surrey: Soncino Press, 1943), p.182.
13 J.H. Hertz, 'Opening Address of the Chief Rabbi', *1932 CAJP*, p.8.
14 J.H. Hertz, *Ancient Semitic Codes and the Mosaic Legislation* (London: Publications for Society for Jewish Jurisprudence, 1928), p.213.
15 J.H. Hertz, 'Opening Address by the Chief Rabbi', *1925 CAJP*, p.7.
16 J.H. Hertz, 'Jewish Learning – Old and New', *SAS*, II, p.48.
17 Hertz, 'Opening Address of the Chief Rabbi', *1932 CAJP*, p.8.
18 J.H. Hertz, *The Celebration of the Chief Rabbi's Silver Jubilee, 21 March, 1938* (London: The Chief Rabbi Presentation Committee, 1938), pp.13f.
19 D.L. Sowden, 'In The Transvaal Till 1899', G. Saron and L. Hotz (eds), *The Jews in South Africa: A History* (Cape Town: Oxford University Press, 1955), pp.161f.
20 *JC*, 18 Jan. 1946.
21 Jeremy Schonfield has suggested in conversations with the author that it was the Chief Rabbi who made this comment about himself rather than it being something said of him by one of his ministers, as has been suggested in a number of other sources. See, for example, Ephraim Levine, 'Memoir', in I. Epstein (ed.), *Joseph Herman Hertz 1872–1946: In Memoriam* (London: Soncino Press, 1947), p.12.
22 Hertz, 'Opening Address by the Chief Rabbi', *1932 CAJP*, p.9.
23 Hertz, 'Opening Address by the Chief Rabbi', *1923 CAJP*, p.19.
24 Ibid., p.3.
25 Hertz, *The Pentateuch and Haftorahs*, p.936.

6 PROGRESSIVE CONSERVATIVE JUDAISM, PART II: IN ANGLO-JEWRY

1 *JC*, 18 April 1913.
2 J.H. Hertz, 'Installation Sermon', reprinted in *SAS*, I, p.7.
3 Ibid., p.10.
4 Ibid., p.8.

5 J.H. Hertz, *Affirmations of Judaism* (London: Oxford University Press, 1975), p.159.
6 J.H. Hertz, 'Religion and Life', A Sermon Preached at the New West End Synagogue Shabbat Bereshit 18th October 1919, in *SAS*, I, p.289.
7 J.H. Hertz, 'Traditional Judaism: An Appeal for the Jewish War Memorial', *A Sermon Preached at the New West End Synagogue Shabbat Bereshit 18th October 1919* (London: Office of the Chief Rabbi, 1919), p.7.
8 J.H. Hertz, 'Opening Address by the Chief Rabbi' at the *1932 Conference of Anglo-Jewish Preachers* (London: Office of the Chief Rabbi, 1932), p.10.
9 For example, the Golders Green United Synagogue was founded in 1917, Cricklewood in 1931, Kenton in 1932, Finchley, Highgate and Hendon in 1935, Kingsbury and Ilford in 1936, Hampstead Garden Suburb in 1937, Edgware in 1938. This period, in addition, saw a growth in the synagogues of the Union of Orthodox Hebrew Congregations, created in 1926, but these represented far smaller numbers, in terms of both synagogues and population.
10 *MBJ*, p.256.
11 In 1939 Selig Brodetsky, the Zionist candidate, was elected president of the Board of Deputies, confirming the growing control which the Zionists had exercised over the board for some years. By 1921, Zionist council members had come to be elected to the United Synagogue Council, urging the donation of money by that institution to the Zionist cause. However the Honorary Officers overruled these requests, as they continued to be dominated by the Cousinhood, indeed four of the eleven were members of the League of British Jews; see D. Cesarani, 'The Transformation of Communal Authority in Anglo-Jewry, 1914–40', in D. Cesarani (ed.), *The Making of Modern Anglo-Jewry* (Oxford: Basil Blackwell, 1990).

7 JOSEPH H. HERTZ, CHIEF RABBI OF THE UNITED HEBREW
CONGREGATIONS OF THE BRITISH EMPIRE

1 A. Newman, *The United Synagogue 1870–1970* (London: Routledge and Kegan Paul, 1976), p.157. It should be noted that the conflicts between Hertz and Waley Cohen were not continuous and did not extend into every sphere. There were often prolonged periods of agreement between the two. Moreover, notwithstanding his own criticisms of the Chief Rabbi, Waley Cohen was always quick to defend Hertz from the reproach of others.
2 J.H. Hertz, 'The Recall to the Synagogue', *Sermon Preached at the Hampstead Synagogue 17th August, 1940 by the Chief Rabbi* (London: Office of the Chief Rabbi, 1940), p.6.
3 Ibid., p.7.
4 'The Recall to the Synagogue', *Address by the Chief Rabbi at the United Synagogue Conference, 25th July, 1940 by the Chief Rabbi* (London: Office of the Chief Rabbi, 1940), pp.4f.
5 J.H. Hertz, 'Opening Address of the Chief Rabbi' at the *1927 Conference of Anglo-Jewish Preachers* (London: Oxford University Press, 1927), p.2.
6 Henriques, *RWC*, p.385.
7 Quoted by Henriques, *RWC*, p.344, from a letter of Hertz to Waley Cohen dated 22 Sept. 1924.
8 Quoted by Henriques, *RWC*, p.346, from a letter of Hertz to Waley Cohen without reference to date.
9 Newman, *United Synagogue*, p.157.
10 Henriques, *RWC*, p.348.

11 As quoted in the *JC*, 18 April 1913. Hertz also referred to this event in various letters in which he sought to defend his religious authority. See, for example, letter to Lionel de Rothschild dated 14 July 1940 held in LMA, Acc.2805/4/5/54.

12 From a letter to Lionel de Rothschild dated 11 Nov. 1940 in LMA, Acc.2805/4/5/54. The Chief Rabbinate Conference had resolved to adopt the summary of a chief rabbi's duties that had been composed during the 1890 elections. This had stated 'it is almost impossible to enumerate in detail the whole of the duties which have to be performed by a Chief Rabbi. These duties are naturally of a complex character and being not exclusively religious, it may be fairly said they touch upon every point which concerns the religious, moral, and general welfare of the community.' (From the minutes of a meeting of the Sub-Committee on 28 April 1912, in LMA, Acc.2712/1/143.)

13 J.H. Hertz, 'The First Pastoral Tour to the Jewish Communities of the British Overseas Dominions', in *SAS*, II, p.328. The Tour, in addition to its goal of rejuvenating the contact between the Chief Rabbinate and the far-flung communities of the Empire, was also viewed as opportune at that time for the potential it offered to collect donations towards the Jewish War Memorial.

14 Ibid., p.337.

15 Ibid., p.346.

16 The proposal also considered the creation of thirteen equal months of 28 days. See J.H. Hertz, *The Battle for the Sabbath at Geneva* (London: Oxford University Press, 1932), for a more detailed description.

17 Ibid., p.11.

18 Ibid., p.12. Hertz reproduced the letter sent to him by Abram Simon of the Central Conference of American Rabbis which requested that Hertz 'be gracious enough to add our protest as Jews in America to the ones which you have already forwarded, and select such methods of presentation of our statement as you deem best under the circumstances' (p.38). Hertz was joined in a Jewish delegation by Grand Rabbi Israel Levin; Rabbi Fuerst of the Agudas Yisroel, Vienna; Dr Lewenstein of Zurich and Mr Lucien Wolf.

19 From Address reproduced in Hertz, *The Battle for the Sabbath at Geneva*, p.24.

20 Letter reproduced in J.H. Hertz, *Early and Late; Addresses, Messages and Papers* (Surrey: Soncino Press, 1943), p.227.

21 He delivered a lecture at the West London Synagogue in 1925 and 1935. In 1934, when a ceremony was held for the opening of an extension to the West London Synagogue, Hertz attended, as guest of honour, and addressed a sermon to the community. With the dayanim of the London Bet Din he was present at the funeral of Joel Blau, Senior Minister of the West London Reform Synagogue in 1927, and attended the Memorial service for Morris Joseph in 1930. Incidentally, Hertz had frequently praised Joseph's key work, *Judaism as Creed and Life* (London: Macmillan and Co., 1903), praising its value as a clear expression, in English, of Jewish life, regardless of its author's Reformist theology. See, for example his 'Opening Address by the Chief Rabbi' at the *1932 Conference of Anglo-Jewish Preachers* (London: Office of the Chief Rabbi, 1932), or *Affirmations of Judaism* (London: Soncino, 1975), p.188.

22 Quoted in A. Kershen and J. Romain, *Tradition and Change: A History of Reform Judaism in Britain 1840–1995* (London: Vallentine Mitchell, 1995), p.159.

23 Since the 1960s, more precise work has been carried out by demographers that have charted certain changes that have occurred in the Anglo-Jewish population. In addition, synagogue affiliations have been monitored to demonstrate the religious breakdown of the community according to synagogue groupings. See for example, B. Kosmin and S. Waterman, *British Jewry in the Eighties:*

A Statistical and Geographical Guide (London: Board of Deputies of British Jews, 1986). The changes in synagogal affiliation that occurred during the Chief Rabbinates of Hertz's successors are considered further in the epilogue.

24   Kosmin has noted that after one generation the fertility patterns of the eastern European immigrants were transformed to more closely match the pattern of the host society, whose fertility patterns were replicated amongst the native community. See B. Kosmin, 'Nuptiality and Fertility Among British Jews', in D.A. Coleman (ed.), *Demography of Immigrants and Minority Groups in the United Kingdom* (London: Academic Press, 1982), p.259.

25   Marriages performed in Sephardi synagogues accounted for 1.6 per cent of marriages between 1921 and 1940 and 2.5 per cent in 1965. These figures are derived from Barry A. Kosmin, 'Localism and Pluralism in British Jewry 1900-80', *Transactions of the Jewish Historical Society of England*, 28 (1982); S.J. Prais and M. Schmool, 'Statistics of Jewish Marriages in Great Britain: 1901–1965', *JJS*, 9, 2 (Dec. 1967); S.J. Prais, 'Polarisation or Decline? A Discussion of Some Statistical Findings on the Community', in S.L. Lipman and V.D. Lipman (eds), *Jewish Life in Britain 1962–77* (New York: K.G. Saur Publishing Inc., 1981); and S.J. Prais, 'Synagogue Statistics and the Jewish Population of Great Britain, 1900–70', *JJS*, 14, 2 (Dec. 1972).

26   Kosmin, 'Localism and Pluralism in British Jewry 1900-80', pp.114f.

8 FORCES OF POLARIZATION

1   *JC*, 19 Feb. 1926. For further consideration of the development of the Gateshead community, see Louis Olsover, *The Jewish Communities of North-East England, 1755–1980* (Gateshead: Ashley Marks Publishing, 1981), pp.221–50; A. Levy, *The Story of Gateshead Yeshiva* (Taunton: Wessex Press, 1952); M. Dansky, *Gateshead: Its Community, its Personalities, its Institutions* (Michigan: Targum Press, 1992).

2   See for example Bernard Homa, *Orthodoxy in Anglo-Jewry 1880-1940* (London: Jewish Historical Society of England, 1969), pp.27; 33ff.

3   From Victor Schonfeld, *Memorandum on the possibility of co-operation between the Dalston and Adath Yisroel Congregations*, 26 October 1924, in LMA, Acc.2805/4/5/1.

4   Julius Carlebach, 'The Impact of German Jews on Anglo-Jewry: Orthodoxy, 1850–1950', in W.E. Mosse *et al.* (eds), *Second Chance: Two Centuries of German-Speaking Jews in the United Kingdom* (Tubingen: J.C.B. Mohr [Paul Siebeck], 1991), p.419. The Hirschian influences and the nature of the separatism practised by right-wing Orthodox communities in Britain are examined in greater detail in Chapter 11.

5   See Alderman, 'Power, Status and Authority in British Jewry: the Chief Rabbinate and Shechita', in G. Alderman and C. Holmes (eds), *Outsiders and Outcasts: Essays in Honour of William J. Fishman* (London: Duckworth, 1993), for further consideration of these events.

6   Correspondence between Hertz, Robert Waley Cohen and the UOHC regarding the Slaughter of Animals Act and the creation of this Rabbinical Commission can be found in LMA, Acc.2805/4/1/93.

7   See R. Bolchover, *British Jewry and the Holocaust* (Cambridge: Cambridge University Press, 1993), p.70 and T. Endelman, *Radical Assimilation* (Bloomington, IN: Indiana University Press, 1990), p.204. Some 50,000 came from Germany, with the remaining 5,000 from Austria and Czechoslovakia.

8   A. Newman, *The United Synagogue 1870–1970* (London: Routledge and Kegan Paul, 1976), p.107.

9   A.J. Kershen and J.A. Romain, *Tradition and Change: A History of Reform Judaism in Britain 1840–1995* (London: Vallentine Mitchell, 1995), p.167.

10 They did not actually sever their links from the Liberal movement until 1989 yet differed from the other affiliated synagogues throughout this period.

11 'Hendon Adath Yisroel Congregation: The First Twenty Years' (self-published pamphlet).

12 Additional examples of synagogues created by refugees from Nazi Europe or served by Rabbis from communities in Germany and Austria include the Hampstead Adath Yisroel Congregation, which became associated with the UOHC in 1938, and appointed J. Ansbacher, previously Rabbi in Wiesbaden, as their rabbi in 1941. The Edgware Adath Yisroel, established in 1941, appointed Rabbi E. Konigshofer of Hamburg as their rabbi. The Jewish Centre Synagogue, which became known as the Merkaz HaTorah, had been founded in 1930 by the Agudas Yisroel Movement, and the arrival of refugees from Austria, in particular, swelled its membership during the war years. The Agudas Yisroel, founded in 1912, was a union of separatist Orthodox Jews from eastern and western Europe who opposed the Zionist Mizrachi Movement, which was Orthodox yet willing to cooperate with non-Orthodox Jews. The Zeirei Agudas Yisroel Beth Hamedrash, which was established during the war, was also designed for refugees affiliated to the Agudas Yisroel Movement; their rabbi was Yaakov Teitelbaum from Vienna. The Beis Hamedrash Torah Etz Chaim was created in 1941 by a number of Viennese refugees who had been members of the Adass Jisroel Synagogue in Vienna, which had been led for a number of years by a son-in-law of the Hatam Sofer, Solomon Spitzer. In Vienna, this congregation had been separatist and utterly opposed to innovations, following the principles of the Hatam Sofer. In London these principles continued to be applied by the community's Viennese Rabbi, S. Baumgarten.

13 Julius Carlebach, 'Impact of German Jews', p.421. Carlebach notes that a number of the rabbis involved in Gateshead institutions came from Central Europe: Moses Loeb Bamberger from Bad Kissingen, Rabbi Abraham Kohn from Nuremberg, Rabbi S. Wagshal, born in Austria and raised at the *Adass Jisroel* in Berlin, and Rabbi A. Gruner who had studied at the yeshivah in Frankfurt am Main established by Solomon Breuer.

14 Newman, *United Synagogue*, p.107.

15 Born in 1886, he studied at the yeshivot of Telz, Mir and Slobodka. His *Chazon Yechezkiel*, a commentary on the *Tosefta*, established his reputation. See *JC*, 24 Sept. 1976.

16 A prohibition against eating the sciatic nerve meant porging – the removal of this nerve from the hindquarter – was required before the meat could be sold. See the *JC*, 12 July; 19 July; 2 Aug. 1935, see also Alderman, *MBJ*, p.357.

17 *JC*, 28 June 1935.

18 *RWC*, p.385.

19 *JC*, 2 Aug. 1935.

20 *RWC*, p.386.

21 Judith Hertz and Solomon Schonfeld married in 1940.

22 Solomon Schonfeld studied at the Yeshivot of Nitra and Mir. He gained his doctorate from the University of Koenigsberg.

23 Recorded by Newman in his *United Synagogue*, p.157.

24 From the notes of this meeting, held on 5 June 1941, in LMA, Acc.2805/4/5/54.

25 From a letter dated 7 May 1942 in LMA, Acc.2805/4/5/54.

26 From letters in the LMA, Acc.2805/4/5/54, specifically, a letter to the Editor of the *JC* dated 12 Feb. 1943 discussing his actions and the intervention of the

Honorary Officers of the United Synagogue into this matter at the Home Office.

27 D. Kranzler and G. Hirschler (eds), *Solomon Schonfeld: His Page in History* (New York: Judaica Press, 1982), p.25.

28 Noted by Homa in his *Orthodoxy in Anglo-Jewry* (London: Jewish Historical Society of England, 1969), p.46.

29 *MBJ*, p.356.

30 'Beth Din: Appointment of Dayan, Interview between the representatives of the Federation of Synagogues and the Honorary Officers of the United Synagogue', 30 May 1935, in LMA Acc.2712/15/0053.

31 In comments made by Waley Cohen to the *Jewish Chronicle* these views can be seen to be repeated, as he was recorded to have stated that 'What they [the Honorary Officers of the United Synagogue] desired and what was obviously necessary was that the office should be filled by a man of outstanding reputation and standing as a Dayan in the London Bet Din, who would carry weight throughout Jewry.' *JC*, 28 June 1935.

32 Various minutes contained in LMA Acc.2712/15/0053 detail how Abramsky had procrastinated over accepting the appointment as dayan when initially approached the previous year. He expressed concerns about the standard of kashrut supervision carried out by the London Bet Din. He suggested he could not work within those parameters and made it clear that he wished to implement more stringent standards.

33 Letter dated 12 June 1935 contained in LMA Acc.2712/15/0053.

34 *JC*, 27 Sept. 1935.

35 This was the opinion expressed by Revd Isaac Levy in an interview with the author.

36 When making the appointment, it had been made clear to Abramsky that he was expected to minister to the community as a whole and not just its right-wing sector. See further LMA Acc.2712/15/1161, which contains a letter from the United Synagogue to Abramsky, dated 3 June 1935, setting out the conditions and duties of the office. See also a hand-written report initialled by Philip Goldberg, dated 31 December 1934, expressing concern that Abramsky would be influenced by those outside the mainstream of the United Synagogue. The note foresaw that 'Rabbi Abramsky's backers were implacable people who would first find fault with one thing in Anglo-Jewry, and then another. They would never be satisfied with anything but an ultra-Orthodoxy for which Anglo-Jewry had no desire', LMA Acc.2712/15/1161 (c). See also the statement to the *Jewish Chronicle*, 28 June 1935, following Abramsky's appointment, which further stressed the perceived importance of a Dayan ministering to all sections of the community.

37 Hertz, 'The Recall to the Synagogue', *Address by the Chief Rabbi at the United Synagogue Conference, 25th July, 1940* (London: Office of the Chief Rabbi, 1940), p.5.

38 Newman, *United Synagogue*, p.156.

39 Hertz's objections to the creation of this Committee, which he believed was intended merely to increase the influence of non-Orthodox sections of the community at the expense of the authority of Orthodox Judaism, are collated in LMA, Acc.2805/4/5/54. The material includes a memorandum highlighting the difficulties Hertz believed the Committee would pose and letters to Robert Waley Cohen and Lionel de Rothschild from 1940 and 1941 expressing his objections.

40 During the Second World War, Waley Cohen appointed Bentwich and Montagu, respectively representing the Reform and Liberal Movements in Anglo-Jewry, as the co-chairmen of conferences convened to discuss Jewish

education during the War.
41   *JC*, 28 June 1935.
42   B. Kosmin, 'Localism and Pluralism in British Jewry: 1900-80', in *TJHSE*, 28 (London: Jewish Historical Society of England, 1982), p.113.

9 'PAPAL INFALLIBILITY': THE ELECTION OF A NEW CHIEF RABBI

1   *JC*, 18 Jan. 1946.
2   Reprinted in I. Epstein (ed.), *Joseph Herman Hertz 1872–1946: In Memoriam* (London: Soncino Press, 1947), p.41.
3   See for example *JC*, 10 Jan. 1947, in which a letter was published suggesting that the United Synagogue might be seeking to employ undemocratic methods to appoint a new Chief Rabbi.
4   *JC*, 6 Dec. 1946.
5   A. Newman, *The United Synagogue 1870–1970* (London: Routledge and Kegan Paul, 1976), pp.179f.
6   Dayan Lazarus served as temporary Chief Rabbi during the interregnum.
7   *Welcoming Address*, included in the catalogue collating material related to the 1948 election of a Chief Rabbi in LMA, Acc.2712/11/40.
8   The importance of retirement had already been demonstrated during the Chief Rabbinate of Nathan Marcus Adler, whose illness had prevented him from fulfilling his duties from 1879. Hermann Adler had been appointed to temporarily take over the duties of his father at that time until he assumed the role officially following Nathan Adler's death. The ill health experienced by Hertz towards the end of his life and the difficulties this caused exacerbated the perception that a retirement age should be introduced. The debates concerning the introduction of these conditions are contained in LMA, Acc.2712/11/40.
9   Once again, as in previous elections of a chief rabbi, the United Synagogue sought to exert its authority over proceedings and create a most uneven distribution of votes amongst the synagogal bodies involved in the election. Whilst ninety-three United Synagogue representatives were invited to join the Electoral College, only ninety-one other invitations were issued. The Federation was allocated just three votes to represent their seventy synagogues and 15,000 members. In their defence, the United Synagogue simply restated claims made at the election of the previous Chief Rabbi that the financial responsibility for the office rested predominantly on them. Whether money should have been allowed to override democracy remained a moot point. The impact that this would have on the Chief Rabbi's ability to claim to be representative of a broader spectrum of the Anglo-Jewish community did not appear to be considered.
10   From the minutes of the Committee meeting on 30 Nov., 1947 contained in LMA, Acc.2712/11/40.
11   The proposal was passed by the United Synagogue Council at a meeting in March.
12   Quoted in *JC*, 27 Feb. 1948.
13   *RWC*, pp.341ff.
14   *JC*, 14 March 1947.
15   This was opened in 1941 and in 1954 became the Institute of Jewish Studies.
16   See for example Newman, *United Synagogue*, p.181; Alderman, *MBJ*, p.361; David Cesarani, *The Jewish Chronicle and Anglo-Jewry 1841–1991* (Cambridge: Cambridge University Press, 1994), p.200. The emphasis placed on the national origins of a future chief rabbi is acknowledged in each of these sources.

17 The letter, contained within Chimen Abramsky's personal collection of his father's letters, was addressed to Mikhael Rabinowiecz.
18 See above references to his interview with the *JC*, 28 June 1935.
19 See for example Newman, *United Synagogue*, p.181. Kopul Rosen (1913–1962) born in London, studied in the city's Etz Chaim Yeshivah before travelling to the Mir Yeshivah in Lithuania. He served as rabbi of the Higher Crumpsal Synagogue in Manchester from 1938 until 1942, was appointed Communal Rabbi of Glasgow in 1942, and in 1944 accepted the position of Principal Rabbi of the Federation of Synagogues in London. In 1948 he left the rabbinate to establish Carmel College, a Jewish Boarding School that remained in existence until 1997.
20 He was actually to die aged 49.
21 *JC*, 14 March 1947.
22 *JC*, 18 Jan. 1946.
23 Quoted by A. Newman, *Commemoration of the Centenary of the Birth of Chief Rabbi Dr. Joseph H. Hertz* (London: United Synagogue, 1972), from an unsent letter addressed to Ewen Montagu.

10 ISRAEL BRODIE

1 A. Newman, *The United Synagogue 1870–1970* (London: Routledge and Kegan Paul, 1976), p.181.
2 He wrote a thesis on Anan, the founder of Karaism.
3 See the *JC*, 4 June 1948.
4 This correspondence from September 1962, relating to the use of urns to heat water during the Sabbath, is contained in the collection of correspondence between these two offices held in LMA, Acc.2805/6/1/16.
5 Newman, *United Synagogue*, p.183.
6 John Shaftesley, 'Israel Brodie, Chief Rabbi: A Biographical Sketch', in H.J. Zimmels, J. Rabbinowitz and I. Finestein (eds), *Essays Presented to Chief Rabbi Israel Brodie on the Occasion of his Seventieth Birthday* (London: Soncino Press, 1967), p.xxviii. It should be noted that in the *JC* on 11 June 1948 it was recorded that Brodie had expressed concern at the introduction of the Lay Advisory Committee. Notwithstanding his eagerness to avoid dispute he was perturbed at this explicit diminution of his powers. This led him to assert that despite his willingness to consult with that body he did not wish to be bound to follow their advice. Newman, in *United Synagogue*, has suggested that: 'He objected not to consulting with others, but with having to do so. Sir Robert's reply was friendly, conciliatory, but quite firm, insisting that there could be no alteration in the conditions of appointment', p. 182.
7 *JC*, 14 March 1947.
8 I. Brodie, *A Word in Season: Addresses and Sermons 1948–1958* (London: Vallentine Mitchell, 1959), p.11.
9 I. Brodie, 'Sermon by the Very Reverend Rabbi Israel Brodie on the occasion of his Installation as Chief Rabbi of the United Hebrew Congregations of the British Commonwealth of Nations', The New Synagogue, London, Mon. 21st Sivan, 5708, 28 June 1948, in *A Word in Season*, p.79.
10 Ibid., p.81.
11 I. Brodie, 'Repentance and Renewal', Overseas radio broadcast on the Jewish New Year, 23 Sept. 1949, in *A Word in Season*, p.22.
12 I. Brodie, 'Installation Sermon', in *A Word in Season*, p.82.
13 I. Brodie, 'Historical Judaism – Challenge to our Times', sermon at Hampstead Synagogue, 1 Dec. 1951, in *A Word in Season*, p.185.

14 I. Brodie, 'The New Year', Overseas broadcast, Sept. 1950, in *A Word in Season*, p.29.

15 I. Brodie, 'Australian Broadcast', May 1952, in *A Word in Season*, p.146.

16 I. Brodie, 'Strangers in Egypt', 5 April 1955, in *A Word in Season*, pp.57f. It is interesting to note that Brodie's hopes for the State led to the introduction of a conspicuous universalism in his thought. In an address directed at an audience containing both Jews and non-Jews he affirmed 'my profound belief that as the years went by it would be more and more realised that *Israel's renewal has been decreed for a universalistic end in behalf of mankind as a whole.* Israel's legacy to the world in the past has been in the form of an imperishable Book: perhaps in the future Israel's contribution would be in the form of a pattern of group and individual living embodying the ethical teachings of the Law and the Prophets' [my emphasis]. From 'Broadcast in Cape Town', June 1950, in *A Word in Season*, p.141. Brodie recognized that the concerns of Anglo-Jewry were merely a symptom of the struggles that faced all humanity in this period. It was thus that he came to view the creation of an ideal state, a nation that could truly provide a 'light unto the nations', as an essential factor in the salvation of the human race.

17 Brodie, 'Historical Judaism – Challenge to our Times', p.188.

18 I. Brodie, 'Liberty and Toleration', Annual Dinner of the Union of Orthodox Hebrew Congregations, New York, 14 June 1956, in *A Word in Season*, p.192.

19 Brodie, *A Word in Season*, p.79.

11 RIGHT-WING ORTHODOXY

1 Solomon Schonfeld, 'Steadily Forward', 25th Anniversary Address to the UOHC, April 1951, reprinted in *Message to Jewry* (London: Dr Solomon Schonfeld Silver Jubilee Committee, 1959), p.216.

2 The first *mikveh* – ritual bath – in the North West London area was established in Hendon by the UOHC in cooperation with local congregations in 1946.

3 S. Schonfeld, 'Role of the Orthodox Union', in *JC*, 20 Aug. 1954, reprinted in *Message to Jewry*, p.217.

4 Letter from Victor Schonfeld to J.C. Gilbert dated 8 May 1925, quoted by J. Carlebach in 'The Impact of German Jews on Anglo-Jewry: Orthodoxy 1850–1950', in W.E. Mosse (co-ordinating ed.), *Second Chance: Two Centuries of German-speaking Jews in the United Kingdom* (Tubingen: Mohr Siebeck, 1991), p.419.

5 Draft of letter from Victor Schonfeld to J.C. Gilbert dated 9 May 1924, quoted by Carlebach, ibid., p.420.

6 See S.R. Hirsch, *Gesammelte Schriften von Rabbiner Samson Raphael Hirsch* (Frankfurt am Main: J. Kauffmann, 1908), vol.4, pp.239–310; R. Liberles, *Religious Conflict in Social Context: The Resurgence of Orthodox Judaism in Frankfurt Am Main, 1838–1877* (Westport, CT: Greenwood Press, 1985), pp.201ff; Hermann Schwab, *The History of Orthodox Jewry in Germany, 1830–1945* (London: Mitre Press, 1950), pp.73ff.

7 See for example Jakob Petuchowski, *Prayerbook Reform in Europe: The Liturgy of European Liberal and Reform Judaism* (New York: World Union for Progressive Judaism, 1968). For general histories of German Jewry in this period see Michael A. Meyer (ed.), *German-Jewish History in Modern Times* (New York: Columbia University Press, 1996–98), vols 2 and 3; Peter Pulzer, *Jews and the German State: The Political History of a Minority, 1848–1933* (Oxford: Blackwell, 1992).

8   *Der Austritt aus der Gemeinde* (Frankfurt am Main: J. Kauffmann, 1876).
    Also reproduced in Hirsch, *Gesammelte Schriften von Rabbiner Samson Raphael
    Hirsch*.
9   Hirsch's judgement in this matter was questioned. A public and, at times,
    belligerent debate occurred between Hirsch and Rabbi Seligman Baer
    Bamberger, the Wuerzberger Rav, who championed the cause of those who
    opposed the principle of secession. There were several important halakhic
    issues, as well as questions of authority, at the heart of their debate. The
    Wuerzberger Rav questioned whether the heresy of the Reformers was wilful
    or, in fact, accidental and also suggested that second generation Reform Jews
    might not be liable to a charge of heresy since it could be argued that they
    didn't know any better – they could be viewed as *tinok shenishbah* (a child
    raised by gentiles) or *minhag avoteikhem beyadeikhem* (following the customs of
    their fathers) – see Babylonian Talmud, Shab. 68b, Chul. 13b. See Liberles,
    Religious Conflict in Social Context, pp.219ff. See also *Historia Judaica*, 10, 2 (New
    York: Oct. 1948,), pp.99–146, which contains the following three essays on this
    subject: Saemy Japhet, 'The Secession from the Frankfurt Jewish Community
    under Samson Raphael Hirsch', (the author is only identified in the editor's
    note); Isaac Heinemann, 'Supplementary Remarks on The Secession from
    the Frankfurt Jewish Community under Samson Raphael Hirsch'; Jacob
    Rosenheim, 'The Historical Significance of the Struggles for Secession from
    the Frankfurt Jewish Community'.
10 S. Schonfeld, *Jewish Religious Education: A Guide and Handbook with Syllabuses*
    (London: National Council for Jewish Religious Education, 1943), p.34.
11 Liberles, *Religious Conflict in Social Context*, p.113. For other studies of Hirsch's
    thought see, for example, Noah Rosenbloom, *Tradition in an Age of Reform:
    The Religious Philosophy of Samson Raphael Hirsch* (Philadelphia, PA: Jewish
    Publication Society of America, 1976), though see also a review of this work
    by Mordechai Breuer, 'On Noah H. Rosenbloom, "Tradition in an Age of
    Reform – the Religious Philosophy of Samson Raphael Hirsch"', *Tradition*,
    XVI, 4 (1977), pp.140–9; Jacob Rosenheim, *S. R. Hirsch's Cultural Ideal and our
    Times*, trans. E. Lichtigfield (London: Shapiro, Vallentine and Co., 1951).
12 Following Solomon Breuer's death in 1926, his son Raphael hoped to succeed
    his father but the community rejected the more Hungarian-influenced Ortho-
    doxy that he advocated. Generally, the Breuer family introduced a narrower
    Orthodoxy to Hirsch's community, the *Israelitische Religionsgesellschaft* (IRG),
    including the introduction of a yeshiva following the Pressburg model. See *The
    Living Hirschian Legacy: Essays on 'Torah im derekh eretz' and the Contemporary
    Hirschian Kehilla* (New York: Feldheim, 1988); Charles Liebman, 'Orthodoxy in
    American Jewish Life', in R. Bulka (ed.), *Dimensions of Orthodox Judaism* (New
    York: Ktav, 1983); Samuel Heilman, 'The Many Faces of Orthodoxy, Part I',
    Modern Judaism, 2, 1 (Feb. 1982), pp.23–51; Steven M. Lowenstein, *The Mechanics
    of Change, Essays in the Social History of German Jewry* (Atlanta: Scholars Press,
    1992), pp.201–14.
13 Carlebach, 'The Impact of German Jews on Anglo-Jewry: Orthodoxy
    1850–1950', p.419.
14 Note on p.167, in essay by Isaac Breuer, 'Samson Raphael Hirsch', in L. Jung
    (ed.), *Jewish Leaders 1750–1940* (New York: Bloch Publishing Company, 1953).
15 Joseph Elias, *The World of Rabbi S. R. Hirsch: The Nineteen Letters about Judaism*
    (Jerusalem: Feldheim Publishers, 1995), p.312.
16 Hirsch's *Adass Jisroel* (IRG) synagogue in Frankfurt had relatively lenient
    halakhic requirements for its members. Although the by-laws of the com-
    munity stated that officers of the synagogue had to observe the Sabbath,

Festivals and laws of Kashrut, the only requirement of members was that they had to be circumcised, had to be married by recognized Jewish authorities, and had to ensure that their sons were circumcised.

17 *JC*, 20 Aug. 1954, reprinted in Schonfeld, *Message to Jewry*, p.217.
18 B. Homa, *Orthodoxy in Anglo-Jewry 1880–1940* (London: Jewish Historical Society of England, 1969), p.32f.
19 'The Union of Orthodox Congregations', in *JC*, 4 May 1951, reprinted in Schonfeld, *Message to Jewry*, p.213.
20 Ibid., p.212.
21 Quoted in Schonfeld, *Message to Jewry*, p.230.
22 *JC*, 20 Aug. 1954, reprinted in Schonfeld, *Message to Jewry*, p.217.
23 I. Brodie, 'Opening Address' at the 1953 CAJP, in *A Word in Season: Addresses and Sermons 1948–1958* (London: Vallentine Mitchell, 1959), p.161.
24 C. Bermant, *Troubled Eden: An Anatomy of British Jewry* (London: Vallentine Mitchell, 1969), pp.128–9.
25 Schonfeld, *Message to Jewry*, p.222.
26 Reprinted in Brodie, *A Word in Season*, p.457.
27 'Jewry in the North-East', reprinted in Brodie, *A Word in Season*, p.418. See also his comments in A. Levy, *The Story of Gateshead Yeshiva* (Taunton: Wessex Press, 1952), where he stated his view that the yeshiva served 'as a reservoir of Jewish Orthodoxy in this country … to constitute that nucleus of learned Jewish laymen which can assure the maintenance of Orthodoxy in our communities. The Gateshead Yeshiva deserves the moral and material support of the Anglo-Jewish Community.'

12 THE JACOBS AFFAIR

1 See L. Jacobs, *Helping With Enquiries: An Autobiography* (London: Vallentine Mitchell, 1989) (hereafter *HWE*), p.117. The article, entitled 'The United Synagogue, Progressive Conservatism', was published in *The Jewish Review*, 11 June 1954.
2 Quoted by Jacobs in *HWE*, p.61.
3 Jacobs married in 1944.
4 B. Williams, *The Making of Manchester Jewry: 1740–1875* (Manchester: Manchester University Press, 1976), p.325.
5 *HWE*, p.95.
6 Ibid., p.103.
7 Ibid., p.104. The New West End Synagogue became a constituent member of the United Synagogue in 1879, one of the earliest synagogues to be associated with the new synagogal movement.
8 *JC*, 13 May 1960, report on Annual Meeting of New West End Synagogue. Ewen Montagu took over as United Synagogue President in 1954, succeeding Frank Samuel who had served from 1953–54 following Robert Waley Cohen's resignation.
9 *JC*, 11 May 1962.
10 Isidore Epstein was born in 1894 in Kovno, Lithuania. He arrived in England with his parents in 1911 but went to Continental Europe to receive his yeshivah training before returning to England to study at the University of London. He served as a congregational rabbi of the Middlesborough Hebrew Congregation between 1921 and 1928 before accepting a teaching position at Jews' College.
11 *JC*, 24 July 1959

12   From an interview with the author.
13   As reported in the *JC*, 22 Dec. 1961.
14   From interview with the author.
15   *We Have Reason to Believe* (London: Vallentine Mitchell, 1995), p.4.
16   Quoted in *HWE*, p.130. Since the publication of his *We Have Reason to Believe* Jacobs had also published *Jewish Values* in 1960.
17   Recorded in the *JC*, 11 May 1962.
18   See for example *The Times*, 30 Dec. 1961. Coverage of what became known as Stage II of the Affair, the events of which are detailed below, was closely covered in a number of the broadsheet papers of the British Press including *The Times* and *Sunday Times* and *The Sunday* and *Daily Telegraph*, between March and May 1964.
19   *JC*, 2 Feb. 1962.
20   Jacobs has explained that he was invited to consider taking up a position at the JTS before he was appointed lecturer at Jews' College. To prevent him considering a move to America following his resignation from the College, the Society had been established. *HWE*, pp.120; 144ff. William Frankel, editor of the *JC* in this period, and a friend of Jacobs, has recounted that the post at Jews' College and the promise of the Principalship had initially been made in order to dissuade him from leaving England in 1959 to accept a post at the JTS. See Frankel's 'Traditional Alternatives', *JC*, 26 Sept. 2003, New Year Section, p.xi.
21   It seems significant to note that Pearl left England to assume the pulpit of a Conservative Synagogue in Riverdale, New York. It is also interesting to consider Frankel's suggestion that, conscious of Pearl's desire to leave, a motivation amongst those who helped facilitate his move was the thought that a ministerial opening at the New West End could provide an opportunity to invite Jacobs back. See Frankel, 'Traditional Alternatives', p.xii.
22   C. Bermant, *Troubled Eden: An Anatomy of British Jewry* (London: Vallentine Mitchell, 1969), p.248.
23   *HWE*, pp.114f.
24   Quoted by Jacobs in his *HWE*, pp.160f. Isaac Wolfson was elected president of the United Synagogue following Ewen Montagu's resignation in December 1962.
25   *JC*, 6 March 1964.
26   Quoted by Jacobs in his *HWE*, p.180.
27   Comment made by Rabbi A in an interview with the author.

13 INTERPRETATIONS OF THE JACOBS AFFAIR

1   A point he claims was admitted to him by Grunfeld at a later date, *HWE*, p.136.
2   See above, Chapter 12, n.19, regarding the Dayanim's statement to the *JC*, 2 Feb. 1962.
3   *JC*, 5 Jan. 1962.
4   *JC*, 2 Feb. 1962.
5   *JC*, 10 July 1959.
6   Both Rabbi A and Isaac Levy made this point in interviews with the author. Rabbi Rayner, in a conversation with the author, confirmed this position, recalling how Jacobs had told him that it was his review of *Jewish Values* that set in motion the events of the Jacobs Affair.
7   J. Rayner, 'Guide to Jewish Piety', *Liberal Jewish Monthly* (Tabernacles, 1960), p.160.

8   Montagu's statement was reprinted in the *JC*, 26 Jan. 1962.
9   *JC*, 2 Feb. 1962.
10 *HWE*, p.172.
11 *HWE*, p.159.
12 *JC*, 29 Dec. 1961.
13 William Frankel was born in 1917 in the East End of London, the child of Galician immigrants. He was trained as a barrister but joined the staff of the *JC* in 1955 serving initially as the paper's general manager before taking on the role of Editor, in which job he remained until 1977.
14 See D. Cesarani, *The Jewish Chronicle and Anglo-Jewry 1841–1991* (Cambridge: Cambridge University Press, 1994), pp.216ff, for further treatment of this subject.
15 See further William Frankel, 'Anglo-Jewish Attitudes and Minhag Anglia', in S. Massil (ed.), *The Jewish Year Book 2000* (London: Vallentine Mitchell, 2000). See also Cesarani, *The Jewish Chronicle*, pp.213f.
16 Frankel, 'Anglo-Jewish Attitudes', p.48.
17 Ibid., pp.47f.
18 *JC*, 13 March 1959.
19 Reprinted by Brodie in his *The Strength of my Heart: Sermons and Addresses 1948–1965* (London: G.J. George & Co. Ltd., 1969), p.345.
20 Quoted by Jacobs in *HWE*, p.128.
21 A. Newman, *The United Synagogue 1870–1970* (London: Routledge and Kegan Paul, 1976), p.186.
22 Ibid., p.174.
23 Ibid., p.186.
24 *The Times*, 30 Dec. 1961. Jacobs has stated that he was informed that this view was provided by Ephraim Levine, the minister of the New West End before Jacobs' initial appointment to the Synagogue.
25 It should be noted that in many respects the actions of William Frankel at the *JC* coincided with those of the spiritists.

14 A RE-INTERPRETATION OF THE JACOBS AFFAIR

1   Jacobs, *HWE*, p.127. For an additional analysis of Jacobs' own understanding of the Jacobs Affair see also, L. Jacobs, *Beyond Reasonable Doubt* (London: Littman Library, 1999), particularly Chapter 1.
2   *JC*, 24 July 1959.
3   It is worth considering the extent to which this approach can be found to characterize much of modern Jewry. See for example A. Eisen, *Rethinking Modern Judaism: Ritual, Commandment, Community* (Chicago: University of Chicago Press, 2000).
4   For examples of Hertz's opposition to Biblical Criticism see his *The Pentateuch and Haftorahs: Hebrew text, English Translation and Commentary* (London: Soncino, 1975), pp.554f; 397ff. See also Harvey Meirovich, *A Vindication of Judaism: The Polemics of the Hertz Pentateuch* (New York: Jewish Theological Seminary of America, 1998), pp.49–58, for a more detailed analysis of Hertz's reasons for opposing Biblical Criticism. For further consideration of changing attitudes to the notion of *Torah min hashamayim* see, for example, M. Kellner, *Must a Jew Believe Anything* (London: Vallentine Mitchell, 1999); Marc B. Shapiro, *The Limits of Orthodox Theology: Maimonides' Thirteen Principles Reappraised* (Oxford: Littman Library of Jewish Civilization, 2004); Haym Soloveitchik, 'Rupture and Reconstruction: the Transformation of Contemporary Orthodoxy', *Tradition*, 28, 4 (1994), pp.64–130; M. Friedman, 'Life

Tradition and Book Tradition in the development of Ultra-Orthodox Judaism', in H.E. Goldberg (ed.), *Judaism Viewed From Within and From Without* (Albany: SUNY Press, 1986).

5 Reprinted in I. Brodie, *The Strength of my Heart: Sermons and Addresses 1948–1965* (London: G.J. George & Co. Ltd., 1969), p.348.

6 In opposing the activities of the Reform movement many Orthodox rabbis set themselves against any innovation in Traditional Judaism, fearful of the effects of emancipation. There had been 116 signatories to a declaration from Orthodox rabbis attacking the activities of Reformers at the Brunswick Rabbinical Conference of 1844. In 1871, 133 Orthodox rabbis had signed a protest against the Reform Rabbinical Conference held in Augsburg. Moses Sofer, known as the Hatam Sofer (1762–1839), became established as the leader of Orthodox Rabbis in Hungary and across Central Europe who were opposed to interaction in the modern world. He famously adapted the Talmudic dictum *Chadash asur min haTorah* – the new is prohibited by Torah law – to insist that all innovations perceived to be in line with the spirit of the times were to be rejected. He was joined in this opposition by rabbis such as Jacob Lorbeerbaum (1760–1832), who was rabbi in the Prussian-governed Polish town of Lissa and Akiva Eger (1767–1837), father-in-law of Moses Sofer, who was rabbi in Posen. In 1819 they took the lead in gathering responsa from twenty-two rabbis against the reforms instituted at the creation of the Hamburg Temple. For further consideration of Hungarian Orthodoxy see J. Katz, *A House Divided: Orthodoxy and Schism in Nineteenth Century European Jewry* (New Hampshire: Brandeis University Press, 1998); M. Silber, 'The Emergence of Ultra-Orthodoxy: The Invention of a Tradition', in J. Wertheimer (ed.), *The Uses of Tradition: Jewish Continuity in the Modern Era* (New York: JTSA, 1998), pp.23–84. See also J. Katz, 'Toward a Biography of the Hatam Sofer', in Francis Malino and David Sorkin (eds), *From East and West: Jews in a Changing Europe, 1750–1870* (London: Blackwell, 1990). His sons took up his cause, his eldest son Abraham Samuel Benjamin took over his position as Rabbi of Pressburg and head of the yeshivah there, which his father had established. His second son Simeon, as has already been noted, was a founder of the Machzike Hadath movement, which fought for the defence of Orthodox Judaism. One of his sons-in-law, Solomon Spitzer, was rabbi of the Adass Jisroel Synagogue in Vienna, also known as the Schiff Shul, which was a bastion of Orthodoxy for Viennese Jewry.

7 From an interview with the author.

8 Jacobs, *We Have Reason to Believe* (1995), pp.142f.

9 Reprinted in Brodie, *The Strength of my Heart*, p.351.

CONCLUSION

1 Comments of Solomon Schonfeld, as quoted above in Chapter 11, see n.22.

2 T.M. Endelman, *Radical Assimilation in English Jewish History: 1656–1945* (Bloomington, IN: Indiana University Press, 1990), p.207.

3 Ibid., p.208.

EPILOGUE

1 *A Time for Change: United Synagogue Review* (London, Stanley Kalms Foundation, 1992), p.2. The review became popularly known as the Kalms Report in recognition of Stanley Kalms' leading role in directing the team conducting the research into the United Synagogue.

2   Ibid., p.4.
3   Ibid., p.3.
4   Ibid., p.208.
5   Ibid., p.97.
6   Ibid., p.32.
7   'Spiritual Leadership – The Heritage of Priest, Prophet and King', Installation Address delivered at St John's Wood Synagogue, London, on 11 April 1967, in I. Jakobovits, *The Timely and the Timeless: Jews, Judaism and Society in a Storm-tossed Decade* (London: Vallentine Mitchell, 1977), p.56.
8   He had been joined by his brother, George, soon after arriving in London. As was noted above, in Chapter 8, following his family's arrival in England his father, Julius Jakobovits, was appointed a Dayan on the London Bet Din during the Second World War.
9   Jakobovits acknowledged that he had intended to study science at university, but was dissuaded from pursuing this career path by his father, who persuaded him to enter the rabbinate.
10 See Michael Shashar, *Lord Jakobovits in Conversation* (London: Vallentine Mitchell, 2000), pp.23f.
11 For a fuller account of Jakobovits' life, see C. Bermant, *Lord Jakobovits: The Authorized Biography of the Chief Rabbi* (London: Weidenfeld and Nicholson, 1990). See also G. Tessler, *Amelie: The Story of Lady Jakobovits* (London: Vallentine Mitchell, 1999), for an account of Amelie Jakobovits' life.
12 Shashar, *Lord Jakobovits in Conversation*, p.18.
13 Bermant suggests that Jakobovits' view of university departments in Jewish Studies was that: 'They leave nothing unquestioned … At best they are religiously neutral and are not geared to generate Jewish commitment.' *Lord Jakobovits: The Authorised Biography*, p.202.
14 Jakobovits obtained his doctorate in 1956. He subsequently established a reputation as a pioneer and leading, albeit rather conservative, halakhist, in the field of Jewish medical ethics. See his *Jewish Medical Ethics: A Comparative and Historical Study of the Jewish Religious Attitude to Medicine and its Practice* (New York: Philosophical Library, 1959).
15 'Samson Raphael Hirsch: A Reappraisal of his Teachings and Influence in the Light of our Times', in Jakobovits, *Timely and Timeless*, p.257.
16 'Halakhah in Modern Jewish Life', in Jakobovits, *Timely and Timeless*, p.283.
17 See, for example, 'Human Rights and Human Duties', Address delivered to the Institute of Directors, November 1976, in Jakobovits, *Timely and Timeless*, pp.125–9.
18 Chapter 11, n.11 and n.12 above.
19 See *Der Pentateuch, Übersezt und Erlautext von Samson Raphael Hirsch, Genesis*, (Frankfurt am Main: J. Kauffmann, 1920), pp.77ff, where Hirsch states: אין תורה אם אין דרך ארץ (p.79). See Sol Roth, *The Jewish Idea of Culture* (New Jersey: Ktav, 1997), for further consideration of the nature of Hirschian thought on this issue.
20 J. Elias, *The World of Rabbi S. R. Hirsch: The Nineteen Letters about Judaism* (Jerusalem: Feldheim Publishers, 1995), p.247.
21 Jakobovits, 'Samson Raphael Hirsch', p.257.
22 Ibid., p.254.
23 Bermant, *Lord Jakobovits: The Authorised Biography*, p.178.
24 See, for example, newspaper comments on Jakobovits' peerage cited in Bermant, *Lord Jakobovits: The Authorised Biography*, pp.1f.
25 See, for example, Hirsch, *Neunzehn Briefe uber Judentum von Ben Uziel* (Altona: J.F. Hammerich, 1836), 'Nie war land und boden sein einigungsband, sondern die gemeinsame aufgabe der Thauroh', p.79.

26 Shashar, *Lord Jakobovits in Conversation*, pp.134, 157. See also, for example, I. Jakobovits, *'If Only my People ...' Zionism in my Life* (London: Weidenfeld and Nicolson, 1984), pp.136ff.

27 Shashar, *Lord Jakobovits in Conversation*, p.157.

28 Jakobovits, *If Only My People*, p.36.

29 'Letter to my Colleagues', quoted in ibid., p.114.

30 Quoted by Jakobovits from a letter to the Chief Rabbi of Haifa, Shear Yashuv Cohen, a personal friend, in his *If Only My People*, p.109.

31 'Conformity and Diversity in the Jewish Historical Tradition', Lecture delivered at the Inauguration of the Immanuel Jakobovits Chair in Jewish Law at Bar Ilan University, April 1974, in Jakobovits, *Timely and Timeless*, p.264.

32 Ibid.

33 See, for example, Jakobovits' comments in Shashar, *Lord Jakobovits in Conversation*, pp.175f: 'The *yeshiva* heads are generally stringent, because their world consists of their studies and students, and therefore they tend to be very strict. They do not relate well to the observant population at large. Relying on those who are not practising rabbis but rather are great scholars does not appear to be suitable to me. If we do not restore to ourselves the status of rabbis who are involved in life and are present among their congregation, and are therefore responsible for the problems life raises, but rather rely solely upon those individuals for whom the *halachah* is their entire life, the *halachah* will not be able to develop.'

34 Shashar, *Lord Jakobovits in Conversation*, p.120.

35 Ibid., p.62.

36 See above, Chapter 11, n.5.

37 Bermant, *Lord Jakobovits: The Authorized Biography*, p.188.

38 Jakobovits, 'Spiritual Leadership – The Heritage of Priest, Prophet and King', p.55.

39 'Life-line to survival', from the foreword to *Let My People Know*, reproduced in Jakobovits, *Timely and Timeless*, p.198.

40 *JC*, 5 Nov. 1971.

41 See for example 'The Evolution of the British Rabbinate Since 1845: Its Past Impact and Future Challenges', in Jakobovits, *Timely and Timeless*, p.275. He also supported the educational activities of the Lubavitch, although not their interference in Israeli politics.

42 Kalms, *A Time for Change*, p.271. See also, B. Kosmin and S. Waterman, *British Jewry in the Eighties: A Statistical and Geographical Study* (London: Board of Deputies of British Jews Research Unit, 1986). Kosmin and Waterman contend (p.31) that these percentage shifts are relevant despite the general numerical decline in overall synagogue membership that could have been expected to distort the applicability of the figures.

43 Bermant, *Lord Jakobovits: The Authorised Biography*, p.88, referring to Wolfson's chairmanship of Great Universal Stores.

44 A. Newman, *The United Synagogue 1870–1970* (London: Routledge and Kegan Paul, 1976), p.187.

45 Quoted in 'The Making of a Chief Rabbi', *Quest*, 2 (London: New London Synagogue, 1967), p.14.

46 The pro-Israel stance that had undermined his candidacy during the previous Chief Rabbinate elections, also continued to raise concerns amongst the Anglo-Jewish leadership. See above, Chapter 9.

47 Letter dated 14 April 1965, *JC*, 14 May 1965.

48 Jakobovits, 'Spiritual Leadership – The Heritage of Priest, Prophet and King', p.54.

49 Ibid., p.55.

50 Ibid., p.57.

51 Jakobovits claims, in Shashar, *Lord Jakobovits in Conversation*, p.73, that agreement was nearly reached with the Reform community over issues of personal status, on a model similar to that employed by the *Gross Gemeinde* in Berlin, but ultimately it failed to come to fruition.

52 'Shall your Brothers go to War ...?', Address delivered on the outbreak of the Six-Day War at the Royal Albert Hall, June 1967, in Jakobovits, *Timely and Timeless*, p.3.

53 *JC*, 22 Oct. 1971.

54 *JC*, 26 Nov. 1971.

55 Shashar, *Lord Jakobovits in Conversation*, p.74.

56 Bermant, *Lord Jakobovits: The Authorised Biography*, p.131.

57 Ibid., p.214.

58 'Milestones and Millstones', Address delivered at the Centenary Service of the United Synagogue, July 1970, in Jakobovits, *Timely and Timeless*, p.65.

59 Ibid., pp.63f.

60 The four appointed were Rabbis Berger, Ehrentreu, Kaplin and Lerner. See Bermant, *Lord Jakobovits: The Authorised Biography*, pp.102f.

61 Shashar, *Lord Jakobovits in Conversation*, p.128.

62 Kalms, *A Time for Change*, pp.39f.

63 *JC*, 30 Sept. 1983.

64 Ibid.

65 *HWE*, p.220. Jacobs' New London Synagogue had produced a spin-off in 1974 with the creation of the New North London. This was followed by the 1984 establishment of an additional Masorti synagogue in Edgware. In 1984 the Masorti Assembly of Synagogues was formed to create a loose affiliation between the initial three synagogues.

66 See Alderman, *Anglo-Jewry: A Suitable Case for Treatment* (London: Royal Holloway and Bedford New College, 1990), pp.6f; *MBJ*, pp.375f.

67 See above, Chapter 11, n.17.

68 'The Evolution of the British Rabbinate Since 1845 – Its Past Impact and Future Challenges', in Jakobovits, *Timely and Timeless*, pp.274f.

69 Quoted from a letter written by Jakobovits to Irving Greenberg, in Jeffrey M. Cohen (ed.), *Dear Chief Rabbi: From the Correspondence of Chief Rabbi Immanuel Jakobovits on Matters of Jewish Law, Ethics and Contemporary Issues 1980–1990* (New Jersey: Ktav, 1995), pp.237–8.

70 Alderman has frequently decried the viability of the Chief Rabbinate. In his view, religious polarization has undermined the idea that there is an undivided Anglo-Jewish community which could be represented by a single Jewish view. Both the Board of Deputies and the Office of Chief Rabbi inappropriately seek to maintain this fiction. See, for example, Alderman, *Anglo-Jewry: A Suitable Case for Treatment*; 'The British Chief Rabbinate: A Most Peculiar Practice', *European Judaism*, 23, 2 (1990); and a number of his, sometimes vitriolic, columns in the *Jewish Chronicle*.

71 S.J. Prais, 'Polarisation or Decline? A Discussion of some Statistical Findings on the Community', in S.L. Lipman and V.D. Lipman (eds), *Jewish Life in Britain 1962–77* (New York: K.G. Saur Publishing Inc., 1981), p.4.

72 Ibid., p.6. Sociologist, Charles Liebman, in his 'Extremism as a Religious Norm', in *Journal for the Scientific Study of Religion*, 22, 1 (March 1983), has argued that the strengthening of more extremist religious viewpoints is to be expected in Orthodox groups. He asserts that 'it is not religious extremism but religious moderation that requires explanation'. He defines extremism,

in terms that resonate with the features found to exist in right-wing Orthodoxy in Britain, as 'the desire to expand the scope, detail and strictness of religious law; social isolation; and the rejection of the surrounding culture'. He contends that: 'The decline of the religious community permits the break-through of extremist tendencies. This is facilitated by the decline of the secular culture with which the religious moderates were associated' (p.75). With the United Synagogue in decline, Victorian values rejected, and the ideas of the surrounding society widely viewed as vacuous, all the factors were in place in Anglo-Jewry for the rise of religious extremism.

73 Kalms, *A Time for Change*, pp.240f.
74 Ibid., p.37.
75 Hertz, 'Religion and Life', A Sermon Preached at the New West End Synagogue Shabbat Bereshit 18th October 1919, in *SAS*, I, p.289, as quoted above in Chapter 6, n.6.

Bibliography

Adler, C. (ed.), *The Jewish Theological Seminary of America: Semi-Centennial Volume* (New York: JTS, 1939)

Adler, H., *Anglo-Jewish Memories and Other Sermons* (London: George Routledge and Sons Ltd., 1909)

Adler, N.M., *Laws and Regulations for all the Synagogues in the British Empire* (London: Office of Chief Rabbi, 1847)

Alderman, G., *The Jewish Community in British Politics* (Oxford: Oxford University Press, 1983)

Alderman, G., *The Federation of Synagogues 1887–1987* (London: The Federation of Synagogues, 1987)

Alderman, G., *London Jewry and London Politics 1889–1916* (London: Routledge, 1989)

Alderman, G., *Anglo-Jewry: A Suitable Case for Treatment* (London: Royal Holloway and Bedford New College, 1990)

Alderman, G., 'The British Chief Rabbinate: A Most Peculiar Practice', *European Judaism*, 23, 2 (1990), pp.45–58

Alderman, G., *Modern British Jewry* (Oxford: Oxford University Press, 1992)

Alderman, G., 'Power, Status and Authority in British Jewry: the Chief Rabbinate and Shechita', in G. Alderman and C. Holmes (eds), *Outsiders and Outcasts: Essays in Honour of William J. Fishman* (London: Duckworth, 1993), pp.12–31

Alderman, G., 'British Jews: Religious Community or Ethnic Minority?', in J. Webber (ed.), *Jewish Identities in the New Europe* (London: Littman Library, 1994), pp.188–92

Alderman, G., 'Anglo-Jewry and its Present Discontents', *The Jewish Quarterly*, 158 (Summer, 1995), pp.21–25

Alderman, G., 'The Chief Rabbinate: An Excursion into Myth-Making', *Judaism Today*, 3 (1995–96), pp.36–41

Anonymous contribution, 'The Making of a Chief Rabbi', *Quest*, 2 (1967), pp.10–17

Berger, P.L., *The Heretical Imperative: Contemporary Possibilities of Religious Affirmation* (New York: Doubleday, 1979)

Berkovitz, J.R., *The Shaping of Jewish Identity in Nineteenth-Century France* (Detroit: Wayne State University Press, 1989)

Bermant, C., *Troubled Eden: An Anatomy of British Jewry* (London: Vallentine Mitchell, 1969)

Bermant, C., *The Cousinhood: the Anglo-Jewish Gentry* (London: Eyre and Spottiswoode, 1971)

Bermant, C., *Lord Jakobovits: The Authorised Biography of the Chief Rabbi* (London: Weidenfeld and Nicholson, 1990)

Bolchover, R., *British Jewry and the Holocaust* (Cambridge: Cambridge University Press, 1993)

Brenner, M., V. Caron and U. Kaufmann (eds), *Jewish Emancipation Reconsidered: the French and German Models* (Tübingen: Mohr Siebeck, 2003)

Brenner, M., R. Liedtke and D. Rechter (eds), *Two Nations: British and German Jews in Comparative Perspective* (London and Tübingen: Mohr Siebeck, 1999)

Breuer, J. (ed.), *Fundamentals in Judaism: Selections from the Works of Rabbi Samson Raphael Hirsch and Outstanding Torah-True Thinkers* (New York: Feldheim, 1949)

Breuer, M., *Judische Orthodoxie im Deutschen Reich, 1871–1918: Sozialgeschichte einer Religiosen Minderheit* (Frankfurt am Main: Judischer Verlag bei Athenaum, 1986)

Brodie, I., *A Word in Season: Addresses and Sermons 1948–1958* (London: Vallentine Mitchell, 1959)

Brodie, I., *The Strength of My Heart: Sermons and Addresses 1948–1965* (London: G.J. George & Co. Ltd., 1969)

Brook, S., *The Club: The Jews of Modern Britain* (London: Constable and Company Ltd., 1989)

Brotman, A.G., 'Jewish Communal Organisation', in J. Gould and S. Esh (eds), *Jewish Life in Modern Britain* (London: Routledge, Kegan & Paul, 1964), pp.1–17

Carlebach, J., 'The Impact of German Jews on Anglo-Jewry: Orthodoxy 1850–1950', in W.E. Mosse (co-ordinating ed.), *Second Chance: Two Centuries of German-speaking Jews in the United Kingdom* (Tübingen: Mohr Siebeck, 1991), pp.405–23

Carmy, S. (ed.), *Modern Scholarship in the Study of Torah: Contributions and Limitations* (New Jersey: Jason Aronson, 1996)

Cesarani, D. (ed.), *The Making of Modern Anglo-Jewry* (Oxford: Basil Blackwell, 1990)

Cesarani, D., 'The Transformation of Communal Authority in Anglo-Jewry, 1914–40', in D. Cesarani (ed.), *The Making of Modern Anglo-Jewry* (Oxford: Basil Blackwell, 1990), pp.115–40

Cesarani, D., 'Dual Heritage or Duel of Heritages? Englishness and Jewishness in the Heritage Industry', in Tony Kushner (ed.), *The Jewish Heritage in British History: Englishness and Jewishness* (London: Frank Cass, 1992), pp.29–41

Cesarani, D., *The Jewish Chronicle and Anglo-Jewry 1841–1991* (Cambridge: Cambridge University Press, 1994)

Cesarani, D., 'Jewish Emancipation: From Teleology to a Comparative Perspective', in M. Brenner, R. Liedtke and D. Rechter (eds), *Two Nations: British and German Jews in Comparative Perspective* (London and Tubingen: Mohr Siebeck, 1999), pp.63–66

Cesarani, D. (ed.), *Port Jews: Jewish Communities in Cosmopolitan Maritime Trading Centres, 1550–1950* (London: Frank Cass, 2002)

Cohen, J.M. (ed.), *Dear Chief Rabbi: From the Correspondence of Chief Rabbi Immanuel Jakobovits on Matters of Jewish Law, Ethics and Contemporary Issues 1980–1990* (New Jersey: Ktav, 1995)

Cohen, N., 'Trends in Anglo-Jewish Religious Life', in J. Gould and S. Esh (eds), *Jewish Life in Modern Britain* (London: Routledge, Kegan & Paul, 1964), pp.41–54

Cohen, S., 'The South African Zionist Federation and the South African Jewish Board of Deputies: Samuel Goldreich and Max Langermann', in M. Kaplan and M. Robertson (eds), *Founders and Followers: Johannesburg Jewry 1887–1915* (Cape Town: Vlaeberg Publishers, 1991), pp.197–210

Cohen, Steven M., *American Modernity and Jewish Identity* (New York and London: Tavistock Publications, 1983)

Cohen, Stuart A., *English Zionists and British Jews: The Communal Politics of Anglo-Jewry, 1895–1920* (Princeton, NJ: Princeton University Press, 1982)

Cowen, A., *New London Synagogue: The First Twenty Years* (London: New London Synagogue, 1984)

Cowen, Anne and Roger Cowen (eds), *Victorian Jews through British Eyes* (Oxford: Littman, 1986)

Cromer, G., 'Intermarriage and Communal Survival in a London Suburb', *The Jewish Journal of Sociology*, XVI, 2 (Dec. 1974), pp.155–70

Dansky, M., *Gateshead: Its Community, its Personalities, its Institutions* (Michigan: Targum Press, 1992)

Davis, M., *The Emergence of Conservative Judaism: The Historical School in 19th Century America* (Philadelphia, PA: The Jewish Publication Society of America, 1963)

Dorff, Eliot, *Conservative Judaism: Our Ancestors to Our Descendents* (New York: United Synagogue of Conservative Judaism, 1997)

Drachman, B., *The Unfailing Light: Memoirs of an American Rabbi* (New York: Rabbinical Council of America, 1948)

Duschinsky, C., *The Rabbinate of the Great Synagogue, London, from 1756–1842* (London: Oxford University Press, 1921)

Eisen, A., *Rethinking Modern Judaism: Ritual, Commandment, Community* (Chicago: University of Chicago Press, 2000)

Elias, J., *The World of Rabbi S. R. Hirsch: The Nineteen Letters about Judaism* (Jerusalem: Feldheim Publishers, 1995)

Ellenson, D., 'Church-Sect Theory, Religious Authority and Modern Jewish Orthodoxy: A Case Study', in M.L. Raphael (ed.), *Approaches to Modern Judaism* (Chico, CA: Scholars Press, 1983), pp.63–83

Ellenson, D., *Tradition in Transition: Orthodoxy, Halakhah, and the Boundaries of Modern Jewish Identity* (Lanham, MD: University Press of America, 1989)

Ellenson, D., *Rabbi Esriel Hildesheimer and the Creation of Modern Jewish Orthodoxy* (Tuscaloosa, AL: The University of Alabama Press, 1990)

Ellenson, D., 'German Jewish Orthodoxy: Tradition in the Context of Culture', in J. Wertheimer (ed.), *The Uses of Tradition: Jewish Continuity in the Modern Era* (New York: Jewish Theological Seminary of America, 1998), pp.5–22

Endelman, T.M., 'Comparative Perspectives on Modern Antisemitism in the West', in David Berger (ed.), *History and Hate: The Dimensions of anti-Semitism* (Philadelphia: JPS, 1986), pp.95–114

Endelman, T.M., 'The Englishness of Jewish Modernity in England', in J. Katz (ed.), *Toward Modernity: The European Jewish Model* (New Jersey: Transaction, 1987), pp.225–67

Endelman, T.M., *Radical Assimilation in English Jewish History: 1656–1945* (Bloomington, IN: Indiana University Press, 1990)

Endelman, T.M. (ed.), *Comparing Jewish Societies* (Ann Arbor, MI: University of Michigan Press, 1997)

Endelman, T.M., *The Jews of Georgian England: Tradition and Change in a Liberal Society, 1714-1830* (Ann Arbor, MI: University of Michigan Press, 1999)

Endelman, T.M., *The Jews of Britain 1656–2000* (Berkeley, CA: University of California Press, 2002)

Epstein, I., *Joseph Herman Hertz 1872–1946: In Memoriam* (London: Soncino Press, 1947)

Epstein, I., *The Faith of Judaism: An Interpretation for our Times* (London: Soncino Press, 1954)

Feiner, S. and D. Sorkin (eds), *New Perspectives on the Haskalah* (London: Littman, 2001)

Feldman, D., *Englishmen and Jews: Social Relations and Political Culture, 1840–1914* (New Haven, CT: Yale University Press, 1994)

Finestein, I., 'The Lay Leadership of the United Synagogue Since 1870', in S. Levin (ed.), *A Century of Anglo-Jewish Life 1870–1970* (London: United Synagogue, 1971), pp.29–41

Finestein, I., *Post-Emancipation Jewry: The Anglo-Jewish Experience* (The Seventh Sacks Lecture) (Oxford: Oxford Centre for Postgraduate Hebrew Studies, 1980)

Frankel, J., and S.J. Zipperstein (eds), *Assimilation and Community: The*

Jews in Nineteenth-Century Europe (Cambridge: Cambridge University Press, 1992)

Frankel, W., 'Anglo-Jewish Attitudes and Minhag Anglia', in S. Massil (ed.), *The Jewish Year Book 2000* (London: Vallentine Mitchell, 2000), pp.45–50

Frankel, W., 'Traditional Alternatives', in *Jewish Chronicle*, 26 September 2003, New Year Section, pp.xi–xiv

Friedlander, A.H., 'The German Influence on Progressive Judaism in Great Britain', in W. Mosse *et al.* (eds), *Second Chance: Two Centuries of German-speaking Jews in the United Kingdom* (Tübingen: Mohr Siebeck, 1991), pp.425–35

Friedman, M., 'Life Tradition and Book Tradition in the development of Ultra-Orthodox Judaism', in H.E. Goldberg (ed.), *Judaism Viewed From Within and From Without* (Albany: SUNY Press, 1986)

Friedman, M., 'The Lost Kiddush Cup: Changes in Ashkenazic Haredi Culture – A Tradition in Crisis', in J. Wertheimer (ed.), *The Uses of Tradition: Jewish Continuity in the Modern Era* (New York: Jewish Theological Seminary of America, 1998), pp.175–86

Gainer, B., *The Alien Invasion: The Origins of the Aliens Act of 1905* (London: Heinemann, 1972)

Gartner, L.P., *The Jewish Immigrant in England, 1870–1914*, 2nd edn (London: Simon Publications, 1973)

Goldberg, D. and E. Kessler (eds), *Aspects of Liberal Judaism: Essays in Honour of John D. Rayner* (London: Vallentine Mitchell, 2004)

Gould, J. and S. Esh (eds), *Jewish Life in Modern Britain* (London: Routledge, Kegan & Paul, 1964)

Goulston, M., 'The Status of the Anglo-Jewish Rabbinate, 1840–1914', in *The Jewish Journal of Sociology*, X, 1 (June 1968), pp.55–82

Green, Nancy L., 'The Modern Jewish Diaspora: East European Jews in New York, London and Paris', in Todd Endelman (ed.), *Comparing Jewish Societies* (Ann Arbor, MI: University of Michigan Press, 1997), pp.113–34

Grunfeld, I., *Judaism Eternal: Selected Essays from the Writings of Rabbi S.R. Hirsch*, in 2 vols (London: Soncino Press, 1956)

Grunfeld, I., 'Introduction', in I. Levy (trans.), *The Pentateuch – Translated and Explained by S.R. Hirsch*, in 5 vols (Gateshead: Judaica Press, 1976), pp.viii–xxx

Guttman, A., *The Struggle Over Reform in Rabbinic Literature During the Last Century and a Half* (New York: The World Union for Progressive Judaism, 1977)

Haberman, J., 'Herbert Loewe's Apologia for Traditional Judaism: An Unorthodox Defence of Orthodoxy', in idem, *Aquinas and Maimonides: A Contemporary Appraisal* (New York: Ktav, 1979), pp.119–47

Hebblethwaite, B.L., *The Problems of Theology* (Cambridge: Cambridge University Press, 1980)

Heilman, S.C., 'The Many Faces of Orthodoxy', *Modern Judaism*, 2, 1 (1982), pp.23–51

Heilman, S.C., 'The Many Faces of Orthodoxy, Part II', *Modern Judaism*, 2, 2 (1982), pp.171–98

Heilman, S.C., *Defenders of the Faith: Life Among the Ultra-Orthodox* (New York: Schocken, 1992)

Heilman, S.C. and S.M. Cohen, *Cosmopolitans and Parochials: Modern Orthodox Jews in America* (London: University of Chicago Press, 1989)

Heilman, S.C. and Menachem Friedman, 'Religious Fundamentalism and Religious Jews: The Case of the Haredim', in Martin Marty and Scott Appleby (eds), *Fundamentalisam Observed* (Chicago: University of Chicago Press, 1991), pp.197–264

Heinemann, I., 'Supplementary Remarks on The Secession from the Frankfurt Jewish Community under Samson Raphael Hirsch', *Historia Judaica*, 10, 2 (Oct. 1948), pp.123–34

Helmreich, W.R., *The World of the Yeshiva: An Intimate Portrait of Orthodox Jewry* (New Haven: Free Press, 1986)

Henriques, R., *Sir Robert Waley Cohen 1877–1952: A Biography* (London: Secker & Warburg, 1966)

Hertz, J.H., *The Jew as a Patriot: A Plea for the Removal of the Civil Disabilities of the Jews in the Transvaal* (Johannesburg: 1898)

Hertz, J.H., *Bachya: the Jewish Thomas à Kempis, a Chapter in the History of Jewish Ethics* (New York: Jewish Theological Seminary of America, 1898)

Hertz, J.H., 'Bachya and "The Duties of the Heart"', Appendix in *The sixth biennial report of the Jewish Theological Seminary of America* (New York: Press of Philip Cowen, 1898)

Hertz, J.H., *Inaugural Sermon at Congregation Orach Chayyim, January 13, 1912* (New York: Press of the Hebrew Standard, 1912)

Hertz, J.H., 'Traditional Judaism: An Appeal for the Jewish War Memorial', *A Sermon Preached at the New West End Synagogue Shabbat Bereshit 18th October 1919* (London: Office of the Chief Rabbi, 1919)

Hertz, J.H., 'Opening Address by the Chief Rabbi' at the *1923 Conference of Anglo-Jewish Preachers* (London: Oxford University Press, 1923)

Hertz, J.H., 'Opening Address by the Chief Rabbi' at the *1925 Conference of Anglo-Jewish Preachers* (London: Oxford University Press, 1925)

Hertz, J.H., *Mystic Currents in Ancient Israel* (Liverpool: University Press of Liverpool, 1926)

Hertz, J.H., *Affirmations of Judaism* (London: Oxford University Press, 1927)

Hertz, J.H., 'Opening Address by the Chief Rabbi' at the *1927 Conference of Anglo-Jewish Preachers* (London: Oxford University Press, 1927)

Hertz, J.H., *Ancient Semitic Codes and the Mosaic Legislation* (London: Publications for Society for Jewish Jurisprudence, 1928)

Hertz, J.H., *Fundamental Ideals and Proclamations of Judaism* (New York: Bloch Publishing, 1930)

Hertz, J.H., *The Battle for the Sabbath at Geneva* (London: Oxford University Press, 1932)

Hertz, J.H., 'Opening Address by the Chief Rabbi' at the *1932 Conference of Anglo-Jewish Preachers* (London: Office of the Chief Rabbi, 1932)

Hertz, J.H., *Sermons, Addresses and Studies*, in three vols (London: Soncino, 1938)

Hertz, J.H., *The Celebration of the Chief Rabbi's Silver Jubilee, 21 March, 1938* (London: The Chief Rabbi Presentation Committee, 1938)

Hertz, J.H., 'The Recall to the Synagogue', *Address by the Chief Rabbi at the United Synagogue Conference, 25th July, 1940* (London: Office of the Chief Rabbi, 1940)

Hertz, J.H., 'The Recall to the Synagogue', *Sermon Preached at the Hampstead Synagogue 17th August, 1940 by the Chief Rabbi* (London: Office of the Chief Rabbi, 1940)

Hertz, J.H., 'Response by the Chief Rabbi', *Seventieth Birthday Celebration of the Very Reverend J.H. Hertz – Friends House, 24th September, 1942* (Hertford: Stephen Austin & Sons Ltd, 1942)

Hertz, J.H., *Early and Late: Addresses, Messages and Papers* (Surrey: Soncino Press, 1943)

Hertz, J.H., 'A Vindication of Religion', *Address by Chief Rabbi Hertz at The World Congress of Faiths*, London, 4th June, 1943 (Hertford: Stephen Austin & Sons Ltd, 1943)

Hertz, J.H., *Affirmations of Judaism: Selected Works from the Writings of Chief Rabbi Joseph H. Hertz* (London: Soncino, 1975)

Hertz, J.H. (ed.), *The Pentateuch and Haftorahs: Hebrew text, English Translation and Commentary*, 2nd edn (London: Soncino, 1975)

Hill, M. (ed.), *A Sociological Yearbook of Religion in Britain* (London: SCM Press, 1971)

Hirsch, S.R., *Neunzehn Briefe uber Judentum von Ben Uziel* (Altona: J.F. Hammerich, 1836)

Hirsch, S.R., *Der Austritt aus der Gemeinde* (Frankfurt am Main: J. Kauffmann, 1876)

Hirsch, S.R., *Gesammelte Schriften von Rabbiner Samson Raphael Hirsch*, 6 vols (Frankfurt am Main: J. Kauffmann, 1902–12)

Hirsch, S.R., *Der Pentateuch, Ubersezt und Erlautext von Samson Raphael Hirsch*, 5 vols (Frankfurt am Main: J. Kauffmann, 1920)

Hirsch, S.R., *Judaism Eternal: Selected Essays from the Writings of Samson*

Raphael Hirsch, translated by I. Grunfeld, in 3 vols (London: Soncino Press, 1956)

Hirsch, S.R., *The Collected Writings: Samson Raphael Hirsch*, 8 vols (New York: Feldheim, 1984–95)

The Living Hirschian Legacy: Essays on 'Torah im derekh eretz' and the Contemporary Hirschian Kehilla (New York: Feldheim, 1988)

Holmes, C., *Anti-Semitism in British Society, 1876–1939* (London: Edward Arnold, 1979)

Homa, B., *A Fortress in Anglo-Jewry: The Story of the Machzike Adath* (London: Shapiro, Vallentine, 1953)

Homa, B., *Orthodoxy in Anglo-Jewry, 1880–1940* (London: Jewish Historical Society of England, 1969)

Homa, B., *Footprints on the Sands of Time* (Gateshead: published by the author, 1990)

Hyamson, A.M., *The Sephardim of England: A History of the Spanish and Portuguese Jewish Community, 1492–1951* (London: Methuen & Co., 1951)

Hyamson, A.M., *The London Board for Shechita 1804–1954* (London: The London Board for Shechita, 1954)

Hyamson, A.M., *Jews' College, London 1855–1955* (London: Jews' College, 1955)

Hyman, P., *From Dreyfus to Vichy: The remaking of French Jewry, 1906–1939* (New York: Columbia University Press, 1979)

Hyman, P., *The Emancipation of the Jews of Alsace: Acculturation and Tradition in the Nineteenth Century* (New Haven and London: Yale University Press, 1991)

Jacobs, L., *We Have Reason to Believe* (London: Vallentine Mitchell, 1957)

Jacobs, L., *Jewish Values* (London: Vallentine Mitchell, 1960)

Jacobs, L., *Principles of the Jewish Faith: An Analytical Study* (London: Vallentine Mitchell, 1964)

Jacobs, L., *Faith* (London: Vallentine Mitchell, 1968)

Jacobs, L., *A Jewish Theology* (London: Darton, Longman & Todd, 1973)

Jacobs, L., *A Tree of Life: Diversity, Flexibility, and Creativity in Jewish Law* (New York: Oxford University Press for Littman Library, 1984)

Jacobs, L., *Helping With Enquiries: An Autobiography* (London: Vallentine Mitchell, 1989)

Jacobs, L., *God, Torah, Israel: Traditionalism Without Fundamentalism* (Ohio: Hebrew Union College Press, 1990)

Jacobs, L., *Religion and the Individual: A Jewish Perspective* (Cambridge: Cambridge University Press, 1992)

Jacobs, L., *We Have Reason to Believe* (fourth edn) (London: Vallentine Mitchell, 1995)

Jacobs, L., *Beyond Reasonable Doubt* (London: Littman Library, 1999)

Jakobovits, I., *Jewish Medical Ethics: A Comparative and Historical Study of the Jewish Religious Attitude to Medicine and its Practice* (New York: Philosophical Library, 1959)

Jakobovits, I., *Prelude to Service: A Selection of Statements, Letters and Interviews prior to his installation as Chief Rabbi of the United Hebrew Congregations of the British Commonwealth of Nations* (London: Office of the Chief Rabbi, 1967)

Jakobovits, I., *Journal of a Rabbi* (London: W.H. Allen, 1967)

Jakobovits, I., *The Timely and the Timeless: Jews, Judaism and Society in a Storm-tossed Decade* (London: Vallentine Mitchell, 1977)

Jakobovits, I., 'An Analysis of Religious Versus Secularist Trends in Anglo-Jewry, Especially During the Past Fifteen Years', in S.L. Lipman and V.D. Lipman (eds), *Jewish Life in Britain 1962–77* (New York: K.G. Saur Publishing Inc., 1981), pp.33–48

Jakobovits, I., *'If Only my People ...' Zionism in my Life* (London: Weidenfeld and Nicolson, 1984)

Jakobovits, I., *From Doom to Hope: A Jewish View on 'Faith in the City', the Report of the Archbishop of Canterbury's Commission on Urban Priority Areas* (London: Office of the Chief Rabbi, 1986)

Jakobovits, I., *New Priorities on the Orthodox Agenda* (London: Office of the Chief Rabbi, 1989)

Jakobovits, I., 'Preserving the Oneness of the Jewish People: Can a Permanent Schism be Averted?', *Tradition*, 24, 2 (Winter 1989)

Japhet, S., 'The Secession from the Frankfurt Jewish Community under Samson Raphael Hirsch', *Historia Judaica*, 10, 2 (Oct. 1948), pp.99–122

Jones, S., T. Kushner and S. Pearce (eds), *Cultures of Ambivalence and Contempt: Studies in Jewish– Non-Jewish Relations* (London: Vallentine Mitchell, 1997)

Joseph, M., *Judaism as Creed and Life* (London: Macmillan and Co., 1903)

Jung, L. (ed.), *Jewish Leaders 1750–1940* (New York: Bloch Publishing Company, 1953)

Kalms, S., *A Time for Change: United Synagogue Review* (London, Stanley Kalms Foundation, 1992)

Kaplan, M. and M. Robertson (eds), *Founders and Followers: Johannesburg Jewry 1887–1915* (Cape Town: Vlaeberg Publishers, 1991)

Katz, J. (ed.), *Toward Modernity: The European Jewish Model* (New Jersey: Transaction, 1987)

Katz, J., 'Toward a Biography of the Hatam Sofer', in Francis Malino and David Sorkin (eds), *From East and West: Jews in a Changing Europe, 1750–1870* (London: Blackwell, 1990), pp.223–66

Katz, J., *A House Divided: Orthodoxy and Schism in Nineteenth Century European Jewry* (New Hampshire: Brandeis University Press, 1998)

Kellner, M., *Must a Jew Believe Anything* (London: Littman, 1999)

Kershen, A.J. and J.A. Romain, *Tradition and Change: A History of Reform Judaism in Britain 1840–1995* (London: Vallentine Mitchell, 1995)

Kessler, E., *An English Jew: The Life and Writings of Claude Montefiore* (London, Vallentine Mitchell, 2002)

Klier, J. and Shlomo Lambroza (eds), *Pogroms: Anti-Jewish Violence in Modern Russian History* (Cambridge: Cambridge University Press, 1991)

Klugman, Eliyahu Meir, *Rabbi Samson Raphael Hirsch: Architect of Torah Judaism for the Modern World* (New York: Artscroll Series, Mesorah Publications, 1996)

Kosmin, B., 'Localism and Pluralism in British Jewry: 1900–80', in *Transactions of the Jewish Historical Society of England*, 28 (1982), pp.111–23

Kosmin, B., 'Nuptiality and Fertility Among British Jews', in D.A. Coleman (ed.), *Demography of Immigrants and Minority Groups in the United Kingdom* (London: Academic Press, 1982), pp.245–61

Kosmin, B. and C. Levy, *Jewish Identity in an Anglo-Jewish Community: The Findings of the 1978 Redbridge Jewish Survey* (London: Board of Deputies of British Jews Research Unit, 1983)

Kosmin, B. and S. Waterman, *British Jewry in the Eighties: A Statistical and Geographical Study* (London: Board of Deputies of British Jews Research Unit, 1986)

Kranzler, D. and G. Hirschler (eds), *Solomon Schonfeld: His Page in History* (New York: Judaica Press, 1982)

Kushner, T., *The Persistence of Prejudice: Antisemitism in British Society during the Second World War* (Manchester: Manchester University Press, 1989)

Kushner, T. (ed.), *The Jewish Heritage in British History: Englishness and Jewishness* (London: Frank Cass, 1992)

Kushner, T., *The Holocaust and the Liberal Imagination: A Social and Cultural History* (Oxford: Blackwell, 1994)

Kushner, T., *We Europeans? Mass-Observation, 'Race' and British Identity in the Twentieth Century* (Aldershot and Burlington, VT: Ashgate, 2004)

Leigh, M., 'Reform Judaism in Britain 1840–1970', in D. Marmur (ed.), *Reform Judaism* (London: RSGB, 1973), pp.3–50

Levin, S.S. (ed.), *A Century of Anglo-Jewish Life 1870–1970* (London: United Synagogue, 1971)

Levine, E., 'Memoir', in I. Epstein (ed.), *Joseph Herman Hertz 1872–1946: In Memoriam* (London: Soncino Press, 1947), pp.1–32

Levy, A., *The Story of Gateshead Yeshiva* (Taunton: Wessex Press, 1952)

Levy, B.B., 'On the Periphery: North American Orthodox Judaism and Contemporary Biblical Scholarship', in D. Sperling (ed.), *Students of the Covenant* (Atlanta, GA: Scholars Press, 1992)

Liberles, R., 'The Origins of the Jewish Reform Movement in England', *Association for Jewish Studies Review*, 1 (1976), pp.121–50

Liberles, R., *Religious Conflict in Social Context: The Resurgence of Orthodox Judaism in Frankfurt Am Main, 1838–1877* (Westport, CT: Greenwood Press, 1985)

Liebman, C., 'Orthodoxy in American Jewish Life', in R. Bulka (ed.), *Dimensions of Orthodox Judaism* (New York: Ktav, 1983)

Liebman, C., 'Extremism as a Religious Norm', *Journal for the Scientific Study of Religion*, 22, 1 (March 1983), pp.75–86

Lipman, V.D., *Social History of the Jews in England 1850–1950* (London: Watts and Co., 1954)

Lipman, V.D. (ed.), *Three Centuries of Anglo-Jewish History* (Cambridge: The Jewish Historical Society of England, 1961)

Lipman, V.D., *A History of the Jews in Britain Since 1858* (Leicester: Leicester University Press, 1990)

Lipman, S.L. and V.D. Lipman (eds), *Jewish Life in Britain 1962–77: Papers and Proceedings of a Conference held at Hillel House, London on March 13, 1977 by the Board of Deputies of British Jews and the Institute of Jewish Affairs* (New York: K.G. Saur Publishing Inc., 1981)

Loewe, H., 'The Orthodox Position', from idem, *Essays on Problems in Jewish Orthodoxy by Members of Cambridge University*, series of pamphlets (Cambridge: W. Heffer & Sons Ltd., 1915)

Loewe, R., *The Position of Women in Judaism* (London: SPCK, 1966)

London, L., 'Jewish Refugees, Anglo-Jewry and British Government Policy, 1930–1940', in D. Ceserani (ed.), *The Making of Modern Anglo-Jewry* (Oxford: Basil Blackwell, 1990), pp.163–90

Lowenstein, Steven M., *The Mechanics of Change, Essays in the Social History of German Jewry* (Atlanta: Scholars Press, 1992)

McLeod, H., *Religion and Society in England, 1850–1914* (London: Macmillan, 1996)

Malino, F. and D. Sorkin (eds), *From East and West: Jews in a Changing Europe, 1750–1870* (London: Blackwell, 1990)

Marmur, D. (ed.), *Reform Judaism: Essays on Reform Judaism in Britain* (London: RSGB, 1973)

Maybaum, I., *The Office of a Chief Rabbi* (London: RSGB, 1964)

Meirovich, H., *A Vindication of Judaism: The Polemics of the Hertz Pentateuch* (New York: Jewish Theological Seminary of America, 1998)

Meyer, M.A. (ed.), *German-Jewish History in Modern Times*, 4 vols (New York: Columbia University Press, 1996–98)

Meyer, M.A., *Response to Modernity: A History of the Reform Movement in Judaism* (New York: Oxford University Press, 1988)

Montefiore, C.G., *Liberal Judaism: An Essay* (London: Macmillan, 1903)

Montefiore, C.G., *Outlines of Liberal Judaism: For the use of Parents and Teachers*, 2nd edn (London: Macmillan, 1923)

Montefiore, C.G. and H. Loewe, *A Rabbinic Anthology* (London: Macmillan and Co., 1938)

Montefiore, C.G., *An English Jew: The Life and Writings of Claude Montefiore*, selected, edited and introduced by E. Kessler, 2nd edn (London: Vallentine Mitchell, 2002)

Mosse, W.E. (coordinating ed.), *Second Chance: Two Centuries of German-speaking Jews in the United Kingdom* (Tübingen: J.C.B. Mohr [Paul Siebeck], 1991)

Neusner, J., 'Scripture and Mishnah: Authority and Selectivity', in F.E. Greenspahn (ed.), *Scripture in the Jewish and Christian Traditions: Authority, Interpretation Relevance* (Abingdon, Nashville: Parthenon Press, 1982), pp.64–87

Newman, A., 'Setting the Scene: Anglo-Jewry in 1870', in S.S. Levin (ed.), *A Century of Anglo-Jewish Life 1870–1970* (London: United Synagogue, 1971), pp.1–12

Newman, A., *Commemoration of the Centenary of the Birth of Chief Rabbi Dr. Joseph H. Hertz* (London: United Synagogue, 1972)

Newman, A., *The United Synagogue 1870–1970* (London: Routledge and Kegan Paul, 1976)

Newman, A., 'The Chief Rabbinate and the Provinces, 1840–1914', in J. Sacks (ed.), *Tradition and Transition: Essays Presented to Chief Rabbi Sir Immanuel Jakobovits to celebrate twenty years in office* (London: Jews' College Publications, 1986), pp.217–26

Newman, A., *The Board of Deputies of British Jews 1760–1985: A Brief Survey* (London: Vallentine Mitchell, 1987)

Norman, E.R., *Church and Society in England, 1770–1970: A Historical Study* (Oxford: Clarendon Press, 1976)

Novak, D., *Law and Theology in Judaism* (New York: Ktav, 1974)

Novak, D., *Halakhah in a Theological Dimension*, Brown Judaic Studies Series no.68 (Chico, CA: Scholars Press, 1985)

Olsover, L., *The Jewish Communities of North-East England, 1755–1980* (Gateshead: Ashley Marks Publishing, 1981)

Ornstien, P., *Historical Sketch of the Beth Hamedrash* (London: 1905)

Paneth, P., *Guardian of the Law: the Chief Rabbi, Dr. J.H. Hertz* (London: Allied Book Club Ltd, 1943)

Paul, G., 'The Value of Controversy in Communal Life', in S.L. Lipman and V.D. Lipman (eds), *Jewish Life in Britain 1962–77* (New York: K.G. Saur Publishing Inc., 1981)

Petuchowski, J., *Prayerbook Reform in Europe: The Liturgy of European Liberal and Reform Judaism* (New York: World Union for Progressive Judaism, 1968)

Philipson, D., *The Reform Movement in Judaism* (New York: Ktav Publishing House, Inc., 1967)

Prais, S.J., 'Synagogue Statistics and Jewish Population of Great Britain,

1900–70', *Jewish Journal of Sociology*, XIV, 2 (Dec. 1972), pp.215–28

Prais, S.J., 'Polarisation or Decline? A Discussion of Some Statistical Findings on the Community', in S.L. Lipman and V.D. Lipman (eds), *Jewish Life in Britain 1962–77* (New York: K.G. Saur Publishing Inc., 1981), pp.3–16

Prais, S.J. and M. Schmool, 'Statistics of Jewish Marriages in Great Britain: 1901–1965', *The Jewish Journal of Sociology*, IX, 2 (Dec. 1967), pp.149–74

Prais, S.J. and M. Schmool, 'The Size and Structure of the Anglo-Jewish Population, 1960–65', *The Jewish Journal of Sociology*, X, 1 (June 1968), pp.5–34

Pulzer, Peter, *Jews and the German State: The Political History of a Minority, 1848–1933* (Oxford: Blackwell, 1992)

Rabinowitz, L.I., 'The Transvaal Congregations', in G. Saron and L. Hotz (eds), *The Jews in South Africa: A History* (Cape Town: Oxford University Press, 1955)

Raphael, Marc Lee (ed.), *Approaches to Modern Judaism*, no.49 of Brown Judaic Studies series (Chico, CA: Scholars Press, 1983)

Raphael, Marc Lee, *Judaism in America* (New York: Columbia University Press, 2003)

Rayner, J., 'Guide to Jewish Piety', *Liberal Jewish Monthly* (Tabernacles, 1960), p.160

Rosenbloom, N.H., *Tradition in an Age of Reform: The Religious Philosophy of Samson Raphael Hirsch* (Philadelphia, PA: Jewish Publication Society of America, 1976)

Rosenheim, J., 'The Historical Significance of the Struggles for Secession from the Frankfurt Jewish Community', *Historia Judaica*, 10, 2 (Oct. 1948), pp.135–46

Rosenheim, J., *S.R. Hirsch's Cultural Ideal and our Times*, trans. E. Lichtigfield (London: Shapiro, Vallentine and Co., 1951)

Roth, C., *The Federation of Synagogues 1912–1937: A Record of Twenty Five Years* (London: The Federation of Synagogues, 1937)

Roth, C., *History of the Jews of England* (1st edn) (Oxford: Oxford University Press, 1941)

Roth, C., *The Great Synagogue: London 1690–1940* (London: E. Goldston, 1950)

Roth, C., 'Britain's Three Chief Rabbis', in L. Jung (ed.), *Jewish Leaders 1750–1940* (New York: Bloch Publishing Company, 1953), pp.477–90

Roth, C., *Essays and Portraits in Anglo-Jewish History* (Philadelphia, PA: Jewish Publication Society of America, 1962)

Roth, C., 'The Haskalah in England', in H. J. Zimmels, J. Rabbinowitz and I. Finestein (eds), *Essays Presented to Chief Rabbi Israel Brodie on the Occasion of his Seventieth Birthday* (London: Soncino Press, 1967), pp.365–76

Roth, S., *The Jewish Idea of Culture* (New Jersey: Ktav, 1997)

Rubinstein, W.D., *A History of the Jews in the English-Speaking World: Great Britain* (London: Macmillan, 1996)

Ruderman, D., 'Was there an English parallel to the German Haskalah?', in M. Brenner, R. Liedtke and D. Rechter (eds), *Two Nations: British and German Jews in Comparative Perspective* (London and Tübingen: Mohr Siebeck, 1999), pp.15–43

Ruderman, D., *Jewish Enlightenment in an English Key: Anglo-Jewry's Construction of Modern Jewish Thought* (Princeton and Oxford: Princeton University Press, 2000)

Ruderman, D., 'Was there a "Haskalah" in England? Reconsidering an old question', in S. Feiner and D. Sorkin (eds.), *New Perspectives on the Haskalah* (London: Littman, 2001), pp.64–85

Rudolph, B.G., *From a Minyan to a Community: A History of the Jews of Syracuse* (Syracuse, NY: Syracuse University Press, 1970)

Sacks, J., (ed.), *Tradition and Transition: Essays Presented to Chief Rabbi Sir Immanuel Jakobovits to Celebrate Twenty Years in Office*, (London: Jews' College Publications, 1986)

Sacks, J., *Traditional Alternatives: Orthodoxy and the Future of the Jewish People* (London: Jews' College Publications, 1989)

Sacks, J., (ed.), *Orthodoxy Confronts Modernity* (Hoboken, New Jersey and London: Ktav Publishing House in assoc. with Jews' College, 1991)

Sacks, J., *The Persistence of Faith: Religion, Morality and Society in a Secular Age* (London: Weidenfeld and Nicolson, 1991)

Sacks, J., *Crisis and Covenant: Jewish Thought after the Holocaust* (Manchester: Manchester University Press, 1992)

Sacks, J., *One People? Tradition, Modernity, and Jewish Unity* (London: Littman Library of Jewish Civilization, 1993)

Sacks, J., *Will We Have Jewish Grandchildren? Jewish Continuity and How to Achieve It* (London: Vallentine Mitchell, 1994)

Sacks, J., *Community of Faith* (London: Peter Halban, 1995)

Saron, G. and L. Hotz (eds), *The Jews in South Africa: A History* (Cape Town: Oxford University Press, 1955)

Saron, G., 'The Long Road to Unity', in G. Saron and L. Hotz (eds), *The Jews in South Africa: A History* (Cape Town: Oxford University Press, 1955)

Schechter, S., 'Four Epistles to the Jews of England', in idem, *Studies in Judaism* (London: Adam and Charles Black, 1908)

Schonfeld, S., *Jewish Religious Education: A Guide and Handbook with Syllabuses, for use by Teachers, Group Leaders and Parents* (London: National Council for Jewish Religious Education, 1943)

Schonfeld, S., *Message to Jewry* (London: Dr Solomon Schonfeld Silver Jubilee Committee, 1959)

Schorsch, I., 'Zacharias Frankel and the European Origins of

Conservative Judaism', *Judaism*, 30, 3 (Summer 1981), pp.344–54

Schwab, H., *The History of Orthodox Jewry in Germany, 1830–1945*, trans. by Irene R. Birnbaum (London: Mitre Press, 1950)

Schwartzfuchs, S., *A Concise History of the Rabbinate* (Oxford: Blackwell, 1993)

Shaftesley, J.M., 'Israel Brodie, Chief Rabbi: A Biographical Sketch', in H.J. Zimmels, J. Rabbinowitz and I. Finestein (eds), *Essays Presented to Chief Rabbi Israel Brodie on the Occasion of his Seventieth Birthday* (London: Soncino Press, 1967), pp.xi–xxxix

Shaftesley, J.M., 'Religious Controversies', in S.S. Levin (ed.), *A Century of Anglo-Jewish Life 1870–1970* (London: United Synagogue, 1973), pp.93–113

Shapiro, Marc B., *Between the Yeshiva World and Modern Orthodoxy: The Life and Works of Rabbi Jehiel Jacob Weinberg, 1884–1966* (London: Littman Library, 1999)

Shapiro, Marc B., *The Limits of Orthodox Theology: Maimonides' Thirteen Principles Reappraised* (Oxford: Littman Library of Jewish Civilization, 2004)

Sharot, S., 'Secularization, Judaism and Anglo-Jewry', in Michael Hill (ed.), *A Sociological Yearbook of Religion in Britain* (London: SCM Press, 1971), pp.121–40

Sharot, S., 'Religious Change in Native Orthodoxy in London, 1870–1914: The Synagogue Service', *JJS*, 15, 1 (June 1973), pp.57–78

Sharot, S., 'Religious Change in Native Orthodoxy in London, 1870–1914: Rabbinate and Clergy', *JJS*, 15, 2 (December 1973), pp.167–87

Sharot, S., 'Native Jewry and the Religious Anglicization of Immigrants in London: 1870–1905', *The Jewish Journal of Sociology*, XVI, 1 (June 1974), pp.39–56

Shashar, M., *Lord Jakobovits in Conversation* (London: Vallentine Mitchell, 2000)

Silber, Michael K., 'The Emergence of Ultra-Orthodoxy: The Invention of a Tradition', in J. Wertheimer (ed.), *The Uses of Tradition: Jewish Continuity in the Modern Era* (New York: JTSA, 1998), pp.23–84

Simon, J.I., 'Pulpit and Platform: Hertz and Landau', in M. Kaplan and M. Robertson (eds), *Founders and Followers: Johannesburg Jewry 1887–1915* (Cape Town: Vlaeberg Publishers, 1991), pp.182–96

Sklare, M., *Conservative Judaism: An American Religious Movement*, augmented edn (New York: Schocken, 1972)

Sklare, M. and J. Greenblum, *Jewish Identity on the Suburban Frontier: A Study of Group Survival in the Open Society*, 2nd edn (Chicago: Chicago University Press, 1979)

Soloveitchik, H., 'Rupture and Reconstruction: The Transformation of Contemporary Orthodoxy', *Tradition*, 28, 4 (1994), pp.64–130

Sorkin, D., *The Transformation of German Jewry, 1780–1840* (Oxford: Oxford University Press, 1987)

Sowden, D.L., 'In The Transvaal Till 1899', in G. Saron and L. Hotz (eds), *The Jews in South Africa: A History* (Cape Town: Oxford University Press, 1955)

Sperling, S.D. (ed.), *Students of the Covenant: A History of Jewish Biblical Scholarship in North America* (Atlanta, GA: Scholars Press, 1992)

Temkin, S., 'The Chief Rabbinate: A British Institution', *Jewish Heritage*, 10, 1 (Summer 1967)

Temkin, S., 'Orthodoxy with Moderation: A Sketch of Joseph Herman Hertz', *Judaism*, 24, 3 (Summer 1975), pp.278–95

Temkin, S., *Isaac Mayer Wise: Shaping American Judaism* (Oxford: Oxford University Press, The Littman Library, 1992)

Tessler, G., *Amélie: The Story of Lady Jakobovits* (London: Vallentine Mitchell, 1999)

Trachtenberg, H.L., 'Estimate of the Jewish Population of London in 1929', *Journal of the Royal Statistical Society*, XCVI, (1933), pp.87–98

Umansky, E., *Lily Montagu and the Advancement of Liberal Judaism: From Vision to Vocation* (New York: E. Mellen Press, 1983)

Wertheimer, J. (ed.), *Tradition Renewed: A History of the Jewish Theological Seminary*, 2 vols (New York: Jewish Theological Seminary of America, 1997)

Wertheimer, J. (ed.), *The Uses of Tradition: Jewish Continuity in the Modern Era* (New York: Jewish Theological Seminary of America, 1998)

Williams, B., *The Making of Manchester Jewry: 1740–1875* (Manchester: Manchester University Press, 1976)

Zimmels, H.J., J. Rabbinowitz and I. Finestein (eds), *Essays Presented to Chief Rabbi Israel Brodie on the Occasion of his Seventieth Birthday* (London: Soncino Press, 1967)

Many of the archives of the institutions of the Jewish community in Britain are held together at the London Metropolitan Archives, in Clerkenwell, London. This collection includes the archives of the United Synagogue, the office of Chief Rabbi, the London Bet Din, the Federation of Synagogues, the former Jews' College, and the Board of Deputies. Additional archival material is contained in the Parkes library at the University of Southampton, which includes the private papers of J.H. Hertz and some of the papers of Israel Brodie.

Index